Dear Reader,

Event planning is a diverse career choice. People from different backgrounds and education levels are drawn to it, and there is a scope of diversity in the types of careers in event planning. With its many career paths to choose from, event planning and its different schedules and work environments attracts a variety of people.

Now is a great time to be an event planner. The industry is booming with potential and growing strong roots, but much uncharted territory still remains in the way of policies and resources. Paving your way in a new career is challenging, but blazing the trail can be even more daring.

My love of the restaurant and hospitality field helped me parlay event planning into a career. My first position as a special events coordinator made me realize more resources are needed to benefit event planners just starting out, so I jumped at the opportunity to author this book.

As I wrote, I tried to include academic information as well as conceptual principles in the subject matter. This is what I feel has made me a better event planner. Writing this book has reminded me why I love this profession, and I truly hope you will as well.

Jennifer Mancuso

THE

EVERYTHING
Series

The handy, accessible books in this series give you all you need to tackle a difficult project, gain a new hobby, or even brush up on something you learned back in school but have since forgotten. You can read cover to cover or just pick out information from the four useful boxes.

 Alerts: Urgent warnings

 Essentials: Quick and handy tips

 Facts: Important sound bytes of information

 Questions: Solutions to common problems

When you're done reading, you can finally
say you know EVERYTHING®!

EDITORIAL
Innovation Director: Paula Munier
Editorial Director: Laura M. Daly
Executive Editor, Series Books: Brielle K. Matson
Associate Copy Chief: Sheila Zwiebel
Acquisitions Editor: Kerry Smith
Associate Development Editor: Elizabeth Kassab
Production Editor: Casey Ebert

PRODUCTION
Director of Manufacturing: Susan Beale
Production Project Manager: Michelle Roy Kelly
Prepress: Erick DaCosta, Matt LeBlanc
Interior Layout: Heather Barrett,
Brewster Brownville, Colleen Cunningham

Visit the entire *Everything*® series at www.everything.com

THE
EVERYTHING®
GUIDE TO BEING AN
EVENT PLANNER

Insider advice on turning your creative
energy into a rewarding career

Jennifer Mancuso

A adamsmedia
Avon, Massachusetts

Dedication
This book is dedicated to the three best events of my life: Ed, Grace, and Harper.
Much dedication is owed to my family who encouraged my love of reading and writing.

An Everything® Series Book.
Everything® and everything.com® are registered trademarks of F+W Media, Inc.

Published by Adams Media, a division of F+W Media, Inc.
57 Littlefield Street, Avon, MA 02322 U.S.A.
www.adamsmedia.com

ISBN 10: 1-59869-417-0
ISBN 13: 978-1-59869-417-8

Printed in the United States of America.

10 9 8 7 6 5 4 3 2

Library of Congress Cataloging-in-Publication Data
Mancuso, Jennifer.
The everything guide to being an event planner / Jennifer Mancuso.
p. cm. – (An everything series book)
Includes bibliographical references.
ISBN-13: 978-1-59869-417-8 (pbk.)
ISBN-10: 1-59869-417-0 (pbk.)
1. Special events—Planning I. Title.
GT3405.M36 2007
394.2068–dc22   2007015887

This book is available at quantity discounts for bulk purchases.
For information, please call 1-800-289-0963.

Contents

Top Ten U.S. Cities for Event Planning

1. **New York City:** For city-goers, there is no place like the Big Apple to host and elaborate events.

2. **Los Angeles:** With its many celebrities and actors, the City of Angels will be sure to keep you busy as an event planner.

3. **Miami:** This sunny, wealthy, beach community attracts many clients.

4. **San Francisco:** This hilly community known for its hippies and gorgeous views has been compared most often to a European city.

5. **Boston:** With its charm and history, this city has many opportunities for event planners.

6. **New Orleans:** Mardi Gras is a draw to thousands of tourists every year, making this city a spectacular event location.

7. **Las Vegas:** This city is rumored to have more wedding chapels than any other. For this reason alone, Las Vegas makes the Top Ten list.

8. **Philadelphia:** Much like Boston, Philadelphia is a destination that attracts clientele interested in history and culture.

9. **Washington, D.C.:** Politicians and socialites—along with event planners who enjoy working with high-profile clients—spend a lot of time in this city.

10. **San Diego:** Coastal views and wealthy inhabitants make San Diego an obvious target on the event-planning map.

Introduction

Imagine sipping champagne with celebrities, shaking hands with politicians, or walking down the runway holding hands with top designers. Now imagine yourself changing into a second outfit hours before an event because you got a butter stain on your new dress. Or imagine looking through the phone book to try and find live reptiles, or playing therapist to a mother and daughter minutes before a wedding. If you can picture yourself in any of these scenarios, you can picture yourself as an event planner.

From small dinners to gala affairs and every occasion in between, the public is looking to experts to organize their events into grand occasions. As a result, clients are calling on event planners to coordinate the most splendid affairs, creating an all-time high demand for event planners.

Businesses of all sorts are on the search for an organized person to market their company. In addition to organizing functions, an event planner attracts new clients, increases revenue, and develops marketing strategies. The candidate who can do these things can be an asset to any company. Many fields now employ event planners on staff, and event-planning companies have more work than imaginable. Businesses, from large corporations to smaller restaurants, are exploring new ways to attract qualified applicants, so it is a great time to consider event planning as a career.

Event planners have many types of backgrounds and beginnings, from florists to caterers to MBAs. The event-planning career path you choose may depend upon the skills you have already developed or skills that you would like to develop. You may also choose a position based upon scheduling and convenience. Event planners can choose to work in a corporate setting or nightclub depending on the hours they prefer.

A career in event planning can be rewarding both financially and emotionally. The compliments and accolades you will receive will be tremendously satisfying. The profession can be stressful at times, but seeing your client and her guests enjoying the event you dedicated your time to makes it worthwhile.

This book will give you the tools and resources you need to begin your career. Whether you are just considering event planning or you have a few years in the industry, using these tools can help you succeed in your new endeavor. This book outlines the types of career paths available to you as an event planner, different ways to break into the business, and the types of events you may be designing. Understanding the process of event planning will give you the foundation to start your career.

As an event planner you must be creative, motivated, and detail oriented. You will lend your style, imagination, and methods of executing to all types of events. To have a passion for cuisine, organization, and people is what it means to be in this occupation. Won't you join me as we journey down the road to becoming an event planner?

Acknowledgments

Special thanks to Jack Bardy and the team at the Beehive. Chris, Kristen, Brielle, and Lisa, my editor—I thank you for the momentum to get this project off of the ground. Many thanks to Matt Demers for thirty lashes. Great friends in Kenmore Square who have supported me during this endeavor deserve thanks as well.

Further gratitude is owed to Lolo, Anne Agen from I Soci salon, Jeanette, Peter, Chip, Christa Linzey and Rebecca Alssid from Boston University, Nick Cohen, Stuart Horowitz and the team at the Hotel Commonwealth, Nina Jung, Beth Grossman, my team of babysitters, and my crew of friends for your love, support, and pens.

Chapter 1

An Introduction to Event Planning

IF YOU HAVE EVER had the desire to be a part of the top social events in your city, event planning is an excellent career path to take. The life of an event planner is filled with socializing and networking with people from all walks of life. As an event planner you will find doors opening in your social life as well. That said, it is also a very challenging position that involves many skills, including organizing, marketing, and hospitality. This chapter offers a general introduction to what's involved in a career as an event planner.

What Is Event Planning?

Simply put, an event planner is a person who plans social events professionally. Event planners are employed in many industries and settings, from restaurants, hotels, banquet halls, and party planning companies to *Fortune* 500 corporations and mom-and-pop operations. Event planners are also known as event coordinators, special event coordinators, or private event coordinators. For the purpose of this book, all of these titles will be referred to as simply event planner.

Many businesses have a single person or a core of people responsible for their calendar of events. Restaurants use a planner to book large groups coming in and to book private rooms. Hotels use a planner to book their function rooms. Hospitals, colleges, and corporations use a team of planners to coordinate functions for their doctors, professors, and staff respectively. The career path you choose as an event planner might be based upon your past experience, creativity, and prior education.

Event planning is fast becoming the most popular major among college freshmen in the restaurant and hospitality industry. There is also an increased demand within businesses to establish this position internally to streamline communications between different departments. For these reasons, the number of event planner jobs are at an all-time high, and the options within this field are bountiful.

 **Question**

How will becoming an event planner impact my social life?
In many communities event planners not only plan functions but also attend them as well. Fundraisers, restaurant and nightclub openings, as well as press-related events are some of the many different invitations on an event planner's social calendar. Many companies employing event planners expect them to attend these events.

A career in event planning can be accessed through education or hands-on experience, which makes it a great field for beginners as well as seasoned professionals looking to make a career shift. As you begin your career, you will meet event planners from different backgrounds and with different levels of experience. It is a fast-paced career in which you will be meeting new people and learning new things every day. The more experience you have, the easier it will be for you to increase your income potential.

Important Characteristics

An event planner is the main point person or contact for social and business events. You might be hired by a client looking to book a function or be employed within a business in which your main goal is overseeing the company's social and business calendar. As an event planner booking a function, you will find that oftentimes your point of contact is another event planner.

Event planners must be extremely organized. You will deal with so many details, both large and small, and your organizational techniques will be tested on a daily basis. As an event planner, you will also need to be a good communicator. So much of the success of an event comes from your ability to relate the needs of your client to chefs, staff, and vendors. Communication skills are a must for this career. Other positive attributes include:

- Calm demeanor
- Sociability
- Friendliness
- Efficiency
- Leadership
- Ability to be a team player
- Creativity

By using positive qualities that you may already possess, you will become a more attractive hire as you build your client base, interview for a job, and establish contacts. A positive reputation is very important for success as an event planner. Potential clients and employers may ask for letters of recommendations or references from your past experiences. To succeed as an event planner you must be trustworthy, generous, and patient. Your clients need to know they can trust you with their most important moments, whether that means coordinating a board meeting or planning a wedding. They should know that you have their best interest in mind.

Much of event planning involves the client's budget and expenditures. Often you will be asked to entertain events in the client's private residence. You need to remember that you are responsible for the actions of yourself and your staff. You will be accountable to the client if budgets go over or if any damage occurs to personal belongings. Accidents are bound to happen, and it is best to be honest and correct the problem rather than make excuses and lay blame on someone else. Offering to dry-clean a guest's dress after a server spills wine on it is a better solution than not acknowledging it at all. The dry cleaning bill will be a few dollars, which is nothing compared to an unhappy client. This will only increase your accountability with your client and employer.

Helpful Experiences and Specialties

It is likely that interests or hobbies in your past can be a springboard to event planning. If you enjoy entertaining friends in your home, this may have led you to the idea of event planning. The same can be said of a love of cooking, baking, and gardening. Perhaps you have a passion for wine, fashion, art, or music. These are all hobbies that can be useful in an event planner's career.

In fact, many careers in the hotel, restaurant, and hospitality industry also make for a seamless transition into event planning. Because employment in these areas usually entails dealing with the general public, you'll learn the etiquette, phone skills, and public speaking skills you'll need to effectively deal with guests and complaints.

It is possible that upon entering the field of event planning you will find a specialty within the field. A fashion enthusiast may gravitate to the creative department of a party planning company where she can coordinate china, linens, and centerpieces. An amateur chef may find a calling as a catering manager to develop menus. An art lover will find himself at home booking events for a museum. Even a sports enthusiast can use the similarities between the team environment of organized sports and that of an event planning team to her advantage. While you are deciphering the connection between your hobbies and the specialties of event planning, remember that it may have been these hobbies that attracted you to the field to begin with. It only makes sense now to use your strengths in your new career.

Floral Designer

A floral designer is a specialist in the florist field. A florist might be an employee of a flower shop or a shop owner but usually doesn't have as much experience as a floral designer. A designer is a person who is trained to make flowers into visual art. He may specialize in exotic or rare flowers, and his knowledge is broad and extends well beyond the regional selection of flowers in his area.

The craft of designing flowers includes creating bouquets, centerpieces, and large ornamental decorations. Event planners will call on floral designers when booking weddings, galas, and large festive events such as rehearsal dinners and holiday parties. Designers work closely with event planners to create themes, follow color schemes, and visualize creations that will work within the parameters of chosen venues.

In large party-planning companies, a floral designer is a member of the staff. She is part of the creative department that will brainstorm and work up a proposal that aids in turning clients' dreams to reality. Outside of a party planning company, you will find floral designers at high-end florists. To find a good floral designer, ask for recommendations from other event planners that have similar needs as your own.

Baker or Pastry Chef

A great baker may or may not have a culinary degree. A good percentage of the field has not been formally trained. In lieu of formal education, he may have chosen to travel and work as an apprentice for someone of great reputation and stature. He may also gain experience by working in the garde manger department of a large restaurant. Also known as a pastry chef, members of this field not only must make their creations look aesthetically pleasing but taste magnificent as well. Some pastry chefs specialize in only cakes or decorating cakes.

E ssential

Garde manger is a French term for the place in the restaurant where cold dishes such as salads, cold appetizers, and desserts are plated. A person overseeing this department is referred to as a chef garde manger.

Whichever field of event planning you come to work in, chances are you will have the name of a baker in your Rolodex. Most catering companies, hotels, and restaurants employ their own in-house pastry chef. Still, requests will come from guests asking to bring in their own cakes from their favorite neighborhood bakery.

Alert

When a client brings in a cake from another bakery, it is customary to charge a cake-cutting fee. Typically the fee is $2 to $4 per person, which offsets the labor involved and plateware used. A bistro may charge a lower price; a high-end hotel will most certainly charge more. Some restaurants waive the fee entirely since dessert is taken out of the equation.

Restaurant Maitre D'

Maitre D' is the formal term for a host. The maitre d' of a restaurant usually has some management responsibilities, but his main focus is guest interaction. His duties include answering telephones, greeting and seating guests, and enhancing the guest experience. A maitre d' should exude hospitality, though in popular culture a maitre d' is portrayed as being snooty.

Restaurant Server

Servers used to be referred to as waiters and waitresses. As with a maitre d', a server's role is interacting with the general public, therefore, she needs to handle situations and complaints well. A server should have a fair understanding of the idea of hospitality as she performs her job. She should have a firm understanding of the menu as well as the wine and cocktails that are offered. A server is ultimately the salesperson for the chef and proprietor. She is responsible for "reading" her guests to establish when a couple is looking for a romantic dinner and when a large group wants to be more interactive and involved. She should be attentive yet not obtrusive in her service.

If you have worked in a restaurant as a maitre d' or server prior to being an event planner, chances are you have a basic knowledge of the hospitality field. You have an advantage of having seen some of the many scenarios that can occur when dealing with guests in the food and beverage industry. Thinking on your feet might be second nature by now. With that, you can take these experiences into your new event-planning career.

If you haven't worked in the hospitality field before, don't despair. Every time you have been to a restaurant, had dinner at a friend's house, or attended a function, chances are you have been exposed to elements of this industry. In fact, the next time you have the opportunity to dine at a restaurant, you should make a mental note of the many things occurring around you. The maitre d' might pull out the chair for you or the server may refold your napkin when you return to the table after making a phone call. These are special touches that you might consider implementing once you have a staff of your own.

E ssential

When serving food and beverage, all staff should pull back hair longer than shoulder length. No dangling jewelry or open-toe shoes should be worn. Nails should be groomed with no chipping nail polish. Supply breath mints in employee restrooms and wait stations.

Restaurant Manager

It is possible to become a manager of a restaurant by going to college, though a good portion of people in this field have worked through the ranks and have been promoted to this position. A restaurant manager is someone who oversees the front-of-the-house staff. On some occasions a manager will also oversee the back-of-the-house employees. If the restaurant has a chef or chef owner, he will usually manage the back-of-the-house employees while the restaurant manager concentrates on the front of the house. An MOD is the manager on duty, while GM is the general manager who reports directly to the owner. There can also be an AGM, assistant general manager, and assistant managers.

A restaurant manager's duties include being responsible for the house money and banking, doing employee payroll, overseeing employees, defusing guest complaints, and enhancing the guests' overall experience. A manager is an integral part of the daily opening and closing of the restaurant and is on hand to ensure proper setup and breakdown. A manager is also responsible for keeping up staff morale and the general health of the restaurant. As with a maitre d' or server, a restaurant manager has to think on her feet.

 Fact

In a restaurant, the front of the house refers to employees who work on the front lines in a restaurant. These employees deal directly with guests. Servers, bartenders, hosts, bus people, and food runners all encompass the front-of-the-house team. Back-of-the-house employees are the people who work behind the scenes in a restaurant. Cooks, dishwashers, and prep cooks are all referred to as back-of-the-house staff.

With respect to the hospitality industry, a restaurant service or meal period is like live television. There are no rehearsals and no second takes. The members of the staff of a restaurant are like actors in a play—always onstage. Keep this idea in mind on your future visits to restaurants. Depending on which area of event planning you choose, you may also think of your event as a live performance.

Caterer

A caterer is a chef who specializes in off-site events. Think of caterers as chefs without a permanent home in a restaurant. A caterer may work in a private home, outside venue, or a banquet facility that does not employ an in-house chef. Mobile and rental equipment are used in place of equipment that is not available at the on-site venue. Large catering companies tend to have a storeroom or warehouse that holds much of this equipment.

A catering manager is the person responsible for booking the events for a company. A catering manager is a specialty term for an event planner that is employed by a catering company. Catering managers are responsible for pricing, proposals, and designing menus with the caterer. A catering company will handle the food and beverage portion of an event and staffing but usually is not involved with securing the venue and decorations.

The staff of a catering company will handle all of the production associated with the menu. This includes taking inventory of rental equipment and setting up tables, chairs, and plate settings. The bar, buffet station, and satellite kitchen will all be set up by the catering staff as well.

There are many different ways you may interact with caterers as an event planner. You might decide that being a catering manager is the route you would like to take in your new career. You might also have the opportunity to work alongside catering companies if you are employed by a venue that does not have an in-house chef. If you work for an event-planning company it is likely you may work with a few different catering companies that specialize in different types of cuisine. Another way to work with caterers is in a company setting where catered lunches and boardroom meetings take place.

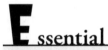

A production team is a group of people in charge of setting up and breaking down an event. Production includes choosing the table settings and orchestrating the table setup by a caterer. Production is also a broad term used to include companies or individuals hired to design a stage and set up lighting and equipment.

Chef

A chef is someone who cooks as a profession. A chef can be the proprietor or co-proprietor of a restaurant. A chef oversees the back-of-the-house employees, designs and tests the menu, and educates the front- and back-of-the-house staff on the menu items.

An executive chef is the highest level of chef in the kitchen. An executive chef may own the establishment or be co-owner. In some cases, an executive chef is given the opportunity to gain sweat equity, a term used to describe a portion of the restaurant that the chef can own by working a certain number of years for the owner. The executive chef oversees his sous chefs (assistant chefs) and trains them on his menu. Other duties of an executive chef include quality control, ordering food and supplies, and doing back-of-the-house payroll.

Communicating with the chef is one of the largest responsibilities of an event planner working in the hospitality business, second only to communicating with the client. It is important to extend the needs of the client to the chef without compromising the quality of the menu and event. For this reason, being the liaison between the client and chef can be challenging. It is important as an event planner to satisfy the wishes of both the chef and client while still meeting their needs

Depending on which field of event planning you're in, these are some of your core group of people and companies that will become your vendors. When you are starting from scratch at a new company, you will want to build a relationship with these vendors. Once you have developed a rapport with your vendors or purveyors, it would benefit you to arrange a stagier (*stagier* is a French term used in the hospitality field and means to follow or shadow someone in a training atmosphere). Knowing as much as you can about all aspects of the business will only benefit you down the road. Learning from a chef will better prepare you for designing a menu with your client. Following a floral designer has its advantages when discussing seasonal flowers for a bride's bouquet. Familiarizing yourself with the skills of a restaurant manager will advance your leadership techniques, which is helpful when working with a staff.

Why Clients Use Event Planners

Clients use event planners for various reasons, out of both desire and necessity. The first reason might be the simplicity of using one point person to organize an event. A client needing assistance planning a large detail-oriented event might be a second reason. Often a business, hotel, or restaurant has appointed one person to coordinate their functions as a service to guests and clients. The goal of an event planner is to be the main point person to organize functions from beginning to end.

Alert

When working for an event-planning company, it is wise to assess your competition. You want to be sure that the services you are offering match or exceed other companies in the field. This can mean the difference between a client using your services or choosing another company. It is worth mentioning in the initial client interview if your company has hosted high-profile events in the past.

People in various fields use event planners. It is important to know the demographics of the area you wish to work in before embarking on your adventure. Imagine you live in an area with a popular mountain community. You have an opportunity to interview for two jobs. One position is at a popular ski resort with a low base salary and high commission for events that you book. The other position is at a large medical facility that needs a planner to organize all social and business affairs and offers a high salary. Which job do you choose? If your goal is to make the most money, you will need to get a sense of the level of commission you can make and weigh the two salaries. You might choose the first position if you are looking to gain experience before starting your own company.

Clients use event planners in all types of settings. A bustling financial district of a city will need a catering company for in-house board meetings. A quaint inn in the country, an ideal place for weddings, will need an event planner to organize its functions. A restaurant with a private dining room will keep its event planner busy because of its close proximity to medical facilities. With the needs of so many clients to be met, your first challenge will be to decide which specialty field of event planning you would like to enter.

Is Event Planning for You?

The first step to becoming an event planner is deciding which industry best fits your lifestyle. As you gain experience in the field you might find that your lifestyle or circumstances may change. The contacts you make will allow you to explore another area of event planning you might not have previously considered. When you are content in your field, you will be happier and more productive in even the most challenging aspects of event planning.

Before you sit in front of a potential employer or potential client, you will need to assess your skills and experience. This will allow you to convey to the employer or client how well you are suited for the job or event. If the job you are interviewing for involves late nights and you are more of a morning person, then chances are this is not the right job for you. If the client you are meeting with is trying to save money and have you design her centerpieces, it will be best to tell her up front that you have no experience in designing flowers. The services you can offer as an event planner will enrich your job performance and put that special touch on the events you book.

At the same time, your skills can be expanded once you are involved in the field. For example, if you are working in a restaurant setting and your knowledge of wine increases over time, you might begin offering wine pairings with a chef's tasting menu. You might have taken a course in floral design and obtained a permit to shop at your local floral market. You can now design the centerpieces for the functions at the hotel you are working for. You are saving the hotel money and making a little extra as well.

Finding your niche will be easier once you gain knowledge of the field. You might be trying to narrow down your options within the many different organizations that employ event planners. Or you might be trying to gain as much experience as possible before starting your own company. Whichever path you take, this book will help you navigate through the different career choices in event planning and detail their rewards and benefits.

Chapter 2

How Events Are Born

EVENTS ARE BORN under many circumstances. An event can be centered on a special occasion such as a birthday, anniversary, or wedding celebration. A fashion show, music concert, or art show can become an event. In the business world, entertaining clients, recruiting new employees, and holiday celebrations can all constitute events. But all events are not created equal. Each individual function will need different time commitments to plan and execute. Whatever the cause for the event, care needs to be taken in the planning stages.

Determining the Client's Needs

In this business you will hear many extravagant ideas and requests from clients. Often the event planner and client can find a common solution to make an idea more mainstream while keeping the creativity. On rare occasions, requests become demands, and these are the ones that take some maneuvering to satisfy the client. Telling a client that his cigar-smoking request might severely restrict your ability to find him a venue that permits smoking might make him realize that he needs the venue more than the cigars.

Reading Your Client

Reading a client is an important skill you will acquire as you gain experience in this field. Reading your clients means picking up subtle clues about their demeanor and personality. These clues can assist you in improving your client's experience. For example, if you are meeting a potential client and she inquires about the costs of everything, from your fees down to the table linen, in your initial interview, you guess she may be money-conscious. Therefore, designing a cost-effective menu with little frills is a sure-fire way to get this client to accept your proposal. The same level of intuitive decision-making will only benefit you and your client through the planning stages.

Processing Information

After your initial meeting with a potential client, it is important to process all of the notes you have taken. When it comes time to begin your research, you will want to keep all of your notes close by. An outdoor garden ceremony will not be well received as a venue for a bride who confessed she has severe allergies. A high-end art museum might not be an ideal location for a family reunion with a large number of children on the guest list. And a suggested menu heavy with steak, pork, and chicken may not appeal to a vegetarian staff for their annual fundraiser.

You will find many ways to get information from your clients. Some information will come in the form of outright requests while other information will be harder to decipher. Placing a value on all of the information, no matter how small, will catapult you into the next level of event planning.

Types of Events

There are many different types of events. The type of position you look for as an event planner will dictate the specific events you will be working with. For an event planner of a party planning company, you will have the largest range of events to work with. As an event planner of a corporation, hospital, or university, your experience will be limited to the specific needs of each organization. When you choose to work for a foundation as an event planner, your skills may be utilized for an annual gala. Once you have narrowed your search to the types of events you are interested in, deciding your career path will be much easier.

Weddings

A wedding is a union between two people who wish to spend their lives together. It is customary to celebrate the union with a celebration among family and friends. A wedding can be small with just two people plus a person to officiate the ceremony such as a priest, rabbi, justice of the peace, or minister. In some states it is legal for a friend or relative to be ordained for one day to perform a wedding ceremony.

Weddings can also be enormous, elaborate events involving a few hundred people or more. The average wedding in this country has two hundred people on its guest list. Weddings are as unique as the couples getting married. As a wedding planner, you must be open to new ideas as well as be familiar with traditional wedding customs of different ethnicities.

Galas

Gala events take place at large venues and often involve a few hundred guests. The occasion for a gala may be to celebrate milestone events such as anniversaries or birthdays or to raise money for various causes. The menu varies from cocktail-party fare to a multi-course dinner. Cocktail or formal attire is required for a gala.

There are many different ways you can be involved in galas as an event planner—working for a nonprofit company and planning its fundraising event; as an event planner for a banquet hall, restaurant, or hotel; or as a planner for a catering company. Chances are as an event planner a gala or two will cross your path in your career.

Large Casual Events

A large casual event is a business or casual gathering involving at least one hundred guests. These events are less formal than galas and take place in the afternoon as well as the evening. A large casual event can be a company picnic, bar or bat mitzvah, or a family reunion. In some cases, children are included on the guest list, which involves diversifying the menu and entertainment.

You will most likely work a large casual event if the venue you are working for is popular among families. A catering manager is a good career choice if casual events interest you. Event-planning companies are also experienced in planning large casual events.

Corporate Events and Dinners

In recent years, many corporations have elected to hire in-house event planners. In this position, you would be responsible for planning meetings, scheduling in-house catering, and coordinating dinners with clients. Any large off-site employee or client event, such as a holiday party, would fall in your domain. As a corporate event planner, you may also be responsible for arranging travel and expense accounts for employees.

E ssential

Many of these events will pique your interest as you consider the field of event planning. Keep in mind your lifestyle, personality, and skills when considering where to concentrate in this industry. You will benefit more from carefully choosing your specialty and will create a sustainable career in the process.

The job description of a corporate event planner or meeting planner is the same in a university or medical setting. Event planners in the hotel and restaurant industry usually form strong relationships with corporate planners. While you may decide to not work for a corporation, it is beneficial for you to familiarize yourself with the position. Whether you decide to work in catering, restaurants, or fundraising, booking corporate events regularly can be lucrative.

Intimate Dinners

An intimate dinner can be held in a private residence or the private room of a restaurant or hotel. Thirty guests or less meets the requirement for an intimate dinner. Dinner can be casual or formal and involves at minimum a three-course meal. Guests can range from family members to clients to colleagues. Hired servers for an intimate dinner should adhere to proper serving etiquette, even in a casual setting.

Private dining rooms in restaurants and hotels are used frequently by members of the corporate, collegiate, and medical communities. While the restaurant and hotel industry plans the bulk of intimate dinners, it is possible you will see a fair amount of intimate dinners while employed by a catering company or personal chef.

Cocktail Parties

A cocktail party takes place during evening hours, and it can work well at a wedding, gala, business, or social event. Various venues can fit such a party since the guest list can span from a handful of guests to a thousand. A typical cocktail party provides seating for about half the guests and serves a menu of passed hors d'oeuvres and appetizers with some stationary items.

Creativity and Individuality in Events

Clients looking for a planner will have distinct visions for their events before you meet. Even those clients who are looking for more traditional affairs enjoy putting their own creative touch on an event. There are many ways to use your creativity in planning an event.

 Fact

"Crowd-pleasing" and "user-friendly" are terms used to describe items such as food and wine that will please most guests. While a cheeseburger is crowd-pleasing, steak tartare (raw beef) may not be. Adventurous and remedial are also buzzwords used to compare gourmet diners to beginners.

Choosing Wine and Pairing with the Menu

Even as Americans become more and more wine and food savvy, there are still those who prefer to leave the choices to the professionals. A client may brag about his wine knowledge and then turn sheepish when asked if his guests would prefer a sauvignon blanc or a chardonnay. You need to remember your responsibility to the guests attending the function (not just the host) to design a menu that is crowd pleasing or user friendly.

E ssential

As you become better informed about the world of wine, it is best to keep things simple for your guests. Wines are said to be more palatable if they are easy to drink. Pairing wine with a three-course meal means you can offer more variety. Offer lighter varietals when serving wine at a cocktail reception. For better value, shop for wines from Italy, Spain, South America, and Australia.

The time will come to sit down with the chef to plan the menu. You will need to convey all of the client information and requests to her before she can design a menu. The chef may include seasonal items or house specialties, but if something doesn't look right to you, it is important to speak up before you propose the menu to the client. The guest is sure to ask questions about the menu, so be certain you have all of the answers.

You can then proceed to the next stage and pair wine with the food. Before you set up a client tasting, have the wines opened and at the correct temperature (35–41 degrees for white and 50–61 degrees for red) so the wines show better. Traditionally, wines were paired with their regional cuisine. Today more and more wine professionals are getting creative with their pairings. To expand your knowledge of wine and cuisine, it may be a good idea to take a wine course.

Themes

A theme is a common idea that runs through the entire event. For a company retreat at a beachside mansion, you could suggest a clambake for the menu. Because the event is happening in August, offer a light white wine and a bucket of different local beers. For decorations, string lights inside the outdoor tent and cover the tables with red-and-white checkered tablecloths. Here you have taken the setting—the beach—and run the theme throughout.

Choosing a Theme

Clients will sometimes choose a theme based upon music, color, or cuisine. Mardi Gras is a popular theme for a party in which you would see Creole cuisine on the menu with a jazz band as entertainment and colorful beads given to guests. For an annual gala fundraiser, a black-and-white ball in which all of the guests are asked to dress in formal attire is an example of a color-themed event. A theme based on a cuisine might be a Mexican fiesta that features a mariachi band.

Organize Your Creativity

When you sit with a client for the initial interview, ask him if he has any ideas for themes. It is likely that he will have a theme in mind and will ask you to expand on it. As you begin your career in event planning, it is a good idea to use a creative notebook. In your notebook, keep a log of different themes as you come across them. You may see themes on invitations, in magazines, or hear about them through other event planners. You can refer to your notebook after your first meeting. Once you have gained experience you can replace your notebook with a scrapbook of your events complete with photos.

Alert

Before your creative meeting with your client, be sure to secure a deposit for your services. Unfortunately, in this business event planners have been taken advantage of by potential clients who are just looking for ideas but not willing to pay you for your services. Narrow potential clients down to serious prospects by submitting a cost proposal and saving your ideas until after a contract is signed.

Decorations

There are many different ways to be creative with decorations in event planning. Traditional ways would be through centerpieces, flower arrangements, party favors, and place settings. Even lighting can play a part in the decorations, with candles for an intimate dinner or spotlights announcing a large music event.

A client's personal taste will influence the decorations for an event. Before suggesting ideas, remember you are trying to keep in line with a theme. Decorations are also a great outlet for your client's personality to show through. A bride may envision a romantic wedding but relent when her film producer fiancée asks for movie-style popcorn buckets filled with giant boxes of candy as the centerpiece. Using different aspects of the client's career, hobby, and even first or last name can be successful ways to suggest decorations. For example, to impress a client you might purchase little bottles of a liquor that share his first name to hand out as favors for his bachelor party.

Jot down ideas regarding decorations in your creative notebook. You can get ideas from books, magazines, and events you have attended. You should also begin researching different ethnicities through cookbooks. Your creativity will be applauded when a client requests a traditional afternoon tea for his wife's birthday and you include finger sandwiches on the menu and a recipe for English biscuits as individual placemats.

Cakes and Desserts

Every event needs to finish with a little something sweet. With their pastel colors and perfect piping, cakes have held center stage at weddings and other large events. Specialty cakes are fast becoming the creative icing on any event. Specialty cake shops nowadays create visual art with their cakes and offer cakes with photographs, ships with a captain, aquariums, flower boxes, and antique cars. You can even order customized cakes online to be shipped to your door.

Some events might not necessarily call for a cake. A cocktail party serving rich, heavy hors d'oeuvres will welcome a shift in the evening when the host presents coffee and sweets. Suggest homemade donuts and serve with coffee ice cream as a twist to the classic breakfast pair. Or dust off the fondue pot and serve with chocolate instead of cheese. Accompany the fondue with fruits and angel food cake for dipping.

Shop around for a specialty bakeshop when you get started as a planner. The likelihood of you needing to order a high-end cake during your career will be quite high. Be certain you keep the bakery's hours and ordering information handy.

E ssential

As the bakery industry grows, so does the price tag of its products. Spending a few thousand dollars on a cake is becoming the norm, which may be a little hard to swallow for your client. Fortunately, bakeries have been forced to get creative in pricing their services. Suggest that the baker make a smaller version of a wedding cake for presentation and serve the guests slices from a sheet cake in the kitchen.

Favors

From birthdays to weddings to showers and everything in between, favors can add a little something extra to an event. Psychologically, it makes a guest feel appreciated for making an appearance at your event. Simply putting a bag in your guests' hands will have them leaving with smiles on their faces. Favors are the final farewell to the evening's creativity.

Traditionally, some cultures have made wedding favors a labor of love with homemade cookies or pastries. Those traditions still hold true for many. For others though, favors are another way for a client to put her own signature on an event that her guests will talk about long after the event has ended. As with the decorations, read your client to determine if she is looking for more conservative ideas for favors. For weddings, the favors should appeal to your male and female guests. Morning bread wrapped with the family recipe and a note from the couple is a great favor that will appeal to all of your guests. Picture frames are also a popular favor at weddings.

Your client may be inclined to be more playful when considering favors and remember to tie in their careers, names, and personalities. In this case, a mini martini shaker and a bottle of liquor might be perfectly suited for the couple that owns a bar. A personalized golf ball and tee would be a great match for the couple who met on a golf course.

Alert

You may be entering event planning as a transition from another career. You may be tempted to customize the stationery, make the centerpieces, and design the flowers if your specialty lies in these areas: Don't. You will not want the added pressure of, say, decorating a cake the day of the event. Find vendors that you trust who will get the job done for you.

Some clients hire event planners based upon their creative ideas in the initial interview. For this reason it is important to stay on top of current trends and research traditional functions. With the right balance of the two, your objective should be to develop your own style and impress even the toughest critics.

The Event Planning Formula

When meeting with a client for the first time, you will need to gather some preliminary information before you can showcase your ideas. This interview will become very important later for your proposal and presentation. You will need to take excellent notes. As soon as you are able after the event, rewrite or type your notes so the meeting is still fresh in your mind. Some questions you may want to ask before you meet are detailed in the following sections.

The Occasion

Usually the first question asked—the reason for the occasion—sets the tone for the rest of the interview. There is a chance you have spoken at length about the occasion in your initial phone conversation with the client. If this is the case, be sure to revisit this detail with the client when you meet. Let them embellish and have your pen ready. A client's romantic idea for her husband's sixtieth birthday will come out in those first few moments of the interview.

When it comes time to respond, you want to convey a genuine excitement to the client about the possibility of the event. You also want to inform the client if you have any experience in the type of event she is looking to hold. Give some detail about the event, but not too much. Hold onto your trade secrets until after she has signed a contract.

If you have not planned an event such as the one she is proposing, be honest. You can then mention other similar events you have planned and your experience.

 Fact

RFP—an industry term—stands for "request for proposal." In the beginning stages of the event planning process a potential client may submit an RFP to get a general idea for an event. An RFP is usually a form letter or generic list of costs associated with functions. Facility planners tend to deal with more RFPs than any other event planner.

The Date

For birthdays and other milestone events such as anniversaries, dates for a client cannot be flexible. Ask for alternate dates for all other events. A guest may not be specific and will be comfortable with any Saturday in March. If a guest is specific, do not push alternate dates. Simply let your potential client know that you will make calls and try to make it happen.

The Time

When choosing a time for the event it is wise not to get too specific. Ask for general times like morning, afternoon, midafternoon, early evening, or late night. There is much left to plan, so not getting too specific on times will benefit you and the client when it comes time to secure a venue.

A little research on your part will help the client decide on the time to hold the event. The venue may be close to a ballpark during baseball season. You will want to research the baseball schedule and make sure to pick a time when the event will not be affected by traffic. Also take traffic and construction concerns into consideration when planning conventions, concerts, and events that meet or let out around rush hour.

Essential

Give yourself and your client a realistic idea of the amount of time it will take to plan his event. You want to seem confident to the client and assure him you can succeed in planning his event. At the same time, agreeing to a timeline of three weeks to plan a company retreat for six hundred employees from all across the country will only set you up for extra stress and possible failure.

The Venue

As in real estate, an event can depend so much on location. If you are interviewing as the event planner for a facility, you are a salesperson representing the venue. You should plan a tour, have copies of the chef's menu available, and perhaps set out light refreshments to give the client an idea of the cuisine. Showcase the facility and make specific mention of added features. In the interview it is acceptable to ask if the potential client has looked at other venues. She may ask for your opinion, in which case you should be honest but gracious. Point out the positives of the other venue, especially if you have a relationship with the event planner. The client will decide without negative commentary from you. The sense of camaraderie you show might sway her opinion.

Refreshments and Menu

Whether you are serving coffee and soda in a board meeting or a seven-course tasting menu with wine pairings in a private dining room, the menu plays a large part in the planning process. You will be tempted to sample many caterers, restaurants, and hotels when you first begin your career. Keep in mind that it is important to develop a small select core of vendors. Your relationships with your vendors, in this case a caterer, will be strengthened if he knows your business is solely with him. The same is true of event planners you may work with in restaurants and hotels.

Once you have established your selection of caterers, restaurants, and hotels, create a folder with all of their information. Include menus, pricing, and photos to show your clients in proposals and presentations. If your client is looking to book a function at a restaurant, arrange to meet her there for afternoon coffee. Call ahead and ask the chef to prepare a small sampling of appetizers so the client may get a better idea of the menu. The restaurant may comp your tasting to entice your business. If this doesn't happen, you should treat the client.

When you first contact a potential client, whether over the phone or in person, you can gain an enormous amount of information. Great event planners use all of this information to create a client-specific event. Using this information can make all of the difference to a client who is looking for originality and creativity in an event. Being aware of your client's needs will allow you to maximize your client's experience.

 Fact

Comp is short for "complimentary." As an event planner you will often enjoy comped items from restaurants you deal with on a regular basis. While comp is a restaurant buzzword, it has carried over to hair and spa services, hotel rooms, and music and theater tickets.

Beginning the Planning Process

Every event needs a beginning. After meeting with the client, preparation should be done for your next meeting. If you are shopping venues for your client, be sure her event needs will match the capacity and style of the venue. Hopefully you have done your homework and your client will be dazzled by the possibilities.

Site Visits

As an event planner working for a planning company, your responsibilities will involve securing a site for the event. Once you have a signed contract, site visits should be planned with your client. A site visit is when you accompany your client to visit different venues. Call ahead to the venues and gather preliminary information for your client. Have your client review the proposals and decide which venues she would like to visit and then be sure to make an appointment. It is not appropriate for the facility planner at the venue to discuss costs with your client, but you may want to gently remind him of this over the phone.

After your client has chosen a venue, be courteous and call each facility's planner and thank him for his time. Taking time out of his day to send you proposals and meet with you deserves a phone call.

Many events call for a secondary venue or a subvenue. If you are planning an event in which the venue closes early, you can suggest an afterparty at another location. To secure a subvenue sometimes is as simple as making a call beforehand. Upscale bars and restaurants make for great second locations.

Double Booking a Date

When confirming dates with the client, be sure to check your own calendar to avoid double bookings. A double booking occurs when you have agreed to plan two events for the same evening. This poses a problem to clients who expect your presence on the day of the event. You might have an assistant or another senior planner who can take the second event if this is the case. If not, refer the client to another event planner whose reputation you trust. It is also important to mention who might fill in for you if an emergency keeps you from the event.

Chapter 3

How to Get Started

THERE ARE MANY ways to get started as an event planner. Perhaps you are on your way into the field via college, or you might be thinking of a career change and are not sure of the best way to make the transition. Starting a new career is a venture filled with both excitement and anxiety. By gaining experience in a savvy manner, you will become a more attractive candidate to employers and clients alike. This chapter will guide you through the beginning stages of this exhilarating career.

Obtaining a Salaried Position

The most common way to start out in event planning is through a salaried position with an established company. The first step to finding a salaried position is to narrow your search by asking yourself these questions:

- What is my ideal work schedule?
- In what social settings am I most comfortable?
- Am I a hands-on type of worker or do I prefer to delegate?
- Am I a self-motivating starter or task-oriented team player?
- Am I looking to put my creative skills to use?
- What type of setting would I enjoy?

If you think of yourself as more of an office person who likes your nights and weekends off, then corporate event planning may be the path for you. Your ideal job will very likely be with a university, corporation, hospital, museum, or fundraising company.

Your Resume

Once you have established your target field, you will need a resume. Your resume should list your education and last three jobs. In addition, you will want to list any events in which you might have previously worked. Being that event planning has such a heavy emphasis on organization, it would also be a good idea to list any office experience that you have had as well as any creative experience. Working alongside a caterer, florist, or photographer would be worth mentioning for creative experience. Jobs in the hospitality industry will also be worth mentioning. Event-planning companies look for assistants with all types of backgrounds. It is also worth mentioning if you have had some experience in public relations, marketing, or advertising.

 Fact

The Internet and newspapers are the most popular places to look for a job. Temp agencies can also be a good resource for a job search in event planning—use them as a final measure since they will deduct part of your income as a fee. A new hotel, banquet facility, or restaurant in your area will be looking for new event planners before the doors even open.

Once you have developed your resume, you will need to have a strategy for interviewing. After you have sent your resume out, it is a good idea to follow up with a call to the general manager, operations manager, owner, or human resources department.

The Interview

Congratulations! You have a job interview. This most likely means your prospective employer is impressed with your resume. Rarely will companies take the time to interview unqualified applicants.

Essential

The outfit you wear to an interview can speak volumes about you to a prospective employer. Dress in neat business attire. Dry-clean your outfit and pick it up two days before the interview. Some event companies are notoriously casual in dress, but you are trying to make an impression. You should leave the jeans, T-shirts, and flip-flops at home.

Before your interview, take some time to research the company interviewing you. The company's Web site should provide you with a brief history of the company. You should also make notes about your experience, work ethic, and job skills. Use these cheat sheets to practice speaking about yourself in the days leading up to the interview. Following is a list of questions frequently asked during an interview:

- How did you hear about this company?
- Can you tell me a little about your job background or experience?
- What about event planning interests you?
- Where do you see yourself in five years?
- What skills can you offer this company?
- Can you describe yourself in a work environment?
- If I were interviewing your family members and former colleagues, what would they likely say about you?

The day of your interview has arrived. Do not be late! Bring a magazine in case you are too early. Ideally you should arrive at the office or meeting place fifteen minutes early for the interview. When sitting across from your prospective employer, be sure to make eye contact. Avoid using filler words such as "like" and "um." Smile and be upbeat upon the first handshake but listen intently while you are being spoken to. The time might come in the interview for you to ask questions. It is important that you have a few questions ready to appear interactive. If your interviewer has been especially thorough, thank her and let her know she has covered everything. Following is a list of questions to ask a prospective employer.

- What are the hours?
- What is an average day like for someone in this position?
- What is the dress code?
- What will I be expected to wear for events?
- Can you tell me a little about the benefits package?

Once the interview has ended, inquire about what happens next in the hiring process. Thank your interviewer for her time and convey the message that you hope to hear back from her. The instant you get home, write your interviewer a thank-you note, and be sure to put your contact phone number on the bottom. If the company is interviewing other applicants, the decision process can take two weeks or longer. It is acceptable to check back after two weeks and inquire about the status of the job.

Starting Your Own Business

Starting your own event-planning business can be very challenging. However, it can be very exciting, rewarding work. There are some scenarios that make going it alone less risky. The level of experience you have when you are starting out may determine which path you choose when starting your own event-planning company.

Starting Small

An event-planning business is unique in that it does not require huge overhead to get started. The client absorbs most of the costs, and very little money comes from your bank account when planning an event. You will be working with many vendors that are equipped with their own facilities, so the space you need is minimal. There are so many businesses these days supporting the event industry, from party rental companies to florists to bakeries to venues, you may find your time is divided between your office and off-site locations.

For these reasons, working from your home is not a bad idea until you have built up your clientele and business. This is also a good idea because you may find yourself with an unsteady income in the early months. Not paying rent for an office or facility space will save you money until you are comfortable with your budget. You might also find that spending money on marketing or going to a trade show is a better investment early on than having an office.

E ssential

When you choose to work from home, it is easy to never close your office. Be certain you strictly adhere to your office hours. For a home office to work for you, it needs to provide you a home life as well. Working around the clock in your home will likely lead to burnout. The key to a home office is a balance between work and rest.

Your home should be the first place to look when setting up an office. The space needs to be large enough for a desk, a computer, wall-mounted shelves, and a filing cabinet. If your personal space is not large enough or just too personal, look elsewhere to set up shop. Here are some options for finding office space outside your home:

- **Ask your vendors:** As long as your business does not conflict, your vendors' facilities would be a great place to set up shop. A caterer may not think it in her best interest to share an office with you because she employs her own event planner, but your florist who has a conference room in her shop may welcome the extra exposure. Also try personal and private chefs who may not have a relationship with a separate event planner, as well as bakeries, small hotels, bed and breakfasts, and photographers.
- **Ask a Realtor:** Occasionally a landlord or homeowner may have a small space that can be the perfect spot for you to set up shop.

- **Ask friends and family:** If a friend who is a massage therapist is looking for a space to put his chair and office, maybe partnering up with him and sharing a larger space will be more cost-effective. Similarly, an arrangement could be made with a family member who is willing to give up a spare bedroom to you for a period of time.
- **Find an art studio:** The artist community in your area might be a resource to explore for an inexpensive alternative to an office space. Artists and photographers seek out large open studios or lofts and may be willing to rent out a corner to an event planner.

Large-Scale Event Planning

You have decided your niche market is large-scale events. Rather than paying for rentals, you have decided to purchase everything that you will need to plan a great event. To get to this point, you may have had to secure an investor or two and develop a business plan. After the initial development stages, you will want to revisit your business plan and establish how many events per year or per month you will need to meet your profit margin.

E ssential

On-call employees are essential for an event-planning company. Unless you have standing events every week, such as catering office lunches, you will come to rely on your on-call employees. On-call staff members call in or are notified when events are taking place. An e-mail list has become the most popular form of communication when announcing your upcoming events to staff.

You have searched for and found a facility that is part warehouse, part kitchen, and part office, complete with a conference room for entertaining clients. Your staff is complete with part-time and full-time junior event planners working under you, and you have a complete back-of-the-house and front-of-the-house staff employed on an on-call basis. To accomplish the needs of your new company, it will take a great deal of networking and marketing.

Partnering Up

Whether you have decided to go small or large scale, it could be in your best interest to find other event planners in the same field or level of industry to partner up with. It may be a casual or more concrete relationship that you develop, but by doing so you can offer your services in an otherwise slow season and collaborate with other planners at the same time.

Get creative when determining a suitable business partner. Note people who have similar experience or who share common interests in the event-planning world. Consider an associate you have worked with in the past and might be looking to make a move from party planning. Think of the fledging chef who would like to expand his personal catering business. Team up with your favorite, trusted photographer who is looking to shoot more specialty events.

Your Niche Market

So you have secured your working space. Next you will need to find your niche market. Again, this will likely be in an area that you may have some experience in. Getting started means you need to get your name out in your community. To do this, you must first have a name and a brand. You might have an idea and a specific marketing plan in mind for your business. Otherwise, there are companies that specialize in brand marketing that you may want to consult for ideas. If you are having a Web site developed (which is strongly recommended), your graphic designer may offer this service and help you develop collateral such as a folder outlining your services and business cards.

Finding Work Outside of Your Business

Assisting other event planners is a way for you to gain more experience while your fledgling company is taking off. For example, the holiday season is a notoriously busy time for restaurants and hotels.

Event planners in these industries frequently hire temporary help to assist through the holiday season. You may be a wedding planner with one wedding planned for the winter and offer your services as an assistant to a hotel or restaurant planner. This way you are gaining experience, adding to your income, and, when appropriate, still marketing your company. While you are getting your business up and running, you should be trying to secure clients while offering your services to other events.

Getting Paid

As an event planner, there are several ways in which you can get paid. One way is to charge an hourly rate for your services. Most large event-planning companies use an hourly method as a system for billing clients.

You will need to provide the client with an estimate of the hours you are planning to work. It is important to convey to the client that you expect to come within 5 to 10 percent of your estimate. If you come under budget, of course the client will be pleased; if you come in higher than your estimate, however, you should be able to provide the client with an explanation of why the overage occurred.

Alert

A single detail can blow the budget on an event. Underestimating can happen quite easily. An estimate is, after all, an educated guess. Always gain client approval before deciding on an event detail. Contact your client with a full report on overages. By suggesting an inexpensive solution to the problem, you will be making the issue less of a problem.

If you are interviewing for a salaried position, the topic of salary will come up with your potential employer. Event planners' salaries can range from $30,000 to $110,000 depending on the position and your region. You will have a better sense of salaries once you begin the interview process.

Not sure what is fair? Nowadays Web sites are available that create formulas for salaries based on geography and specialties. (Two great ones are Salary.com and Payscale.com.) Working in and around cities means a higher income potential. To save on expenses, some event-planning companies set up offices and warehouses outside of a city. This does not mean you should expect a lower salary. A salary should be based on the area you will be working.

Before accepting a position, you must have a firm understanding of comparable salaries in your field. Your employer will likely offer you a salary based upon your experience. If it is lower than you anticipate, ask to renegotiate your salary in six months or counter with a creative bonus program.

Bonus Programs

A bonus is a monetary amount that a prospective employer may offer you in addition to a salary. A bonus is usually performance-based, which in the case of an event planner is based upon sales and business generated. Not all bonuses are monetary. Your employer may also offer incentives that increase the value of your salary, such as:

- Health club membership
- Clothing or retail discounts
- Employee meals
- Trade
- Signing account for meals
- Hotel discounts
- Travel voucher
- Passes to cultural events
- Tickets to music shows and concerts
- Tickets to sporting events

As an example of a monetary bonus, an employer may offer you a base salary of $40,000 plus a 2-percent commission on the business you generate. Some facilities also charge a 5 to 10 percent management fee, and a certain percentage of this may be passed onto the event planner. Other facilities levy a room charge, of which a percentage may be used for a bonus program. Additional incentives can also be factored into a salaried position.

When negotiating bonuses, be wary. Do not let the bonus undermine your base salary. A bonus should be in addition to a competitive salary, not in lieu of one. And always receive information on bonus programs in writing.

Alert

If you are operating within a tight budget, don't let that stop you from establishing a Web site. By strategically linking your Web site to various event sites, you may get more business than you imagined.

Interviewing Other Planners and Potential Clients

Somewhere in your research you will want to interview other planners to get a sense of the fees they charge. While individuals may not be open to discussing their salary outright, you might get a sense of the percentages an event planner quotes from shadowing her for a day.

Need more insight? Enlist the help of friends who might have used planners in the past. Ask your friends and family members to recall the services offered by their planner and the costs associated. If all else fails, you can plan a bogus event in a city far away and get quotes from planners. Do not forget to ask about the planners' experience. Send a thank-you note and tell the planner you decided to go with someone else. You want to reach the event planner before his follow-up call.

Listening to advice, tips, and personal anecdotes other event planners may share is another reason to set up interviews. You should take notes. Learning from your mistakes (or someone else's) is part of the learning process. Other questions to ask an event planner:

- What type of advertisements do you pay for?
- How do the majority of your clients find you?
- How do you find the majority of your clients?
- How did you get your start?

Event Planner Advice

Gaining experience means taking a variety of jobs in the beginning. From time to time you will be presented with an event that isn't in your field. You may want to consider taking the job to gain some valuable experience. You could also meet a vendor you would not have otherwise had the opportunity to meet, or you could meet a future contact. Also, the client that is asking you to plan her mother's seventy-fifth birthday may also have a daughter getting engaged in six months. By spending some time with this client and working up a proposal, you are building your reputation as someone who is professional, patient, and courteous—all worthwhile attributes when clients are shopping for an event planner.

The Value of an Inquiry

Meeting with every client who inquires about your service is also a good way to build your database. You may not value the time you spend with this client when she is inquiring about a holiday party in the spring and you are extremely busy, but when she attends your fall fundraiser because she was on your e-mail list, it can make it all worthwhile.

Getting started means building your resume and preparing for the interviewing process. Getting started can also mean you are building your clientele and setting up your office for your new event-planning business. If you think your experience doesn't translate well to a resume, consider a volunteer program, a co-op, or internships as a way to get started. All of your hard work will pay off when you successfully complete an event for your first client or land your dream job.

Chapter 4

Breaking Into the Business

GAINING CONFIDENCE AND building your resume will be easier as you get more experience in the field of event planning. As you are preparing yourself for your new career, integrating yourself into the industry will help you narrow your job search. This chapter outlines several ways for you to make contacts and gain exposure, such as educational programs, internships, volunteering, and more.

Degree Programs

Colleges and universities that offer event planning as a degree have a broad range in their study programs. College programs usually offer hospitality as a major with event planning a minor. These programs integrate coursework in business, management, and finance into the curriculum. Rather than focus on particular training in specific fields of event planning, these general programs include:

- Hotel management
- Food and beverage
- Travel and tourism
- Convention-meeting planning

Many schools offer associate's and bachelor's degree programs as well as certificate programs in event planning.

Bachelor's Degree

Most senior-level and management positions require a bachelor's degree or two to four years experience in event planning or related fields. Bachelor's degree programs take an average of four years to complete. Students receiving a bachelor's degree will graduate with a comprehensive understanding of all the fields related to the hospitality market.

Along with an applied knowledge of the various aspects of event planning, many graduates also have training in restaurant settings on campus or through internships. Event planning relies heavily on the food and beverage industry. This is an advantage of having a background in a food and beverage program. Some colleges and universities offer paid internships as well as externships.

Associate's Degree

An associate's degree takes about two years to complete. Associate's degrees tend to offer more specialized education in event planning. Consider an associate's degree when you have a specific field in mind. An associate's degree gives the beginner the foundation she needs to get started in event planning. This program will familiarize her with the language used in event planning and give her a basic understanding of the career. Examples of positions obtained through a two-year program are travel coordinator, trade show planner, or casino event planner. With an associate's degree, you can start your career in midlevel management or junior-level positions.

E ssential

Some culinary schools also offer event-planning programs. In a culinary school environment, students are exposed to training in back-of-the-house as well as front-of-the-house environments. Culinary schools often have kitchens as classrooms and restaurants on campus. The culinary school's restaurant is open to the public and often has banquet facilities in which students can observe and train.

Certificate Program

A certificate program in event planning is a great way for a beginner to transition into event planning in a short amount of time. Certificate programs can take as little as ten weeks to complete. A person working in fields related to event planning, such as a vendor position, may consider obtaining a certificate. Upon receipt of your certificate, you will be qualified for various positions, including junior-level event-planning positions or hourly paying jobs in production and development. Some schools offering certificate programs offer job placement as well.

 Fact

According to Salary.com, the average salary for event planners ranges from $26,000 to $88,000. A formal education can also put you on the fast track to the top of your earning potential. In some major metropolitan markets, event-planning executives can make as much as $110,000 at the height of their careers.

Other Benefits of Degree Programs

Some colleges and universities offer a more international scope in their hospitality education programs. Study-abroad programs attract students who would like to combine their education with travel and relocation opportunities in different countries. Studying a second language will also benefit students and make them more attractive on the global hiring stage.

Alumni contacts are a little trade secret and an enormous benefit to getting a degree in event planning. Students a year or two your senior will be established in the field by the time you need an internship or graduate. Faculty and alumni of a university will often keep in close contact when an internship or job opportunity arises for undergraduates. Alumni offices often hire students for various positions to aid in planning events.

Become involved with the events departments on your campus. Chances are your college has more than one events department, depending on the size of your school. The office of student affairs, responsible for all student activities, would be a valuable resource to gain experience. Volunteering at faculty and alumni offices would also be a good place to gain experience. Commencement exercises will always be in need of a production staff, as will parent-student activities that take place throughout the year.

Internships and Co-ops

As a college student, internships will aid you in narrowing down your search for the event-planning position that best suits you. Internships allow you to enter the field for a short amount of time and experience different areas of the business.

 Alert

Before choosing your internship program, consider areas of event planning you are not drawn to immediately. A production position might not be as glamorous as an internship assisting a party planner, but experience in production will prove to be more beneficial when you market yourself for employment. Since these positions are the ones most offered to new planners, you will already have the experience and a leg up on the competition.

There are paid and unpaid internships. Unpaid internships are generally offered to college students on a part-time basis for a semester and allow students to gain perspective in certain environments while being supervised by a professional. As an intern you may get a sense of the responsibilities of a certain position as well as the hours involved. Your university usually will give you and your employer an outline of task-oriented goals you must complete to fulfill the internship requirements and receive academic credit. Some tasks may include:

- Clocking a minimum number of hours (usually one hundred) during the internship
- Gaining a firm understanding of the finances and daily operations of the business
- Submitting a mock proposal, invoice, and budget sample

- Performing a minimum number of hours (thirty) on the phone or doing other guest-related activities

Paid internships are offered more to graduates than undergraduates. The position may be full or part time, and it can sometimes be used as credit toward a degree program. Often a company will keep a paid intern until a position becomes available. This type of internship is beneficial to an employer who is looking for an extra set of hands but may not be able to fully commit to another salaried employee. This type of program allows the employer to observe a potential employee on a trial basis. For a paid intern, the benefit is the ability to gain experience in a specialized field without fully committing to a company.

Some companies also offer cooperative education or externships to university seniors. Co-ops are also offered at universities with trimester programs. Co-ops differ from internships in that students are able to work full time for a semester rather than splitting the time between work and study. Co-op students are usually paid and receive some credit toward a degree program. Companies often look to hire co-op students for full-time positions upon completion of their degree programs.

E ssential

When in an internship, co-op, or externship program, remember to dress and act professionally. You are trying to establish yourself, make contacts, and secure a position while you intern. It may be wise to read a company's employee handbook since you may be just entering the work force and are not familiar with company policy.

Externships can be offered as part of a university's curriculum. Because externships last from a week to a few months, these programs usually do not have monetary compensation or degree credits in return for services. Externships are more of a service a company offers to a student or individual to attract him into a field. The student or individual does little other than observe in an externship. Externships are also a great way to make contacts in a professional field.

Volunteering

Volunteering is a clever way for an event planner to gain experience in many different fields before committing to a full-time career. Volunteering also allows an event planner to build or diversify a resume while also making valuable contacts. Because many companies hire internally before posting jobs externally, you can market yourself while volunteering.

Areas where you may consider volunteering are in the medical, art, and social service communities that are looking for individuals to dedicate their time to fundraising, development, and production.

As a volunteer, you can be involved at the very beginning stages of an event. If you choose a position volunteering for an art museum, your first task may be sending out donation letters to its 5,000-member mailing list. Next you may be involved in events by hosting special member services, such as a cocktail party before the opening of a new exhibit. Finally, you may be asked to participate in the museum's annual fundraiser. Participation may include everything from choosing the invitations to passing out programs the night of the event. By being exposed to all facets of the art museum, you have made your resume more diverse.

Volunteering for just six to twelve months, depending on the experience you obtain, can qualify you for certain event-planning positions. Skills obtained through volunteering can easily be transferred to hourly positions. For example, a job volunteering in development for the events surrounding a summer concert series can help aid you in a similar paid position for an event-planning company.

Stagier Programs

Stagier is the French term for an apprentice. Stagier programs differ from internships because of the lack of formal education associated with an apprenticeship. As a stagier, you will receive specialized training. Where an intern may work in many different offices of an event-planning company, a stagier will work only for the lead creative planner, executive planner, or owner of the event-planning company. A stagier can take on similar responsibilities as an assistant, but because the stagier's primary objective is to act as a shadow, she would not at any time take the place of an assistant.

A stagier position is usually paid, though not very much. The low wage is a result of the hands-on training a stagier receives. Some companies and industries in the United States have adopted stagier programs, but it's not used in the same manner by each company. Internationally, the program trains stagiers in a craft so they may go on to start companies. For this reason, companies that have a stagier program do not hire an apprentice for a permanent position.

Staff Member and Specialty Training

Applying for a position as an event staff member is the easiest way for an event planner to break into the business. As a staff member, you can increase your earning potential and gain experience throughout different fields. In event planning, there are many positions that are needed specifically on an on-call basis. Working on call would be beneficial to those getting started who are in college or those who may not be able to sacrifice a lower-paying job as they transition into this field.

E ssential

For many events taking place in the evenings or on weekends, the demand for temporary staff is quite high. These employment opportunities can be part time or seasonal. A catering company, banquet hall, or hotel is always a good place to find temporary employment on an event staff. The positions in these areas include servers, bartenders, cooks, and production staff.

Specialty training as an event planner will always be advantageous as well. Whether you are just starting out or you are a twenty-year professional, expanding your training can be beneficial to you, your clients, and your company. Expanding your training can include many specialized areas:

Cooking Classes

Knowing your way around the kitchen can enhance your event-planning skills. If a cook burns his hand and cannot work, you can fill in depending on your skill level. Being familiar with a kitchen setting will also better prepare you to design menus.

Signing up for a cooking class is a good idea if you want to increase your knowledge of the culinary arts. In a beginner class you may learn basic kitchen skills and how to prepare simple recipes, while participating in an advanced class can inspire your culinary flair.

Wine Education

There is a seemingly infinite universe of information on wine. A beginner's class will teach you about the different ways wines can taste and ways to distinguish between varietals. Advanced learning will build your understanding about the idea of terroir and how a region's climate and soil contributes to the personality of a wine. Another benefit to a wine class is participating in the many wine tastings. Even if you do not enjoy wine, studying wine can increase your ability to suggest wines to your clients.

Business or Finance Courses

Studying business or finance can equip you with a firm understanding of the business side of the event-planning world. You'll learn about ways to manage your finances as well as the idea of budgets, profit and loss, and business management. No matter how glitzy an event is, it still needs to be properly accounted for on the administrative side.

Team-Building Workshops

Team-building workshops are a great tool for event planners. Methods for conflict resolution are introduced at team-building workshops. Communication techniques are also a highlight at these events. Event planners can translate social skills like trust and delegating to on-the-job management techniques.

Professional Writing Classes

With e-mail being the preferred way to communicate, a professional writing class should be a must for most professional people these days. Professional writing classes can also enhance basic skills you may have learned in school. Drafting a letter, designing a menu, or writing a biography are all writing assignments you may have to tackle in your career.

Photography Classes

Event planners as a profession wield cameras second only to photographers. In this line of work, part of your job will be snapping photos for your guests. Taking a photography class will allow you to learn basic lighting and focusing techniques. And while you may not be a professional with a camera, you will smile knowing your client will have a memorable shot.

Floral Design Training

A walk through a flower market with a client will give you more confidence if you are educated on botanicals. A floral design class will introduce you to annuals, perennials, and topiaries. Knowing what is in season and when will help you help your client decide on bouquets, centerpieces, and boutonnières months before the event.

Where to Find Event Planner Positions

The medical community, nonprofit organizations, and event-planning companies employ some of the positions detailed in the following sections. You may also find these positions exist to varying degrees outside of event-planning companies.

Development

The development staff is overseen by a senior event manager. Once the management team designs the event, the development staff will begin organizing the details for the event. The development team organizes invitations, rentals, and other specifics for an event. In large organizations, the development team can have a few hundred staff members in the department.

Fundraising

The fundraising staff within a company controls the communication with contributors. Members of the staff spearhead donation letter campaigns throughout the year as well as invitations to fundraisers. A senior member of a fundraising team may handle the accounting side of the fundraiser. Obtaining a tax identification number for the organization as well as managing the banking issues might fall under her responsibilities.

Nonprofit companies may appoint a senior staff member solely to liaise with key contributors. His responsibilities would include staying up-to-date with a sponsor using a personalized letter of contribution. Some nonprofit companies may also host events for key contributors that the senior fundraising staff member would organize and host.

Production

Once the development team has organized the event details, the information is passed along to the production team. In the days and weeks before the event, the production team stages the details to fit the venue. The production team may suggest the length of setup time, strategies for setup, and breakdown organization. On the day of the event, the production team is involved in the execution of the entire setup. A senior event manager usually supervises the development team.

Creative Department

The creative department brings the ideas of the event to life. The client will brainstorm with the creative department for concepts and design the event's theme. Once the creative department has met with the client, they set to work and turn inspiration into concrete details.

Once the client approves the details, the creative department partners up with the production team to execute the event.

Event Assistant

The event manager supervises the event assistant. The assistant will work alongside the event manager in an administrative role and may attend the event. While the event assistant usually does not have contact with the client, he is gaining valuable experience. Computer skills, communication techniques, and clerical proficiency are all developed while being an event assistant.

Event Manager

The event manager supervises all departments regarding her event. The event manager is the main point of contact for a client. She directs each department according to the client's needs. The event manager will also attend and supervise the event itself.

Senior Event Manager

An owner or acting partner may hold the title of senior event manager. The senior event manager supervises all of the event managers and steps in when conflict resolution is needed. The senior event manager may manage or supervise the accounting ends of the business. It is possible he may not directly design events on a daily basis but may only work on high-profile affairs.

Breaking into the event-planning industry takes as much creativity as planning an event. You must approach this task with good judgment and a positive outlook. If you are willing to adapt to different environments, you will make the most of each experience.

Chapter 5

The Role of an Event Planner

PART OF THE GLAMOUR of being an event planner is the chance to participate in high-society events. These events can be formal political affairs or high-energy soirees with music and dancing. The role of an event planner can easily become a confusing mix of work and pleasure. This chapter outlines your commitment to your client, how to manage staff, and your general role as an event planner.

Gaining Your Client's Trust

With your new event-planning career comes various new responsibilities. Your client is not only entrusting you with every detail of his event, he is also trusting you to spend his money wisely and within budget. Your responsibility extends to overseeing your vendors' products and managing your staff during the event.

Your client makes an enormous leap of faith when he puts his trust in you. Referrals from past clients will help you gain a potential client's trust. If you are new to this endeavor, the absence of referrals poses a larger problem. Your client will need your assurance that the event will run smoothly. There are certain measures you can take to gain your client's trust throughout the planning of his event.

Sign a Contract

Signing a contract with your client is the first step you can take to gain your client's trust. For your client, a contract is a legal document ensuring your services and costs. For you, a contract is a client's commitment to pay for your services. Deposits are usually taken when both parties sign the contract. Deposits can be a set amount or a percentage of the total service.

Events are extremely detail-oriented affairs; your client may become very detailed as a result. If the client questions the legal language used in the contract, explain terminology using layperson terms. If the client questions the omission of any service you promised to provide, you should offer to rewrite the contract. Using these suggestions in contract negotiations will strengthen your client's trust in you. A sample catering contract is provided in Appendix A.

 **Question**

What measures can I take to stay within the client's budget?
Knowing all of the costs associated with an event will ensure you stick close to a client's budget. This means educating yourself on the prices of rentals, flowers, and photographers and knowing the difference in price between a cocktail party with drinks and a five-course dinner paired with wine.

Refer to Past Experiences

Referring to past experiences similar to your client's event will also help in gaining your client's trust. Perhaps you were not the senior event planner during a past event. Your client will still be comforted to know your experience includes a similar event. You can also refer to past experiences of your company using an associate's experience.

For example, say your client is looking for a venue to plan her daughter's bat mitzvah. She is seeking an event planner with experience in planning bat mitzvahs. You, unfortunately, have not had this specific experience to add to your resume, but your country club has planned several bar mitzvahs in recent months. In your initial meeting with your client, invite your associate who has worked on many bar mitzvahs. When it comes time to discuss the details, your associate can speak on behalf of the country club's experience, assuring the client he will be available to oversee the details and be present the day of the event. Your client will trust you and your establishment because she has witnessed the team dynamic between you and your associate.

E ssential

Be careful when citing past experiences. You never want to mislead your client. If you were a junior event planner on an event, be sure to mention this to your client. But be sure to list all of the details you were responsible for as a junior planner on that event.

Use Positive Language

Using positive language is a great way to gain a client's trust. With positive language comes positive thinking from your client. If you think you can plan a great event, then your client will think the same. Following is a list of words and phrases to build trust in yourself and your client.

- "Certainly"
- "Of course"
- "On the same line of thinking"
- "I'd be happy to"
- "My pleasure"

If you are hesitant about a certain requested detail, mention your apprehension but assure your client you will let him know definitely one way or the other. If a client asks for a helicopter to land on the lawn out front, your initial reaction should be: "I'd be happy to check with the venue."

Positive language isn't meant as a tool to deceive a guest; it should be used in conjunction with honesty. Positive language is meant to reassure your client that his event will be memorable.

Fact

Many venues work on commission. If you are enlisting the help of an associate, be sure to offer some compensation for his time. If you are unsure, ask the advice of the owner or another senior planner to help you decide on a figure.

Anticipating Your Client's Needs

Anticipating a client's needs is crucial for success in the hospitality industry. The line of thinking in restaurants is to make something readily available to the guest before they ask for it. Have a knife on the table before a guest's steak arrives. Present a fresh napkin when a guest's napkin falls off his lap. Refill a guest's water glass when it is half empty. All of these are examples of ways restaurants anticipate guests' needs and increase the level of service. Event planners can do the same to enhance the client experience as well.

Staffing an Event

You may anticipate a client's needs by devising a formula for staffing and referring to it during the planning stages of the event. This document will be helpful when you are meeting with your client. A client may want to scale back on the number of valets for an event, but once you explain the consequences of not being properly staffed—guests waiting twenty minutes or more to enter the event—your client will realize being properly staffed is in the best interest of his guests.

Modifying Products

You can anticipate a client's needs by properly budgeting an event. For example, when a client asks you for a proposal and makes mention of a succulent feast she is envisioning, you should take this into account as you write the menu. To fit within her budget, you may need to modify the products used in the event. Explain to your client you would like to upgrade the menu by offering a filet of beef rather than a sirloin steak. To accomplish this and still remain in your client's budget, you offer downgrading the plate ware, flatware, and glassware.

Transportation and Lodging

Typically, event planners will offer services related to transportation and lodging. By anticipating the client's needs in this case, you are able to avoid mishaps the night of the event. If you ask the client what transportation his guests will need after a cocktail party, you will be opening the lines of communication and ensuring that he appears as a responsible host. Say the client hadn't thought of making any advance arrangements for his guests. What now? You can suggest booking a block of rooms for the client and adding the hotel information to the invitation. You can also suggest renting a shuttle if the guests are headed back to a similar destination. As a final resort, attach the phone number of a taxi company to the favor bags or arrange for a group of taxis to be waiting as guests leave the event.

 **Alert**

If alcohol will be served at the event, be diligent about training your servers and bartenders. TIPS (training for intervention procedures by servers of alcohol) is a certification program used to educate the hospitality industry about the effects of alcohol. Empower your staff to offer water or coffee if a guest is beginning to show signs of intoxication. Also, alert security and valets when alcohol is being served at your event.

Venue Setup

Ultimately you will have more experience than your client when it comes to planning events. Keep this in mind in the early planning stages and have a checklist of items your client will want to consider renting. Mention items he may have missed such as table number cards or candles. Refer to industry standards and do not let him skimp on essential items such as enough glassware. Simply say, "Industry standards suggest you have one martini glass for every guest during a cocktail party."

Have a floor plan accessible if a second site visit cannot be arranged. You will need to talk about the logistics of the dance floor, bar setup, buffet table, and so forth. If your client wants the registration table to be placed in the fire exit, for example, let her know it is a bad idea. Keeping silent about a client's uninformed judgment will reflect negatively on you in the end.

Managing an Event

Part of your role as an event planner is managing the event. Planning a glamorous event will not mean a thing to a client if you cannot execute it. You need to become the eyes and ears of the venue and oversee the setup. You are also the point person for all of your vendors. Being mindful of timing can save you stress during the setup time. When scheduling vendors and staff, be sure you leave enough time to set the stage for the day of the event.

You will need to make yourself available to your staff and your vendors during setup. Questions not covered on a staff itinerary may arise, so be visible at all times prior to the event. The staff and vendors will look to you to solve problems in case of any mishaps. Having a cell phone or walkie-talkie with you is a smart solution if the venue you are working in is particularly large. You will also want to greet your client when she arrives.

The staff you choose for an event ultimately reflects on you as the event planner. Your positive ability to manage a staff will create a better working environment and thus a better event. Treating your staff with respect, delegating tasks efficiently, and being professional will all make you a better manager. Having the right staff in place can make your event run smoother.

Cohosting an Event

Cohosting an event with another planner can be easier because you have a partner, but often the roles between two event planners are not so easily defined. A cohosted event can also result in missed details if you do not work together. You also need to be mindful of each other's schedules and responsibilities. There are many strategies you can employ to successfully cohost an event.

Create a Master Task Board

When partnering up with another planner, all tasks should be outlined on a master board. If you do not share the same office, an e-mail document can be passed easily back and forth. Together you and your partner will create the list detailing every task from beginning stages with the client to the event's end. Divide the list into monthly, weekly, and daily tasks, then divide the list into two separate and equal lists.

E ssential

There are many instances when event planners work together. A facility or hotel event planner or catering manager frequently teams up with event planners from the corporate, medical, and academic fields. Sometimes the share of the workload falls more on one planner. Take every occasion to even the tasks. It shows professionalism and goodwill—key attributes of a planner.

Communicating with Your Cohost

As you conquer the master task board, let your partner know of your progress daily. This can be done through a quick e-mail, phone call, or text message. Even though you have divided the list, one of you may take extra initiative to help the other out. Your partner may think she is doing you a favor by picking up the programs at the print shop only to find out you picked the programs up two days ago.

Meet All Vendors Together

Two heads are better than one. If you trust this old adage, let your new partnership be no exception. When you and your partner meet with each of your vendors and production team, your combined experience will enhance the execution of the event. If you forget a detail, chances are your partner will remember. In addition, as the venue planner, you need to be in meetings with the production crew and staff as your knowledge of the layout of the venue can aid in setup and staffing.

Include Each Other in Decisions

Including the other event planner in your decisions should be done with the same respect, professionalism, and goodwill you afford your client, staff, and vendors. Not including your partner in the decisions will seem sneaky and underhanded. Remember that your objectives are the same: to host a great event. Any added stress or tension between two event planners can jeopardize the quality of the event and your client's experience.

Recognize Mistakes

Take responsibility for mistakes you create and apologize immediately, first to your partner then to the client. When your partner makes a mistake, acknowledge the mistake and move on. Mishaps can and will occur. By being upfront and honest, your mistakes will be forgotten and your good character will take center stage.

Honesty Is a Virtue

The best event planner is an honest event planner. Event planning cannot be successful without honesty. As an event planner, your honesty may be tested on several levels. Following are two examples of challenging situations where your honesty may be called into question.

From the first meeting with the client to the many site visits and menu tastings to the event itself, you will benefit your client most if you are honest from the start. You are entitled to your opinion. For instance, you dislike the magenta tablecloths your client chose. That detail can be kept to yourself. But if on a site visit you are apprehensive about the quantity of guests that can fit in a venue, tell your client. You should question the size of the venue at the start rather than hearing your client complain about it during the follow-up call after the event is over.

A client has requested you count wine and liquor bottles with her at the end of an event. Counting bottles is a theft deterrent you can use to ensure your client is being properly charged for the bottles her guests drank. At first glance you notice a case of wine is missing. You investigate before the client has a chance to notice the missing case.

You quickly interrogate all of the bartenders first. Your interrogation came up with no leads. Your suspicion turns to the back-of-the-house crew, because the wine was being stored next to the kitchen. After interviewing the back of the house, you clear all suspects. Time is running out. The guests are on dessert and your client will be looking to settle the bill. Next on the roster of suspects: the front-of-the-house staff.

Your suspicion falls on two servers. While clearing desserts, the servers in question become anxious and nervous. The said servers try to avoid your questions.

Upon close examination of the employee area, you discover the case of wine among backpacks and jackets. You carry the wine upstairs to meet with your client. The bottles are counted and catastrophe is averted. You settle up with the client who is completely unaware of the theft.

 **Alert**

Disciplining your staff has its boundaries. You would like to keep employee infractions in-house to avoid negative exposure. Sometimes you will be forced to bring in law enforcement. When it comes to theft or drugs, let the police handle the crime.

After the event has ended you confront the two most suspicious individuals. The individuals confess, prompting disciplinary action. You have no choice but to terminate the servers. Theft is not to be tolerated. Because you returned the product to the client, you decide not to involve the police.

Your honesty will be called into question many times as an event planner. Whether it is correcting an invoice or deterring employee theft, being honest will protect your reputation.

Chapter 6

Organization

KEEPING TRACK OF all the details of an event can be a daunting task. However, the more organized you are, the better an event planner you will become. Organization can mean different things to everyone. "An organized mess" is, after all, a famous cliché. But in the event-planning world, being organized means that another event planner, relying on only your notes, can fill in for you if you happen to have an emergency. This chapter includes lots of great tips and strategies for setting up an organizational system for planning events.

Filing Systems

Your system of organization can be just as personal as the events you plan. Tailor a method of organizing to how you work. It is likely you will borrow techniques from other event planners along the way. The steps you take to manage your organization now will set the tone in your career for years to come.

File Cabinet

The first step to becoming organized is purchasing a good old-fashioned file cabinet. A file cabinet is perfect for organizing paperwork. Standard folders with tabs, used in conjunction with hanging file folders, work well in a file cabinet when used for each event. Place a name and date on each folder, and you are on your way.

However, if you are the type of person who follows the "out of sight, out of mind method," this choice may not work for you. Of course, you will still need a file cabinet to archive information from past events. But you, being a visual person, may like to have easier access to your events in progress. Having all of this information in folders on your desk is not ideal. Now what?

Question

How do I choose an organizational system that suits me?
The best way to determine how to organize your event-planning office is to evaluate the way you organize your personal life. If there are items and systems that work in your home life, do not hesitate to carry these over to your workspace.

Shadow Boxes or Cubicles

You would like to keep your events in progress accessible but not just sitting on your desk or atop a filing cabinet. Shadow file holders can be purchased and mounted on the wall. You can also invest in stackable cubicles or a large wall-mounted cubicle. You can organize each holder or cubicle a number of different ways.

One suggestion is labeling them each with a day of the week. All events in progress would be placed in their corresponding day of the week. For example, all functions falling on a Monday would be placed in the Monday holder. For larger offices, the same system can be used with a larger mounted unit, and each cubicle can be labeled with a month. All events in progress in May would be placed in the May cubicle. You could also label each cubicle with a letter of the alphabet, and the folders would be filed under the client's last name.

Try one method and test the waters before you decide which one is right for you.

Spindle

A spindle is a spike used in restaurant kitchens. Orders are spiked on the spindle when the order is completed. Sometimes chefs need to refer back to the order, which is why the orders are spiked rather than thrown away.

Using this same idea, investing in a spindle will help you organize your receipts. As an event planner, you will find yourself buying items for events from time to time. Whether these items are purchased for your company or for your client, keeping your receipts in a central area until the time comes to draw up an invoice will keep you organized.

Your Notes

Taking notes is a big part of your job as an event planner. You should take notes during every meeting and phone call with your client. During the initial phone call, jot notes about dates, times, budget, and costs quoted so you can have this information to refer back to in your initial meeting. Once you have finished your conversation, rewrite or type your notes in a precise format. By rewriting your notes, you will be able to better decipher your handwriting and give more detail to the potential client's inquiry.

 **Alert**

At times you may have to work from your car, an off-site location, or a satellite office. Having a briefcase or a clipboard with a storage compartment makes a great traveling office. Carry pens, a calendar, a calculator, business cards, and a notebook. A copy of your contacts' phone numbers is essential in case of a lost cell phone or computer crash.

Calendars

Calendars will be essential to your career as an event planner. Having at least two calendars that are updated weekly is best for proper organization. One will service your office, and the other should be kept on you for the times you will be working from home or taking calls on the road.

Multiple Calendars

Your office calendar should be the central repository of information for your organization. Your calendar should be filled with your events, client appointments, venue site visits, and vendor visits. When taking calls on the road, write any date information on your secondary calendar, and transfer any appointments to your main calendar. Using different colored pens for different types of appointments can be useful in a large office. Red can be used for all events, blue can be used for client appointments, and black can be used for vendor visits, and so forth.

E ssential

When working with more than one calendar, appointments may be written in one place but not the others. Be sure you devote time each week to reconciling your calendars so each of the calendars is updated.

Noting Inquiries on Your Calendar

The process of booking a client can take several days, if not weeks, to finalize. From the time you take an initial phone call to the initial meeting to a creative meeting, some time has most likely passed before you receive the deposit. For this reason, it is a good idea to write all inquiries on your calendar. This way if you have a potential client for the second Saturday in June, you can let any inquiries for the same day know the date may not be available. This information may affect small catering companies who cannot extend their staff with more than one event per day or a restaurant with only one private room to book. Larger event-planning companies usually can take on more than one event per day. Still, multiple inquiries will affect the house inventory of a large company that may need to outsource items such as plate ware, which will affect the quoting process.

Confirming Dates with Clients

Calendars are also a great way to reconfirm the date with a client. In the initial phone call with a client, you should confirm the date using the day of the week as well as the calendar date. This will eliminate future confusion if a potential client thinks November 20 falls on a Saturday when it really is a Monday. With every interaction about an inquiry, it is a good habit to confirm the date with your client.

Clipboards

Every event planner needs a good way of communicating. Whether you're a catering manager or corporate-meeting planner, some formal method to track the information that flows back and forth is needed. The catering manager needs to communicate with her chef. The corporate-meeting planner needs to communicate with the on-site representative. The clipboard method is commonly used in kitchens and can be used to communicate with chefs and other event planners in your office.

To initiate this technique, you will need to mount seven clipboards on a wall in the kitchen or in your office. Every clipboard is labeled with a day of the week. Every event will be organized on an event sheet that is placed on its corresponding day of the week. For example, all events taking place on a Friday will be placed on the Friday clipboard. The most recent event will be placed on top of the clipboard.

E Alert

It is a good idea to hang additional clipboards. One may be for the pastry chef for specialty orders. Another can be for the service manager for staffing. It is also wise to hang a clipboard to log any changes to the event sheets.

Benefits of the Clipboard Method

For chefs, this method is helpful because it aids in back-of-the-house staffing and ordering products for specialty menus. For associate event planners, the clipboard method helps determine staffing for the front of the house and in-house equipment that may not be available for an existing event. The benefits to using the clipboard method in restaurants and hotels are decreasing the risks of overbooking event space, insuring proper staffing for back-of-the-house and front-of-the-house employees, and ordering appropriate products and rentals.

Disadvantages of the Clipboard Method

The only disadvantage to using the clipboard method is the increase in paper supply since all sheets will need to be duplicated on a copier. One copy is placed on the clipboard in the kitchen and the other is placed in a three-ring-binder or clipboard in the office. This also becomes a factor when updating an event sheet. If a client changes the menus or time, all event sheets will need to be updated or recopied to stay current. Not updating information on event sheets can cause a breakdown in the communication process. For example, if the client has changed from a salad to a soup and the event sheet has not been updated, the chef may order the wrong ingredients. Having a system in place and checking daily with your chef will keep these mistakes from happening.

Photocopy Everything

As an event planner, you are also a facilitator to many vendors, other event planners, and possibly even an accounting department. You will need to be extremely organized to channel specific information to all of the people working on an event. While the chef will be planning the menu and staffing the kitchen, other members of your team may be responsible for aspects of the event. These responsibilities may include staffing for the front-of-the-house employees, ordering wine, or invoicing the client. It is part of your responsibility to have this information readily available to your event-planning team in a BEO (banquet event order) or event sheet. Every time your event sheet or BEO is updated, you will want to photocopy a revised version to send it to the different departments involved in the event.

In addition, you are also responsible for all expenditures you accrue while planning an event. This may mean itemizing a parking receipt to your company or submitting a receipt for flowers to your client. A good practice for event planners to use is to photocopy all necessary documents.

E ssential

Organizing Folders

When planning an event, keep three folders in rotation. The first folder is the master folder to be kept in your office at all times. In this folder you should keep any original notes you have taken, a copy of your rewritten notes, a copy of your client's deposit check, vendor information, and an updated event sheet. The master folder should also hold any contracts relevant to the event.

The second folder is your traveling folder. This is the information you will need to access every day. In this folder you should keep a copy of your rewritten notes, an updated event sheet, vendor information, and a task list for the event. One organizational technique is writing your task list, with due dates, on the front of your traveling folder. This way your tasks will be the first thing you see when picking up this folder. Date each task once it is completed. Other necessary items for your traveling folder are the client contract and vendor contracts.

The third folder is your client folder. Your client may need to have access to any documentation in this folder. Copies of receipts, copies of contracts, and vendor information should be in this folder. Remember, if your company is arranging for your client's flowers, you are allowed to add a surcharge for this service (determined by your company). The receipt for the flowers would not be in the client folder in this case. The client may arrange for the flowers and purchase them herself, in which case the receipt would belong in the client's folder. In another example, the client may arrange for the flowers to be billed through your company. Payment for the flowers would then need to be reimbursed by your client. In this case, you would submit the receipt to your accounting office and to your client, and the receipt would be placed in your client folder.

 Fact

A purchase order (PO) is a legal document used by companies to secure products intended for delivery. The PO lists quantities, buyer information, and delivery information. In event planning, purchase orders are used by some vendors. Once the purchase order is signed by the event planner, it is legally binding.

Which materials are considered necessary? This really depends on which type of event planning you find yourself working.

If you are holding the original document, photocopy the item. The copy is for your client folder, and the original is for your office master folder. Photocopy all receipts and purchase orders from other vendors. This will aid in coordinating deliveries.

Double-Checking Invoices

Before submitting your invoice and the invoices of your vendors to your client, it is a good practice to examine the totals against the original quotes. As an event planner, you have a fiscal responsibility to your client. When the time comes to hand the client her folder with all invoices and receipts, be sure all invoices are correct. This detail ensures your quality as an event planner.

Mistakes on an Invoice

Imagine you are researching your client's invoice and you discover a mistake in the caterer's invoice. The amount in question favors the caterer and is over the quote given to the client. What should you do? The caterer was a recommendation from you to your client. Any sense of impropriety may fall on you as well as the caterer. Your obligation is to the client to correct any mistakes on the invoice. As a courtesy, call the caterer and point out the error. It was most likely a miscalculation and can be easily rectified.

When an Invoice and a Quote Do Not Match

An overage can be the result of an extra service or menu item the caterer offered to supply. Ask the caterer to send over a new invoice explaining the discrepancy in amounts. When the client views the invoice, the client will realize the difference in price came from an additional service he requested.

Be certain the client has approved the additional services. Any amounts charged to the client without his knowledge may not be his responsibility. If the caterer decided at the last minute to hire an additional server without the client's knowledge, the caterer should absorb this extra charge.

 Alert

Store receipts are often printed on a special type of paper called thermal paper. It is important that you photocopy these receipts right away because the ink on the thermal paper fades over time. A photocopied version ensures the accuracy of the receipt even after a few months have passed.

Your Responsibility to Client and Vendor

Remember, you not only have a fiscal responsibility to your client regarding your vendors, but you should also feel a responsibility for the vendor's performance at the event. In most cases, the vendor has come recommended by you. Keep this in mind when following up with your client. Consider your client's feedback, both positive and negative, when it comes time to recommend the vendor again.

On the same note, you are acting as an intermediary between your client and your vendors. You have an obligation to your vendor as well. This obligation is to guarantee your vendor is paid on time, assuming his responsibility to your client is met. Your client and her guests should also treat your vendors and their staff with respect and courtesy during the event.

E ssential

In most cases, vendors are paid a deposit in advance and the balance the night of the event. Event planners are sometimes paid in the same manner. As an additional service, you may offer your client to disburse payment, usually in the form of checks, directly to the vendors. This is one less detail your client will have to worry about during the event.

The Key to Being Thorough

Your office should be neat and tidy. At the very least, it should have some sense of organization, especially if this is the place where you will meet a client for the first time. Training yourself to be thorough requires some discipline.

Give yourself a half hour at the end or beginning of each day to devote to administrative work. Dedicate this time to photocopying, filing, and faxing. Ideally this time would be a half hour before or after your scheduled office hours. Then, once your office hours begin, you are able to focus on phone calls, e-mails, and meetings with clients.

Make this time to organize yourself a priority. Schedule this half hour as you would an appointment you are not allowed to break. Slowing down your hectic schedule to make time for administrative work will make a world of difference in your organizational skills.

Keeping yourself organized throughout the planning process will guarantee you less stress the day of the event. Digging yourself out from a pile of paperwork is not where you want to find yourself the day of the event. Ideally your invoice and all necessary documents are waiting in your briefcase three days before the event, ready for you to hand to the client at the end of the evening.

Chapter 7

Establishing and Maintaining Relationships

AS AN EVENT PLANNER, you will have many opportunities to build relationships during your career. The relationships you nurture may determine how successful you become in the industry. Since event planning has a large role in the hospitality business, your reputation in this industry is very important. This chapter will help you become the ambassador of hospitality, whether the relationship is with your clients, vendors, staff, or other event planners.

The Client Relationship

Clients, and your relationships with them, will vary tremendously. The client relationship can be extremely businesslike or ultracasual and everything in between.

With some clients it will be appropriate for you to wear a business suit to meetings. With other clients you may feel comfortable meeting over cocktails after office hours. The level of your client relationship will be determined by the client's personality, not your own. Until your client relationship has been defined, take steps to ensure you are off on the right foot.

Alert

Meeting with a client after hours may add a level of casualness to your relationship. It is possible to become friendly with a client considering some large events take dozens of hours to plan. Be sure to keep your relationship professional at all times.

The first contact with a client leaves a lasting impression. Your phone etiquette, manners, and communication skills will pave the road to a successful relationship. Adhering to some industry basics will build your communication skills, thus giving you the confidence to interact with your clients.

Professionalism

The field of event planning you enter will dictate the level of professionalism required. In a corporate situation, the dress is typically business attire in a formal business environment. Restaurant event planners adhere to business casual attire within a restaurant's more relaxed environment. Event-planning companies are typically casual around the office. When it comes time for the event, the staff will match dress appropriately for the type of event.

Essential

A staff's uniform is a small but important detail that shouldn't be overlooked during an event. Have staff members dress the same so as to be visible to guests. Black pants and a button-down shirt are an industry standard. Use feminine tailored cuts for the women and leave the ties and bowties for the men.

Within the industry, all event planners should aim for a consistently high level of professionalism. This professional standard can translate to all events, from the very casual to the very formal. Professional does not always mean stodgy. Do not be afraid to allow your personality to mix with your professionalism—great planners have both of these attributes. Follow the tips below to boost your professionalism.

- When a person walks into your office, acknowledge her. Even a mail courier can become a potential client.
- Limit personal conversations in the office.

- Chewing gum is a no-no. Switch to breath mints.
- Always be ready to see a client. Often as an event planner you will be pitching in on event days to help with the workload. The tendency is to dress down when the time comes to load supplies, set up chairs, and decorate tables. Keep a professional appearance at all times.
- Maintain eye contact when talking with a client.
- Keep a calm demeanor. Do not let outside influences or stress affect your day.
- Treat every client like a VIP.

Phone Etiquette

While planning an event with a client, chances are you will be speaking with him over the phone quite a bit. Your client might have even chosen you as his event planner based upon your phone etiquette. There might even be times when the only communication you have with a client is over the phone. In most fields of event planning, proper phone etiquette will be utilized on a daily basis. Here are some basic phone etiquette guidelines:

- Smile when answering the phone—it really makes a difference. If you are hiring a receptionist, his personality should be just as important as his appearance and administration skills.
- Answer the phone by the second ring.
- If a call is waiting on hold, be sure to tell the second caller how long you will be. If you cannot get to the caller in thirty seconds, tell her you will call her back.
- Always ask callers if they mind being put on hold. Most people do not mind being put on hold for a few seconds.
- Pre-empt putting a call on hold by asking the caller for his name and phone number. This way if you are experiencing a heavy call volume, you will not have to put the caller on hold; you can call him back and give him your undivided attention.

- Do not put a call on hold more than twice, and do not keep the call on hold for more than thirty seconds. By offering to call back you are valuing the caller's time.
- Return voice mail messages and e-mails. Leave an outgoing message if you will not be available by phone for a day or more.
- Prioritize your calls. Take any new business calls first. Next, take your existing client's calls followed by your vendor's phone calls. Any marketing, personal, accounting, or sales calls should be taken last.
- If at all possible, make all of your calls from your office phone rather than a cell phone. If you are speaking to a client while driving, you will be distracted and not able to take notes, not to mention the staticky connections and dropped calls that will cause you to lose information. It is also illegal to use a cell phone while driving in some states and jurisdictions.

Manners

When interacting with clients, either over the phone or in person, your manners set the tone for your relationship with your client. Many times in the business world manners often take a backseat to getting the job done. Using good manners as an event planner will have a trickle-down effect, starting with your client and moving down to your vendors and your staff. Here are some basic rules to increase your manners with your client:

- Saying "please" and "thank you" goes a long way.
- Thank your client for his time after a meeting. And thank him for his patience when applicable.
- When communicating with your client, keep to the 9-to-5 rules. No calls outside of this time unless a client specifically requests you call her at home at 7 P.M. This is a good business practice, and even if your clients do not stick to this rule, you should.
- Send an e-mail. It is 7 A.M. and you have forgotten the type of coffee your client requested for his board meeting next

week. What should you do? Send an e-mail apologizing for the missed detail and inappropriate timing of your e-mail. Ask the client to call you as soon as he receives the e-mail.

- Allow minimal interruptions when meeting with a client.
- Be punctual.

Dealing with Difficult Clients

Becoming at odds with a client is easier than you may think. Planning an event can be an emotional experience for some, and when emotions run high a client may not show you her best side. Keeping a level of professionalism and maintaining your composure can help in the most difficult of situations with a client. Follow the suggestions below when dealing with a difficult client:

- **Listen to complaints.** In some cases, a client may need a person to hear her complaints. The complaints may or may not have to do with your performance. You may be performing a great service to your client just by listening to her.
- **Acknowledge complaints.** If the client has a complaint, acknowledge and correct it if possible. This includes any complaints regarding your vendors.
- **Ask your client for suggestions.** You may not know how to repair a relationship with a client, but she may have some ideas. When appropriate, ask a client how she would like to see a problem resolved. Give yourself a day to consider her request. Your client may soften knowing you attempted to fix the problem.
- **Challenge yourself.** Turn the difficult guest into a lifelong client by developing creative ways to win back a difficult client.
- **Exceed the client's expectations.** When the client has stated her needs, add in a few extra services. Offer to pick up the invitations or make guest nametags. With the extra attention, your client is sure to come around.
- **Turn a negative into a positive.** If a client complains to you about details from a past event, use this information to your

advantage. The complaint may have been that there were no vegetarian items on a past event's menu. With information such as this, alert your chef.

- **Walk away from a difficult situation.** There may be a time in your career as an event planner when you may decide to cut your losses and walk away from a client. Open a dialogue with your client by saying, "It seems to me, you are unhappy with my performance." This may give your client a chance to address her difficult behavior or it may give her an opportunity to end the business relationship as well. In the latter scenario, offer to assist her in finding another event planner. Give a courtesy call to the event planner when you refer a difficult client. It is an industry standard.

Keeping in Contact with Clients

Once the event is over, it does not mean your relationship with the client has to end. Keep former clients in communication with your company by sending a newsletter or e-mail blast. The newsletter may include recent press or information about charity events or new employees. A newsletter can be used as a marketing tool when sent ahead of time. If you are attempting to attract business for the holidays, send your newsletter in October to be fresh in the minds of those who are planning holiday parties.

Keep your newsletters interesting as well as informative for your readers. In addition to providing holiday wishes and extended hours, suggest gourmet holiday advice. Add recipes, wine pairings, and festive cocktail recipes to the newsletter.

Handling Subclients

A subclient is a client who is working with your primary client to plan an event. The primary client owns the distinction of paying the final bill, while a subclient mostly aids in the creative process. A few examples of subclients are:

- **A bride planning her wedding with her parents.** The bride is a subclient because her parents are paying for the event.

- **A bride planning her wedding with her future in-laws.** Her fiancé's parents are the subclients because she is not relying on any outside monetary contribution for her wedding.
- **A mother planning a bar mitzvah.** Her son is the subclient in this situation.
- **An administrative assistant planning a dinner for her employer.** In this case the employer is the primary client and her assistant is the subclient.

Having a client relationship with a subclient can be tricky. This holds especially true when the two have completely different creative ideas. You can alleviate this difficult situation by being the intermediary between the two parties.

Having a subclient essentially means you have two clients; one just has more impact on decisions. Discounting the role of the subclient will not benefit either of you. In your initial creative meeting, stay open to the ideas of both the client and the subclient. Take notes and be creative to find solutions that will make both of your clients happy. When possible, involve the subclient in the schedule of events so he will feel included.

 Fact

Working with a subclient may leave you feeling uneasy about the outcome. Having two contacts can lead to miscommunication. This can affect the event in a negative way. Do not be afraid to add an amendment to your contract stating that the signer of the contract has all rights pertaining to decisions about the event.

When working with more than one client, it is good practice to confirm all of the details via e-mail or with a written itinerary. Many ideas and details will flow between you and your clients. It is easy for one of the individuals involved to leave a meeting with a misunderstanding of the sequence of events. Be sure to copy both the client and subclient on all correspondence. Never allow a subclient to make changes to an event without informing your primary client. Be subtle, but you can explain to both parties that you confirm all changes through e-mail. Wait for a response before you put any changes into motion.

Establishing Good Vendor Relations

Having a solid relationship with your vendors can make you more efficient as an event planner. Imagine not having to take the time to choose floral arrangements because your floral designer is always spot on in her creations. Picture a relationship with your caterer in which you can choose a menu without scheduling a tasting because his cuisine is always magnificent. Developing your vendor relations will save you stress and time, both of which you can save for planning more events.

 Question

How can I convince a client that the vendor I recommend is trustworthy?

In some cases, a client may need more than your word when it comes to recommending a vendor. The Better Business Bureau is a good resource for checking a vendor's background. While past references will feature positive client feedback, the Better Business Bureau tracks complaints as well.

The Vendor Cast of Characters

Your vendor list will vary depending on your field of event planning. When shopping for a vendor, ask other event planners for recommendations. You can also ask the company for referrals from other clients in the industry. Be sure to call the company for a full report before you decide to hire a vendor. As with event planners, vendors rely heavily on their reputations to be successful. You might find yourself looking for the following vendors when you begin your career.

- Caterer
- Floral designer
- Specialty baker
- Purveyors, which includes companies selling produce, seafood, meat products, and beverages
- Wine and beer companies
- Liquor distributors
- Labor companies, which includes electricians, general contractors, carpenters, and painters
- Photographers
- Graphic designer or Web designer
- Specialty stationery designer or printing company

Working with an Existing Vendor List

You may also find you are entering into a position with an existing vendor list. Ask your new associates how the relationship between the company and the vendor has been in the past. When appropriate, schedule a meeting with the vendor to introduce yourself. During the meeting you should get an idea of the existing process of ordering, delivering, and billing. You should reserve offering suggestions until you have worked with the company for a few months.

Creating Goodwill among Your Vendors

If your goal is to develop a healthy relationship with a vendor, you must make a conscious effort to show your appreciation. Here are some suggestions to create goodwill and develop your vendor relationships.

- **Offer a drink to your delivery people.** Restaurants have the luxury of offering this service to their vendors. If you are working in an office, keep coffee, sodas, and bottled water on hand for company drivers.
- **Provide vendor meals.** Do so not only for your staff but also for vendors who may be working to set up an event. This simple act encourages staff relationships and builds a sense of community.

- **Have a volunteer day.** Choose a charity and get your company, vendors, and staff involved.
- **Invite vendors to events.** When appropriate, put your vendors on the guest list of an event your company is hosting.
- **Offer your services.** If your wine rep is planning his wife's birthday party, offer to help at no charge.
- **Extend an invitation to company parties.** Holiday staff parties are a great way to integrate vendors into your company.
- **Don't forget the special touches.** If you are the event planner for a hotel and know your baker is celebrating his anniversary, offer a complimentary hotel room. If you are the event planner for a restaurant, you can invite your vendors in for a complimentary meal. Event planners often receive perks such as concert tickets from clients, so remember your vendors if you cannot use the tickets yourself.

Repairing a Relationship with a Vendor

It is possible a relationship with a vendor may strain at some point in your career. You should make every effort to repair the relationship. Misunderstandings often occur in the heat of the moment when staging an event. Tempers and emotions flare at this time between two otherwise calm people. Perhaps a rift was the result. In this case, an apology in your thank-you letter may solve this matter.

Working Toward a Solution

In the instance of larger disagreements, the first step to mending the working relationship is to have a meeting with your vendor. Revisit a disagreement after a few days have passed, to give both parties some clarity. Begin the meeting by addressing the problem, then listen to your vendor's side of the story. Accept your responsibility in the matter and apologize. If warranted, address any issues you may be having with your vendor, and hopefully he will return the apology and you both can continue working together.

Fact

For all vendor and client disputes, it is a good idea to chronicle the circumstances around the event. If a staff member is involved, ask her to write a statement while the details are fresh in her mind. File all statements together in the event's folder for future reference.

Monetary Issues

If the matter involves a monetary issue, try and invite a third party to resolve the dispute. The third party should be someone you both have worked with and trust. Another event planner or vendor would be good choices for a third party. If the matter involves a client and a complaint, you might ask the client how she would like the matter resolved and recommend this to your vendor. For example, your baker created an elaborate cake for your client's twenty-fifth wedding anniversary. The cake was supposed to include four layers, and each layer was to have a different flavor, but one of the flavors was missing. You contact your client, who is asking for a 25-percent refund on her cake. You agree this is a reasonable request and set up a meeting to discuss the matter. The baker agrees to refund the amount with a letter of apology. The solution to this problem has satisfied the three parties involved. Because your baker has rectified the complaint, you can continue your working relationship.

Knowing When to Walk Away

Sometimes a sour vendor relationship has passed the point of repair. If you have followed all the suggested tips for repairing a relationship, it may be time to walk away.

It is best to make a clean break. Do not embellish or gossip to other vendors or event planners. A vendor can also gossip about his experience working for you. Make it a practice not to speak negatively about vendors. Simply stating you used to work with a vendor but no longer do will speak volumes to a client asking for a vendor referral. You will still be dignified in your response and still get your point across.

Nurturing Staff Relationships

Much like developing a solid core of vendors, establishing a dependable staff will help your events run more efficiently. The more dependable your staff, the more work that can be delegated to each staff member. This will lighten your workload significantly so you can do more marketing. Having a dependable staff can also save you stress on the day of the event.

These days it is not enough to simply pay your staff well. The day-to-day atmosphere in your office is almost as important as the salary you are offering. Gaining the reputation for being a great employer can also attract individuals even when the salary you are offering is not competitive. Here are some ways to create a dedicated group of employees.

- **Create a sense of pride in the workplace.** When you take your job seriously and have pride in your career, others will as well. Never speak negatively about an event, clients, vendors, or other employees.
- **Offer benefits.** If possible, offer health insurance to your employees as well as vacation time and 401(k) packages.
- **Offer a competitive salary.** Salaries will vary depending on where you are located. Ask other event planners for salary recommendations. If your company cannot pay a competitive salary, get creative with bonus programs and gratuities.
- **Recognize special occasions.** When possible, celebrate employee birthdays and other special occasions such as anniversaries, the birth of a baby, or the purchase of a new home.
- **Go on a field trip.** Plan a field trip to a setting similar to the industry you're in. A vineyard, brewery, oyster farm, or chocolate factory would be good choices for event staff members in the food and beverage industry.
- **Provide staff meals.** Show your appreciation for your staff by feeding them on event or setup days. Staff meals are also a great time for your staff to socialize and build relationships.

- **Get involved in charitable causes.** Organize your staff to volunteer at a local charity. It is a great way to build camaraderie and help your community.
- **Organize a seminar.** An educational seminar can get your staff excited about furthering their careers in the field. The seminar could include a lecture on calligraphy or cognac. A seminar on savings plans offered by a local banker or a motivational speaker could benefit staff members.
- **Plan an event for your staff.** It can be a holiday party in January (perfectly acceptable in this industry) or a barbeque in June. Celebrate your staff and the accomplishments of your company.
- **Establish trade in your community.** Many companies are willing to create trade accounts. Assess what you have to offer, whether it is a gift certificate to your company or your services for another company's event. Disperse the trade among your staff for good deeds.

When you take the time to nurture your staff, the rewards will come back to you. You will develop a loyal, honest, professional group of people dedicated to working hard for you and your company. Your staff will be your strongest asset when planning and executing successful events.

Considering Other Contacts to Make

Outside of your client, staff, and vendor relationships, there are companies or individuals you may not work with on a regular basis but still want to be on good terms with. Developing a relationship with members of different industries and communities has its benefits.

Event Planners

Collaborating with other event planners in your area is a good practice for many different reasons. The biggest advantage is creating business for each other. Your venue may not be perfect for every client, and there will be times your company cannot take on another client. When this occurs, it would be beneficial for you to refer an inquiry to an event planner in your area. Hopefully when other event planners find themselves in a similar situation the inquiry will come back to you.

Sharing resources with other event planners is another reason to nurture these relationships. The instant your client has requested a midori green martini glass, you will be thankful you have an event planner on speed dial when he has six cases of glasses for you to borrow. Finally, you can come to depend on other event planners for referrals for vendors, purveyors, and labor companies. Event planners share similar needs for events. Why not share similar experiences with each other as well?

Medical Staff

Developing a relationship with members of the medical community in your area is a great channel to explore. The medical community frequently seeks venues for various events during the calendar year. Some examples of events include staff functions, entertaining visiting physicians, and recruitment dinners.

In larger medical communities, locating a point person to market your company to can prove to be difficult. Schedule an appointment with the human resources department in a hospital. The medical community is also a great outlet to turn to when coordinating charity events and volunteer efforts.

Members of the Art Community

The arts community and event planners are always searching for ways to support each other. It may mean a gallery or exhibit opening paired with a cocktail hour. The opportunity may present itself for a book signing and author luncheon. A gala may take place around an annual symphony performance.

Visiting individual theaters, museums, boutiques, and galleries is the best way to make contact with event planners in the art community. Being affiliated with members of the art community has the added benefit of attracting press. Newspapers, magazines, and television are always covering news in the arts. Hosting these events is an easy way to get your company's name in print or on the air.

Chapter 8

Marketing

MARKETING IS THE STRATEGY of attracting new business and securing repeat clients. For most event planners, marketing falls within their job description. The challenging aspect of marketing is discovering new and innovative ways to keep your name in the spotlight. Some event-planning companies and most corporations employ marketing departments. If you decide to work in the corporate sector of event planning, your marketing skills may not be called upon. For all other event planners, prepare to master the art of marketing.

Letters of Reference

As you begin to accumulate events under your belt, start asking clients for letters of reference. A letter of reference in the event planning field can be as informal as a thank-you note from a client or as formal as a character letter from a previous employer. Letters of reference can be used in conjunction with photos from an event or testimonial for an advertisement.

The Goal

The goal of a letter of reference is to build your reputation as a quality event planner. For this reason, the letters should be from positive client experiences. For example, if a client wrote a letter singing your praises but complained about the photographer you recommended, you would not use this particular letter as a letter of reference.

A potential client shopping for an event planner may ask for a past client referral. You can also archive this material to present to future employers. Be sure to date the letters and use the most recent ones when presenting to a client.

Who Should I Ask for a Letter?

Before becoming an event planner, ask your previous employers for a letter. You can suggest your employer include skills or attributes you have mastered that relate to event planning. Also ask your supervisor for any client letters in which you were thanked or named personally. Once you become an event planner, you should approach any satisfied client with a request to write a letter on your behalf. This request can be mentioned at the end of your follow-up call.

Event planners display these letters or quotes from the letters in a number of ways:

- Framed in the office
- In a scrapbook
- On a Web site

Find a creative way to display letters of praise. Or for a more subtle approach, simply state "letters of reference are available upon request" on printed material and brochures.

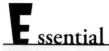

The old adage stating that it is better to give than receive could also refer to thank-you notes. Make a habit of sending notes following an event and you will be sure to receive plenty in return.

Business Cards and Collateral Materials

Collateral items are the tangible marketing pieces that your clients take with them as a way to network your business. Trifold pamphlets, folders, brochures, and business cards are all examples of collateral. You may also decide to pass along items such as pens, refrigerator magnets, or glassware. Be sure to place your company's logo, phone number, and Web address on the item.

Separate from collateral, you may develop a scrapbook to take with you to prospective clients. This book or folder may include the following:

- Pictures of past events from your resume
- Letters of reference from previous satisfied clients
- Thank-you letters from clients, staff, and vendors
- Your biography
- Sample menus you have developed
- A list of recommended vendors with their collateral

Alert

Collateral items are great to pass along as long as they are of good quality. A pen with your logo on it becomes embarrassing if it does not write properly. When ordering items online, ask the company for a sample before placing an order. When the samples arrive, you can check the quality without losing money.

Designing Collateral

When possible, enlist the talent of a professional to design collateral. Resist the urge to order supplies over the Internet if you are not familiar with a printing company. Consulting with a graphic designer will add another level of quality and creativity to your collateral.

Before designing your printed material, think of your target audience. Choose colors, logos, and themes based upon your demographic. For example, wedding event planners might choose a romantic theme for collateral while meeting planners may opt for a classic business image. Party planners will want more festive collateral appealing to a general audience.

How to Dispense Collateral

Again, determine your target audience. Ask yourself which local businesses will be interested in your services. Set up a meeting with a contact person in the company you are soliciting. Write a personal note, and leave your business card if you are unable to meet with someone directly. Remember, the packaging for the materials you are leaving behind is as important as the material itself. Do not forget to consult your graphic designer for a folder to encase your collateral. Use a smart enclosure when packaging your brochures, menus, and business cards. There is a lot of new and creative packaging on the market today. Use richly colored folders with classic fonts for a look that will never go out of style.

 Fact

Some examples of classic fonts: *Edwardwian Script*, *Lucida Blackletter*, *Monotype Corsiva*, and *Snell Roundhand*.

Utilize your vendors to showcase your collateral, as they will be a tremendous resource for marketing your materials. Your vendors will be more inclined to keep your collateral on hand if you agree to return the favor. Ask your network of contacts to keep your material on hand. Your network may include:

- Vendors, purveyors, and labor
- Restaurants
- Other event planners
- Hotels and concierges
- Your city's travel and convention bureau

Online Newsletters
Web sites such as Constantcontact.com make it easy to create newsletters and e-mail blasts with their template and group e-mail list. Build your e-mail list using administrative policies within the company. For example, send confirmation only by e-mail. You can also request e-mail addresses when sending menus or contracts. Every inquiry to your company can become a future e-mail address.

You Are a Marketing Tool, Too

When you are out on the town, always carry your business cards. Seize every opportunity to talk about your business. You never know when you will be seated next to a newly engaged couple at a restaurant or a corporate event planner needing meeting space.

Advertising

Media outlets are a great way to promote your business, but it is a very expensive way to advertise. Before deciding if you are going to advertise, you must determine how much money you can devote to advertising. Most new businesses have a very tight budget when it comes to advertising.

If your advertising dollars are small, you should develop an effective marketing strategy while staying within your budget. First, research the advertising packages in as many media outlets as possible. An advertising package will contain the price for the different types of advertisements offered by each media outlet. When you are meeting with the sales representative for the first time, determine the length of the advertisement versus the cost.

Radio

For example, if a popular radio station's ad costs $750 for a ten-second spot during rush hour, you may be able to spend the same $750 and receive a thirty-second spot during the late evening time slot. The sales representative will help you determine which demographic would be more beneficial for you.

E ssential

In the beginning you may not have the money to spend on a graphic designer. Offer to pay a talented art or photography student to design your collateral. Students will take a fraction of the fee of a professional graphic designer. In exchange a student will add the work to his portfolio.

Magazines

When you consider advertising in a magazine, you will need to compare the prices of the different size advertisements. You will also need to consider the editorial calendar of the publication. For example, a magazine may be printed every month with advertisements costing $600 for a quarter page. Another magazine may be printed every two weeks with quarter-page ads costing $400. It may benefit you to advertise with the monthly publication to save $200 per month. You also need to ask yourself which magazine targets your demographic best. Your sales representative will provide you with demographic information.

 Question

How can I find my demographic?
Demographic is an advertising term used to describe a target market. Just as you have created your niche market, your demographic is usually the same intended audience. A corporate event planner would not use her budget to advertise in a sporting magazine because sporting events are not her demographic.

For wedding planners and banquet event planners, it is wise to focus on advertising in wedding magazines and the Knot.com. Similarly, fundraising event planners working with health events such as walks and marathons should focus on advertising in health magazines. Advertising in trade show publications can also increase your exposure. This type of advertising is short-lived, so it can be relatively inexpensive, but it targets a precise audience. Bridal shows are a good example of trade show advertising. A bridal magazine may sponsor a bridal show, or a local magazine may publish a special bridal edition and couple it with a trade show.

Fact

The positive side to advertising in media is working with a creative department that does the copy and artwork for your advertisement. Media outlets will provide you with this service at no cost. Be sure to confirm with the sales representative what services are provided. Ask to use the same copy and artwork in your collateral to save money.

Trade for Advertising

You may have a small budget when it comes to advertising, so consider trading or bartering your services for advertisement space. For example, as a hotel event planner you can exchange hotel rooms for a magazine company in need of housing for out-of-town clients. As a restaurant event planner you may offer to host a radio station's holiday party in exchange for radio advertisements.

Typically the trade value of your service is equal to the dollar amount of the ad. You can approach many businesses for trade including newspapers, magazines, television, Web sites, and radio. Restaurants and airlines are famous for trade. Trade quotes are often inflated to balance the price of the advertisement. Never discount your prices in a barter situation.

Press Coverage

Successful marketing often entails getting press coverage. Press of all kinds, whether it is print, television, radio, or Internet, will translate into exposure for your business. Finding creative marketing solutions through the press for your company can mean advertising without paying for an advertisement.

Meet the Press

Arts, entertainment, and charity events are among the many types of social events the press cover. The press may cover an event for a celebrity appearance or a political cause. One thing is for certain, when the press is at your event, you want to be sure your company is mentioned.

The first step to securing press at your event is extending an invitation when appropriate. All press should have full access to the event free of charge. Be certain you have indicated the members of the press on all guest lists or provided each with a press pass. With any luck, inviting members of the press will result in a feature article before or after the event. Sometimes, advertising in magazines secures coverage of your event in a feature article or editorial.

Using Awards to Your Advantage

A very popular trend nowadays in the media is to give awards to local businesses in various industries. These "best" awards carry some weight when it comes to advertising. Part of the benefit in winning these awards is the opportunity to gain free advertising through the media. A television station, newspaper, or magazine may be the source of the award. The recipients, whether it is a restaurant, salon, or boutique, are guaranteed exposure when time comes to release the winners. Often the media will dedicate a Web site page to the winners and provide a link to the winners' Web sites. Becoming the recipient of one of these awards also means you can use the award as a marketing tool on your Web site and collateral.

Hosting an Event for Event Planners

In lieu of advertising, there are some crafty ways to target your ideal demographic—other event planners! What is the best way to show off your space to event planners? Throw an event-planners event. With your financial resources, you can team up with vendors and purveyors to host a cocktail reception for planners in your area. Having a vendor donate her time and product with a purveyor also donating his time is ideal. You can design an evening for planners to network and socialize while showcasing your space and services.

Collaborate with Vendors

First, choose a team of your favorite photographers, floral designers, pastry chefs, and caterers if appropriate. If you employ an in-house chef and pastry chef, chances are you will not want to invite another chef. Next, ask your purveyors for donations of food, wine, and alcohol. Explain that the event is for other event planners in the area and the products donated will be featured and promoted during the event. An event such as this will showcase your vendors' and purveyors' products. This event will be a benefit to everyone's marketing efforts.

Restaurant tastings have been increasing in popularity. A restaurant tasting usually takes place in a large open space with many tables. A different restaurant serves a specialty dish at each table, allowing guests to sample from each restaurant. Local breweries and wineries may also be featured at the tables for these events.

Handpick your invites—you can be exclusive without excluding anyone. Use an online service such as E-vite (*www.evite.com*) and follow up with a phone call to add another level of exclusivity to the event. You can mix up the invites to include meeting planners and facility planners. This will create a universal networking environment. Do not forget to invite your vendors and purveyors to the event to network and socialize as well.

Benefits

The benefits to hosting an event for local event planners include:

- Showcasing your space and cuisine to other event planners will increase business.
- The word-of-mouth marketing will extend well beyond the partygoers and create a buzz around the event before and after it takes place.

- Those invited will appreciate the gesture of goodwill you have extended to the event-planning community.
- Volunteers and donors will also appreciate the gesture of goodwill. With any luck, you will have created an air of exclusivity around the event.
- This event will give you the opportunity to not only socialize and network but also market your services.

Alert

When deciding on a date for industry events, pay particular attention to the day of the week. The weekends would be unadvisable since most restaurant and hotel staff work on these days. A Sunday or Monday evening would be a better choice since some restaurants close on these days and it is a slower night for the hotel industry.

A city's business bureau or travel bureau often hosts monthly or quarterly networking meetings for event planners, so it may not be feasible for you to host your own event-planner's reception. In this case, offer to host a function in conjunction with your city's business bureau. The bureau may also use its mailing list to extend the invitation to a large number of event planners around the city. Some might find this disadvantageous since this list may include a small number of planners working on infrequent, smaller-scale events. Large hotels and banquets will be looking to attract planners working on larger-scale events happening more frequently. Also, not all event planners are on the bureau's mailing list; you may exclude a great contact hosting an event such as this.

Collaborating with Industry Members on Events

Many events involve planning with industry members. Industry members may include restaurant, hotel, and hospitality staff, as well as other members of the service industry like salon and retail staff. The time may come for you to collaborate with other members of the industry on events. Market your services by hosting an event with this industry in mind.

The restaurant and hotel industry can be very influential in the food and beverage scene in your area. Purveyors, vendors, liquor companies, and wine representatives all realize industry staff can become salespeople for products. It is the servers, the bartenders, and managers of restaurants, bars, and hotels who are in the position to sell. For this reason, marketing to the restaurant industry is wise if you are an event planner at a restaurant, hotel, nightclub, or banquet facility.

As a general rule, industry staff members are knowledgeable about the trends in cuisine, wine, and cocktails. Hosting an event with a foodie focus will attract many in the industry. (*Foodie* is an industry term describing a person who is knowledgeable about fine food, wine, and spirits.) Some suggestions for an industry event are wine tastings, chef cooking demonstrations, and cocktail samplings. Events can surround a larger event such as a holiday, anniversary, or celebration.

E ssential

The restaurant, hotel, and hospitality industries have always targeted each other's staff. Some restaurants specifically target industry members by staying open late after most restaurants close. Catering to concierges guarantees that hotel guests will receive a referral to retail stores, salons, and restaurants.

In the beginning, choosing marketing opportunities will likely be a challenging task. The best way to decide on the right marketing strategy is by trial and error. Experiment with many types of events and advertising to determine which opportunities are the right match for your company. The more marketing you become involved with, the easier it will become to balance your calendar goals throughout the year.

Chapter 9

Networking

NETWORKING IS MAKING CONTACTS in and out of your prospective industry. These contacts will create the buzz and word of mouth that can make a business successful. When you have the confidence to talk about your company in social settings, you will have mastered the art of networking. This chapter offers lots of suggestions on how to network and grow your business.

Business Bureaus

The city or region where you work may have a greater business bureau, travel bureau, convention center, or visitor's center. This office is the best place to begin your networking activities. The purpose of these centers and bureaus is to provide information to out-of-town businesses and individuals traveling to your area. A city's greater business bureau obtains information about participating businesses and creates a database for recommendations based on a visiting company's specific needs.

Database

The information created by a business bureau is placed in a database. In the interest of event planning, the information obtained may include the following:

- The capacity of a hotel
- The capacity and floor plan of a hotel's function space
- The hours of a restaurant
- The type of cuisine a restaurant serves
- The location of different types of nightlife
- Information on private rooms and meeting space

A visiting company will call the business bureau with specific dates and the needs of its staff while staying in your city. The business bureau will then match the company with local event planners based upon those needs and the company's budget. Typically, local businesses pay a yearly fee to be associated with a business bureau.

Events

The business bureau is a great asset for two reasons: attracting prospective business and utilizing the bureau's database to network with other event planners. A business bureau may host a function specifically for local event planners to network. These events may be held monthly, bimonthly, or quarterly.

As a fledgling event planner, you should attend these events. The idea of networking with other event planners is not to steal clients but to share information and practices. Networking with other professionals will give you the opportunity to hear how they handle legal matters such as contracts and how they attract new business. You may also compare spaces and pricing with other event planners, which can help you refer clients when you are fully booked or cannot accommodate a client for a different reason.

Many different organizations belong to a better business bureau. This means many other event planners may be involved as well. To rise above your competition, keep your information with the bureau current. Make a contact within the bureau and check in with him every so often.

Web Site

Some business bureaus support a Web site for inquiries from visiting companies. As an event planner, members will have the opportunity to bid on events. Once the client has a chance to review the bids, he will choose a venue based upon his company's needs. Occasionally local companies also utilize this service.

E ssential

A business bureau's e-mail list can help you promote large events and fundraisers. Ask your contact at the bureau if the bureau's e-mail list is provided to members. You may be interested in inviting only the event planners and local companies to your event. Remember, some event planners, for different reasons, may not be a member of the business bureau. Completing your invite list may take more effort than depending on the e-mail list of your bureau.

Volunteering Your Time for Fundraisers

Even if an event is not your own, you can still get involved without being the lead event planner. Charitable events attract business and community leaders. Philanthropy can have many benefits, and volunteering is one of those benefits. Volunteering can make you feel good internally while finding support for causes you care about. Involving yourself in a fundraiser will ultimately integrate you in the community. The time you dedicate to a fundraiser can increase your networking skills.

Fundraisers tend to be social events where it may be out of place—yet tempting—to pass out your business card among your city's movers and shakers. Do your best to resist this urge. A well-meaning introduction may offend a potential contact if followed by a slip of the business card. However, you can network subtly by planting a seed with an introduction and a handshake with prospective contacts. Only share your contact information if asked.

Alert

A guest at a fundraiser may not realize he is in your networking sights. For this reason keep conversations with guests brief but make an impact. Even though event planners may be utilizing fundraisers to network with potential clients, a guest may avoid a zealous event planner.

Making the Most of Volunteering

There is a saying in the acting world about no small parts, only small actors. This phrase can be related to event planning as well. When volunteering for an event, offer your time where it is needed. That may mean checking coats or buffing glassware. To make the most out of your volunteer efforts, attempt to work in the forefront and not behind the scenes. To combine volunteering and networking, the best jobs are:

- **Working the registration table.** This is perhaps the best job as it allows you to put a name with prominent members of your community.
- **Passing cocktails.** Use this very social job to introduce yourself to guests.
- **Passing hors d'oeuvres.** Similar to passing cocktails, this job requires conversation. You may begin by talking about the cuisine but end the conversation forging a rapport with a guest.
- **Distributing favors.** It is easier to engage guests in conversation toward the end of the evening. You can make an impression on a guest by asking how her evening was as she is heading out the door. In fact, some restaurateurs argue that the goodbye the guest receives is more important than the greeting the guest received when she first walked in. The goodbye is the very last impression the guest will have of the establishment.
- **Coat check.** Struggling with coats and hangers in a little stuffy room is not very glamorous but it does have its advantages.

Working on the coat check circuit enables you to become a familiar face in a crowd.

Remember Why You Volunteer

Again, try not to be too difficult when the event planner of the fundraiser is passing out jobs. Remember, you are there to volunteer and support a cause first; networking is a bonus. The upside to working behind the scenes is you may be able to join the festivities if your job is finished. Ask the event planner if this is possible to arrange.

Meeting with Other Event Planners

As your confidence in your field evolves, so will your ability to network. It may take a few months in a position, but the time will come when you are ready to leave your comfort zone. All event planners, from party planners to catering managers to meeting planners, can benefit by networking with other planners in their field. Inviting an event planner to lunch at your restaurant will inevitably get you a reciprocal invitation.

The Invitation

Deciding which event planners you should network with is the first step to networking. If you are a meeting planner, invite other meeting planners out for a one-on-one lunch or a tour of your offices. Be mindful of peak seasons, and only send invitations in the slower months. An event planner may be apprehensive about meeting with you, so be sure to assure him it is solely to network and share resources. A personal letter is the best approach.

The Meeting

Set the tone for the meeting. The meeting can be as formal or informal as you choose to make it. Dress according to your company's dress code. Have some collateral and pricing ready for the meeting. Also have an idea of the questions you would like to ask. Here are some examples:

- How long have you been at your company?
- How long have you been in the business?

- Do you network with anyone else in the business?
- Who do you use for flowers, audiovisual equipment, or rentals?
- What are your best resources for this career?

End the meeting on a positive note, promising to refer any overflow business in her direction. Promise to send your new contact any information you discussed in your meeting. Be gracious and offer your services whenever she may be in need.

Using Your Marketing Dollars Creatively

Upon accepting your position, your employer may have offered you some perks to attract clients. One bonus might be an expense account to entertain clients socially after hours. Other bonuses might include a signing account to be used in-house if you are employed by a hotel or restaurant, or being able to entertain using part of the company's marketing budget. A lucky few of you might have a combination of all three bonuses to use. Before you begin your spending, think of creative ways to combine your resources and get the most bang for your buck.

Using Your Company's Marketing Budget

Your company most likely will have set aside resources for marketing in its budget. This budget may be used by the management, marketing department, or event-planning department. The marketing budget is used to attract more business to the company. Determine if these funds are available for your position and if so, what amount has been set aside.

The marketing budget can be used in a few different ways. As stated, this money can be used to host an event for an event planner as a networking campaign. Depending on which field of event planning you are employed in, the marketing budget can be used in a few other ways with your employer's approval:

- **Send a gift certificate from your establishment.** An invitation to showcase your restaurant's private rooms will be that much sweeter if you include a gift certificate. The amount can be as little as cocktails for two or as grand as a five-course chef tasting menu.

- **Cater a luncheon.** As a catering manager with no kitchen, ask the catering chef to prepare some cold, delectable sandwiches for your meeting. State this in your invitation, and refer to your meeting as a picnic lunch at your office.
- **Order in.** As a meeting planner, your first inclination may be to host your new contact outside of the office. Reconsider if you have a nice conference room or boardroom. Make your invitation more tempting by using the lunch hour. You can also mention lunch subtly by asking if your guest has dietary restrictions.
- **Send a gift.** Corporate event planners may send in-house merchandise along with an invitation. If your company manufactures sports equipment, send a seasonal recreational gift along with your invitation. A company jersey (with your logo imprinted on the front) counts double as a marketing and networking tool.

E ssential

There is a chance your position may not have access to the marketing budget. Do not let this deter you from your marketing efforts. If you have a great marketing idea, bring it to your employer.

Using Your Expense Account

The key to using your expense account, especially if it is small, is to use it efficiently. For instance, if there is a new restaurant opening in your neighborhood, you can use this opportunity to invite another event planner. If it is an after-hours meeting, ask your guest if she will be coming straight from work. You can take her cue and dress accordingly.

Another example of using your expense account wisely is to entertain a client at a destination where you are looking to meet the event planner. This will most likely be in a restaurant or a hotel environment. While you will not be able to sit and meet with another event planner at this time, you can at least make the introduction. Call ahead to determine if your contact will be working at the time of your visit. Explain you are bringing in a client and would like to say hello if she is working. Your contact will likely be grateful you are bringing in a client to her restaurant. A second meeting is sure to follow. Casually mention to your client beforehand you intend to make a quick introduction while at the restaurant.

 ## Fact

A signing account is an industry way of describing a program in which an employee, usually management, signs for meals. The meals can be for entertaining clients, family, or friends. A signing account is usually a set amount within a quarter or a year.

Remember to have a dialogue with your employer when using an expense account creatively. Getting approval ahead of time is always a good idea. You can avoid the raised eyebrow when the accounting department processes your receipt if your employer has preapproved your spending. You may need to remind your employer of the benefit of networking and how it leads to more business.

Using Your In-House Expense Account

An in-house expense account or signing account, usually in a restaurant environment, may be used to treat clients, and sometimes friends and family, to dinner. Use your signing account wisely. Rather than treating your friends and family to elaborate meals at your restaurant, use your signing account to invite event planners. If you are a restaurant planner, you can benefit from having meeting planners, corporate planners, and other restaurant planners view your space.

Alert

Be frugal with your money. To make the most of your signing account, invite clients, family, friends, and other event planners into your restaurant for lunch or cocktails. This will be less expensive than dinner, and your signing account will be stretched further. Make certain your servers and bartenders are taken care of each time you comp someone's meal.

Promotions and Coupons

Reaching out to a prospective network contact is always easier if you make the visit worth the contact's time. An invitation is always sweeter if food and cocktails are offered, which is why meeting at a restaurant or café, or catering a luncheon will always secure a positive response. In many cases, fledgling businesses cannot afford such an extravagant marketing budget. If you have started your own company, for example, you may begin your marketing efforts with smaller, more effective measures.

You can begin two ways. One is by offering a coupon of sorts. A coupon is usually a form of collateral which a client needs to present to receive a discount.

The second way to begin a smaller marketing campaign is to offer a promotion of your services. A promotion can be handled a number of ways. Following are some suggestions.

- Offer a client a percentage off of her next event if she refers a friend.
- An advertisement may include an offer for a percentage off an event or service if a client mentions the publication where he saw the ad. This also works for Web site advertising.
- Often new clients are tempted with a promotion to entice business. For example, a promotion can include free linens or a discount from a vendor, such as 10 percent off of floral arrangements.

Alert

Coupons have a less than favorable connotation in the industry. It evokes images of a supermarket dollar-off coupon. Some might think a coupon is a discount because your services are not as good as another event planner's. Avoid the term *coupon* and use *gift certificate* instead. A gift certificate states the same terms as a coupon.

Staying in Touch

Once you have made a new networking contact, add your new contact to all company mailing and e-mail lists to keep him current on events and promotions. You can also reach out to your new contact around the holidays with greeting cards and promotions. Another idea is to attend the same networking events together or agree to meet at an event.

Trade Shows

A trade show is a large-scale event used to showcase specific products or services. Products are set up in booths while event planners are given a floor plan to map out the space. An event-planning trade show may showcase china, flatware, cuisine, wineries, and computer software. The networking benefit to a trade show is meeting with other event planners at the activities around the trade show. As an attendee to a trade show, you may be invited to a meet and greet, a cocktail reception, or a breakfast in the days before and after the trade show.

From a networking perspective, the events around the trade show are as important as the trade show itself. You will have a chance to be more social and interactive at a reception. While at the trade show, event planners will be focusing more on the vendor booths. Other events offered at a trade show might be conferences, seminars, and team-building exercises.

Utilize your time at a trade show and its events wisely. Your time should be spent engaging and interacting with other event planners and vendors. Trade shows are a time for event planners to meet and share in each other's expertise. You may be exposed to different ideas during this time. Keep a journal in your hotel room to chronicle event ideas you will be able to use at a later date.

 Fact

Meet and greet is a term for a reception to introduce event attendees before an event. The reception is usually scheduled on the attendee's arrival date. Typically, the event is scheduled outside of meal periods, and refreshments are served.

Once mastered, networking can be useful for even the most seasoned event planner. You may find you rely on the people who become your network every day for various event-planning issues. Cultivating your networking contacts will integrate you into the community, boost your business, and may even attract other job offers. Most importantly, your business network may double as your support network. A support network is essential for a hectic, stressful, and emotional day in event planning.

Chapter 10

Ethics

ETHICS ARE THE RULES or code of standards that govern how a society or profession behaves. Every day you will confront issues, large and small, that will test your ethics as an event planner. Knowing where you stand on some ethical issues now will better prepare you to face these issues in the future.

Accepting Gifts

Accepting gifts comes with the territory as an event planner. Gifts can come from your employer, your clients, and other event planners. You may even be offered trips as gifts. In some fields accepting gifts is frowned upon, especially if it increases your referral business. In fact, in some contracts it will clearly state the event planner is not to accept gifts of any kind.

When It Is Appropriate

It is appropriate to accept a gift if the gesture comes without strings attached. An example of an appropriate gift is when a client is thanking you for a job well done. Another example of an appropriate gift is when your employer gives you a birthday present. It is also appropriate if a fellow event planner would like to treat you to dinner at her restaurant. Some venues will host an event planner's event to showcase the property. It is appropriate to accept the favor bags given at the end of these events as well.

When to Forgo a Gift

An event planner should reject a gift if she has a contractual agreement with her client not to accept gifts. She should also not accept a gift if it jeopardizes the integrity of her company. For example, an expensive watch accepted by an event planner with the promise of sending a company or venue more business is unethical.

Incentive Programs

Some industries offer incentive programs as a thank-you for referral business. For example, as a wedding planner you refer brides to a hair salon for wedding day hair and makeup. As a thank-you, the salon offers you a free haircut for every ten brides you send. This type of incentive program may not be appropriate if your contract states you cannot accept gifts. The incentive may not be ethical if the salon's services are not satisfactory.

If You Want to Offer a Gift

As a restaurant event planner, you may wish to offer a gift or incentive to promote your venue. The gesture may be a gift card to your restaurant or an invitation to dinner. Such an invitation would entice other event planners to tour your space. Most event planners would not have an ethical issue with this type of gift. But if you are unsure, call and ask. Let the event planner know you are planning on sending some information in the mail with a little token of your gratitude.

Disclosing Gratuities

The exact derivation of tipping, or leaving a gratuity, is unknown. The word *tips* can be an acronym for "to insure proper service," but it is rumored to originate from the phrase "tipping the scales," as in a bribe. Whatever its origin, a tip or gratuity plays a large part in event planning today. It is important you understand how your company handles gratuities and distributes them to staff. It is also important to know the type of gratuities and who is entitled to this money.

Understanding Gratuities

A tip is a gesture or payment for good service. All types of positions in the service industry accept tips. Taxi drivers, bellmen, hairdressers, and valets all accept tips. In the restaurant industry, however, tips are the most prevalent. All countries have different customs regarding gratuities, but in the United States a server receives a tip in a restaurant as part of his salary. A standard gratuity is 10 to 20 percent of the before-tax bill. The tip is then dispersed among the service staff, with a small percentage going to the food runner, bartender, busser, and occasionally the hostess. A server is only instructed to tip out his support staff; the kitchen is not part of the support staff and usually does not get a percentage of the gratuity.

 ## Fact

In most states it is illegal to force a server to tip out his gratuities. Management can only suggest the percentage a server should tip out. It is also illegal for the kitchen staff to receive a part of this tip with the exception being service-related kitchens. A sushi bar or open kitchen are examples of service-related kitchens.

Tips in Event Planning

It is likely your service staff will get compensated in one of two ways. In some banquet halls and catering companies, the servers make a straight hourly wage. The average wage is $15 to $30 an hour for servers and bartenders. The client is charged for the hourly staff in addition to the food and beverage. Quite often the client will give the service staff an extra gratuity for good service. If this tip goes through you or your company, it is important the money goes directly to your staff. Your company cannot benefit or profit from this tip.

The second way a server can be compensated is by a small wage paid by your company. Most servers make minimum wage. In addition to this wage, your support staff will divvy up an automatic gratuity that gets charged to the client. Industry standard is 15 to 20 percent of the food and beverage bill. A company cannot automatically add gratuity to tax or a room charge. Again, the support staff receives the gratuity in its entirety. The tip does not filter down to the kitchen staff.

In some cases, a management fee or administration fee is added to the hourly employee charge. The management or administration fee can also be added to the automatic gratuity. These fees are usually used to compensate the event planner's salary or incentive program. In some cases, a company may choose to charge a higher percentage of gratuities and give a portion to the event planner. For example, an invoice to a client may state a standard gratuity of 21 percent is added to the food and beverage portion of the bill. Out of this portion, the server would receive 18 percent and the event planner would receive 3 percent.

E ssential

Contrary to popular belief, patrons should tip on all food and beverage totals. Expensive bottles of wine should be tipped on in the same manner in which a cheeseburger is tipped. It is standard practice, not just customary, to tip in the United States. A server is taxed 8 percent of her sales by the government even if a patron does not leave a tip.

Ways to Keep Support Staff Honest

Every industry that has products needs to be wary of employee theft. Whether it is a restaurant, a retail establishment, or a hotel, loss prevention is a concern. Fortunately, certain measures can be taken to reduce this concern. Creating an ethical culture in your workplace is one way to instill ethical behavior in your staff. As a manager or an employer, the best preventive measure you can take is being a respectable supervisor. Challenge yourself to being the best manager your staff has worked for. In turn, your staff will rise to every occasion.

Staff Pride and Involvement

Unfortunately, event staff members are not highly regarded in the event industry. Often called "cater waiters," some event planners are uneasy about hiring for these positions due to their part-time and on-call status. Some companies have high staff turnover, which also contributes to theft and low job performance.

Fact

Turnover is the rate at which employees are replaced in a company. A company experiencing low turnover has a stable employee base and rarely has positions available. A company experiencing high turnover is likely to have an unstable employee base. A company with high turnover is always looking to replace employees.

Again, creating a culture of pride in your company may lessen employee turnover. Treat your staff well at events. One way to treat your staff well is to serve staff meals. Forge a sense of community within your staff and organize staff events. Taking your staff out to dinner or on a field trip will increase camaraderie. Organize a volunteering event to improve social awareness and philanthropy among your staff.

Giving Gifts to Your Staff

On occasion award members of your staff with small gifts. Many times after an event extra favor bags will be left behind. Ask the host if you can secure a few favor bags for your staff. Sending your staff member home with a bottle of wine is always a nice token of appreciation. Just be sure you charge the wine to your company and not your client. Be certain any gifts from you are stated to the client to avoid impropriety.

Disciplinary Action

With all of your efforts there still may come a time when a staff member may not use good judgment. An employee coming into work late, repeatedly calling in sick, or not showing up for work may sound some alarms with you. These lapses in judgment may call for disciplinary action. Schedule a meeting with your employee and ask if there are any circumstances causing his unreliability. Address any issues the employee may be having in his personal life and offer solutions.

Fact

Some offenses are cause for immediate termination. Drug use, alcohol abuse, theft, and violence in the workplace are automatic causes for termination. Develop a zero-tolerance policy against these transgressions. Ask the advice of your security team or local police department if the situation escalates beyond your control.

Hopefully after your meeting the employee will feel well regarded and change his negative work behavior. If not, consider suspending the employee for a shift or two. Document each wrongdoing, and after three offenses you usually will have enough cause to terminate the employee.

The worst course of action to take against an employee is no action at all. Turning a blind eye to an employee's faults will only cause a disapproving reaction among the rest of your staff. You may be inadvertently sending a message to your staff that it is acceptable to break the rules.

Conflict Resolution

As an event planner, conflict resolution is a skill you must develop. You will need to defuse arguments or difficult situations that may arise. The conflicting parties will benefit from your calm demeanor and empathy. The goal of conflict resolution is to leave all parties satisfied with a solution.

Conflicts with Clients

When a negative situation presents itself with a client you are put in a unique position. Finding a solution between two parties is quite a test, but when you are one of the two parties, it becomes more challenging. Listen to the client's complaint and offer empathy. Next, ask the client if she has a solution for the complaint. You should consider a reasonable request and attempt to deliver. With unreasonable requests, you can offer to meet the client halfway.

A situation with a client may be out of your control, in which case you should acknowledge her complaint and offer a solution. Send the client a gift card with a note stating, "I am sorry we were unable to see eye to eye on this matter. Please accept this gift card as an apology."

Whichever solution you choose, you should act with haste. Resolve the matter in a timely fashion.

Conflicts Between Clients and Vendors

Complaints are liable to arise between a client and a vendor at some point in your career as an event planner. If the complaint occurs prior to the event, attempt to rectify the situation before the event begins. For example, a floral designer may have used the wrong flowers in an arrangement for an event. With the event hours away, call the floral designer to correct the mistake.

Other complaints may not be as easy to solve. If a vendor has damaged the client's personal property during the setup of an event, the solution may not be as obvious. In this case, reserve judgment until you can assess the situation and speak to both sides. A reputable vendor should be insured specifically for these occasions. Still, offer sympathy to the client and prompt the vendor to at least write a letter of apology.

Conflicts Between Staff Members

Conflicts among staff members range from the simple to the serious. Adopting an open-door policy to mediate between two staff members is always a good idea. Solve staff problems fairly without taking sides and avoid letting the situation escalate out of control. Never tolerate bad language or physical violence. Violence in the workplace is cause for immediate termination and perhaps police involvement.

Conflicts Between Guests

Conflicts between guests will occur during events. Venues such as bars or nightclubs may have more conflicts because alcohol is served. With guest conflicts, simply separating the two guests may solve the disagreement. If a conflict between guests becomes violent, do not attempt to break up the argument, merely call the police. It is preferable to have a security detail at events to avoid guest conflicts altogether.

Social Awareness

Event planners can choose to get involved in a variety of causes. Contributing time and resources to a cause such as hunger is easy for an event planner due to the nature of the business.

Donating Leftovers

A chef working in a restaurant may not have many leftover items. A catering chef may find herself with leftover food because most event chefs order too much food to avoid falling short. As a result, most event chefs have leftover food at the end of an event and have no use for it. Because of specialty items and the timing of events, a caterer cannot use menu items from one event to the next. Leftovers can easily be packaged and sent to a soup kitchen or homeless shelter. Bulk, nonperishable items are best, but check with local shelters for their donation policies.

Many shelters and soup kitchens have strict rules when accepting donations. Again, ask about the food handling policies. Also ask when staff members may be available to sign in the donations. Many events end late in the evening, so be sure to get a hotline phone number so a donation can be made at 1 A.M. if needed.

Donating Products

Supplies from a kitchen can also be donated. Items are replaced every day in kitchens. Misshapen flatware, pots with dings, or knives with a nick simply get thrown out of restaurant kitchens. These items may be recycled and given to homeless shelters or soup kitchens. Call local organizations and inquire about donating supplies.

Looking for a staff volunteer effort? Organize your staff to volunteer at a food bank. Whether it is once a week or once a month, encourage your staff to become involved in a cause directly related to event planning. The service industry can easily lend a hand in a cause such as hunger.

Unfortunately, in the past, groups have not been responsible when donating food to the hungry. Poor food handling has led to organizations becoming very strict when accepting donations, which has led some caterers to avoid the risk of donating leftover food.

Most shelters and soup kitchens will accept nonperishable items such as baked goods. Prepared foods may be checked for safety. A shelter employee may ask when the donation was prepared, has it been refrigerated, and so on and will have guidelines to follow before accepting the donation. To protect your company, contact your local health inspection office before considering donations.

When you decide to donate leftovers, be sure to bring an adequate amount in an appropriate container. A fish tub is ideal because it has a fitted cover and is fairly airtight.

Maintaining a Standard of Professionalism

In this industry, men and women work in notoriously close quarters. The hospitality industry builds relationships as a result. It is not unusual for friends and couples to develop bonds while working together in the business. While it is appropriate to support these relationships, it is also important to adhere to a standard of professionalism.

Sexual Harassment

Sexual harassment has garnered a lot of attention in recent years throughout all professions. Consequently, companies in all industries have developed a no-tolerance policy regarding sexual harassment. In restaurants, an industry known for its late nights and social drinking, sexual harassment seminars are a good idea to establish safe boundaries for employees.

Taking Cues from Human Resources

Your company may have a human resources department, in which case it is a good idea to request a conference or seminar on sexual harassment issues. Smaller companies may not have an on-site human resources department but may consider a consultation with a human resources director. Companies also hire educators to lecture staff members on topics such as sexual harassment.

Becoming a Role Model

As an event planner, you will likely be an owner or manager of a company. Supervising staff members can be a tremendous responsibility, and your staff looks to you to set an example. Therefore, your staff may mimic your behavior, negative as well as positive. Being on time, dressing professionally, and using constructive language all constitute positive behavior.

Your ethical views can be challenged every day as an event planner. But applying good morals in your work environment can encourage positive behavior from your staff, vendors, and clients. Practicing good ethics is contagious and will set the standards for your company. Gaining a reputation for being fair and always making the right decision is a good place to be in this business.

Chapter 11

Legal Matters

SOME KNOWLEDGE OF LEGAL MATTERS will serve you very well in your career as an event planner. Some legal matters, such as contracts, you will work with every day. Other matters, such as permits and insurance, you will need to deal with less frequently. Rarely will you encounter serious legal matters such as nonpayment for services. With a little research, there are steps you can take to protect yourself and your company.

Permits

In your travels as an event planner, you may plan events off-site and outdoors that will require a permit or special license. Concerts, a wedding at a park, and an organized outdoor event may all require special permits. When planning an event at any public venue it is best to assume a permit will be needed.

Athletic fundraising events such as an organized walk, a bike race, or a marathon planned by nonprofit agencies might also need permits. Other outdoor events such as a fair, farmer's market, or a block party may also require some types of permits.

Types of Permits

Permits are required for many reasons. The biggest reason for a permit deals with crowd control. Following is a list of the types of permits you may need when planning a future event:

- A permit for outdoor spaces
- A parking permit
- A sound permit
- A permit for security

- A permit to hang a banner
- A sanitation permit (for portable restrooms)

Permit information can be obtained over the Internet. Most cities and towns have Web sites with information regarding special permits. To obtain a permit, you must fill out the proper paperwork. A permit will most likely be accompanied by a charge or fee. Your local parks and recreation department, town hall, or city hall are good resources for obtaining permits.

Timeline

The time it takes you to obtain a permit can depend on the region where you are planning the event. Some towns may require a few weeks to process a permit, while other cities may take months to process a permit. For example, a small coastal town in Massachusetts may require only a ten-day turnaround time for a permit. It may take four months or longer for a permit to be processed in New York City.

Wherever the location of your event, be sure to proceed with caution until you have the permit. An outdoor permit may not be obtained because the park has been booked, in which case all of the other details you have planned around the park event will need to be changed. If possible, either wait for the permit to be processed or have a backup plan for your first venue.

Contracts

A contract is a legally binding document between two parties. In event planning, the contract is a written agreement that stipulates the client agrees to pay the event planner in exchange of services rendered. An event-planning contract should list specific terms and policies related to the event.

As a new event planner, you may be starting at a company that has contracts in place. If this is the case, take a close look at the language used. Do you understand all of the material? Can you answer questions a guest may ask you about a contract?

You may be starting out as an event planner in a new company or position and have to come up with your own contract. If you are designing the contract, the Internet is a great resource you can utilize to find a contract template. Many Web sites offer different contracts, some you can download for free. You will also find contracts specific to event planning. Use these as a resource to design a specific contract for your company. All event-planning contracts should have similar basic information.

E ssential

Be sure the language is clear and terms and policies on the contract are current. In event planning, it is important to use common language in a contract. Avoid having your contract sound like a team of lawyers wrote it.

Basic Contract Language

An event-planning contract should have basic information regarding the event. If it applies, be sure to include the following in your contract:

- Event date
- Time of event
- Location of event
- The cost of services including room charges
- The cancellation policies
- Charges surrounding a cancellation or a no-show
- Guest count and final count due date
- Billing information
- Server charges, whether by the hour or in gratuities
- Valet arrangements
- Weather cancellations and acts of nature
- Other pertinent details

The contract should be signed by both parties and initialed if on more than one page. Some contracts also include details of the menu and room setup.

Cancellations

A client will occasionally need to cancel or postpone an event she has been planning. Your contract should outline the terms and penalties of cancellations. For example, a client canceling within a week after signing the contract may have no penalties for the cancellation. A client canceling one month prior to his event may forfeit any deposits. A client canceling within one week of the event may forfeit any deposits plus 25 percent of the estimated costs.

 Fact

The estimated costs of an event can be determined by the original quote. For example, an event may have been priced for a dinner for one hundred guests at $100 per person. In the event of a last-minute cancellation, the client would forfeit the deposit of $2,000, plus 25 percent of the estimated cost, an additional $2,500. The total loss to the client would be $4,500.

Cancellation policies vary by the type of event-planning business. The type of event also determines the penalties surrounding the cancellations. For example, when a client has been planning an event for a year or more, the cancellation policy may be stricter: A cancellation made by a client one month before the event may forfeit the deposit and up to 50 percent of the estimated costs.

Breaking a Contract

There are many reasons why a client may break a contract. Relocation, a change in circumstances, and a loss of income may all cause a client to break a contract. In some cases a client may fail to honor the deposit arrangements in the contract. This would also constitute breaking a contract.

Even less rarely, you may be forced to break a contract with a client. Overbooking or emergency situations may cause you to break a contract with a client. Of course, you will have made every effort to keep your obligations to your client. Attempt to have another event planner or company fulfill your obligation in the case of an emergency. You can work out the financial details with your substitute at a later date. If circumstances force you to break a contract, return any deposit to the client and offer referrals to other event planners in your place.

Insurance

Securing insurance is a wise decision. People purchase insurance for their house, car, and life. People buy insurance to protect themselves and investments. Insurance in event planning can protect your events as well.

Special Event Liability Insurance

Insurance for event planning is a good idea for a few reasons. First, insurance protects your office and its belongings against theft or fire. Insurance also protects your events. For example, as the result of a staff member's actions, damage was done to your client's property during an event. Your insurance would cover the damage.

You might also consider using commercial license plates for your vehicle. Commercial insurance for your car will give you more coverage. Commercial plates will allow you to park in designated parking spots, which is convenient if you work in a city.

Your client can also purchase special event liability insurance. As his event planner, you should also strongly urge your client to buy event insurance.

Client Event Insurance

Insurance purchased by a client for his event may cost only a few hundred dollars. It can protect thousands of dollars worth of event costs. Client-event insurance can protect a client's deposits with vendors. If a vendor closes her doors before the event without returning the deposit, event insurance will cover the loss. Also, if a vendor has a fire in his shop—say, a photographer, for instance—the insurance will cover the cost to replace the photographs.

In cases where an event may need to be postponed or cancelled due to weather or unforeseen circumstances, event insurance will cover any charges. It will also cover lost or damaged gifts, damage to the venue, and personal liability.

Certificate of Insurance

Venues usually carry their own insurance, but some require the client to buy additional coverage for certain events. This insurance will protect the venue and client against damage and bodily injury claims. A certificate of insurance is a document outlining the insurance coverage.

Proof of Liability Insurance

Proof of liability insurance is evidence to the venue the client has purchased insurance. Venues are increasingly requesting special event liability insurance for large events like weddings. The venue may also request to be listed on the policy to protect itself against lawsuits. Depending on the insurance carrier in your area, event insurance can start at around $200.

Getting Paid

Assuming you became an event planner to make money, getting paid is most likely high on your objectives list. By signing contracts and taking deposits you are taking steps to ensure you get paid. But what happens if you are having problems securing your fee? It is your client's obligation to pay you after you have completed your service. Steps can be taken to ensure your client's obligation is met.

Enforcing a Contract

If after the event your client has not fulfilled his financial obligation to you, send him an invoice. Let a week pass and attempt to contact your client by phone. If after a few days your client has not responded, contact him by e-mail. In the e-mail, reference your previous attempts to contact him with specific dates. If there is still no response, send a second invoice with a letter registering your concerns. Send the letter certified mail and document your efforts along the way.

Once all efforts have been exhausted, it is time to consider legal action. You may consider taking your client to small claims court or hiring an attorney if the sum exceeds $500. If your vendors have not received payment for services from the client, you may consider taking legal action together against the client.

Credit Card Deposits

In addition to contracts, many event planners also take receipt of a credit card number. A second contract or authorization form may be given to a client to sign. The authorization enables you to charge any cancellation fees as well as unpaid charges to the card. The authorization form details the specifics of the event as well as the cancellation policy.

A charge back from a credit card company results when the customer disputes a charge. During your career, a client may dispute a charge to his credit card. The credit card company will charge back the amount to the client's credit card while an investigation is processed. During the investigation, a merchant representative will contact you for details regarding the charge. Usually when the credit card company receives a copy of the contract and authorization form, the charges will be reversed back in your favor.

Returned Checks

Occasionally you may find a client's check was returned for insufficient funds. Contact your client, again first by phone. It was likely a calculation error. Follow the same manner as you would in enforcing a contract. Before taking legal action however, contact your client's bank manager. Bring a copy of the contract and the returned check. In some cases, a bank can authorize the payment of the check.

If a client has stopped payment on your check, follow the guidelines previously mentioned: Contact the client first with phone contact, then e-mail, and finally a certified letter. Again, bringing a copy of the check and a copy of the contract to the bank manager sometimes ends in good results.

References and Background Checks on Vendors

The event-planning industry relies heavily on vendors. As you begin your event-planning career, it is wise to check a vendor's reliability before beginning a relationship. A client will also want to be assured of a vendor's reliability before she gives a deposit and access to her home. A few tools exist to aid event planners in checking the backgrounds of vendors.

About the Better Business Bureau

The Better Business Bureau is a private nonprofit agency established in 1912. Today 300,000 local offices support the bureau. The bureau was structured to protect consumers against fraudulent companies and products. As a consumer, a person can contact his local Better Business Bureau to lodge a complaint against unfair operations. Once a complaint has been filed, the Better Business Bureau will contact the organization on his behalf and assist in finding a solution.

As an event planner you may wish to check a vendor recommendation before referring him to a client. You can utilize the Better Business Bureau by requesting a reliability report. By contacting the bureau, you can verify that no complaints have been filed against a vendor. The bureau will share the number of complaints for this vendor. You can then decide if you still wish to work with the vendor.

Background Checks

A background check is a safeguard you can take to protect yourself against vendors you may work with. The background check can search criminal records, driving records, and lawsuit history. There are several Internet companies providing background checks. Avoid companies offering cheap or free background checks. Although background checks can be expensive, the information you may receive will provide peace of mind to you and your client.

Checking References

Just as a client may request references before hiring you as an event planner, you should incorporate the same practice with your vendors. Before hiring or recommending a vendor, ask for letters of reference. Contact the references and ask questions specific only to the vendor's performance and reliability. Also contact other event planners in your area and inquire about the vendor's reputation.

Alert

In the event you have a complaint against a vendor, contact your local Better Business Bureau. You would not want another event planner to have the same negative experience with a vendor. Also, if the vendor happens to list you as a potential reference, do not give specific details to your negative experience. Simply saying "I found him unreliable" is a sufficient answer.

References and Background Checks on Your Staff

Selecting a trustworthy, dedicated staff is the cornerstone of a successful event-planning company. When looking to fill positions, you can accept applications (type "standard employment application" into a Web search engine to get forms you can download) or resumes for employment. However a prospective hire applies, always spend time interviewing applicants and call employment references. Occasionally you may also run background checks before completing the interview process.

Interview

Before scheduling an interview with a potential employee, have a list of interview questions prepared. Look for punctuality from the interviewee. Also be prepared to talk about the position, salary, and the company. During an employee interview, do not limit the conversation to previous work experience. Ask the interviewee about his hometown, his family, and even about his interest in the event-planning industry. Candidates who come from large families and who played organized sports tend to be team players in a work environment.

References

Always check references. Before you decide on a candidate as a likely employee, check the references she provided on her application. You will need the permission of the applicant before you make your inquiries. Ask the candidate about any gaps in her employment history as well.

When checking an applicant's references, ask her previous employer questions specific to her job performance. Following is a list of appropriate reference questions:

- Was the employee reliable?
- Was the employee punctual?
- Did the employee work well with others?
- Did the employee complete tasks at hand?
- Did the employee take direction well?
- Would you hire this employee again?

Avoid engaging the employer in details surrounding the employee's personal life. Exchanging certain information can be considered defamation of character.

Background Checks

In this industry, your staff may be filled with full- and part-time employees. On-call employees are also prevalent in this business. For this reason background checks on employees are infrequent. Background checks can be costly for an industry with high turnover, though many high-end event companies will spend the money to check the backgrounds of potential employees. Background checks protect these event-planning companies against hiring felons.

Driving Records

Driving is essential to most members of the event-planning industry. Hiring a staff member who can drive can be necessary to operate an efficient business. Check the driving records of any potential hires. In lieu of paying for a background check, you can request the potential employee supply a copy of his driving record from the motor vehicle department. You are looking to hire an employee without any DUIs (driving under the influence) or moving violations.

As an event planner, you hope for the best but you are also realistic. Accidents will happen, storms will hit, and trusted vendors will have bad days. It's important to focus on finding solutions to any problem. The mark of a great event planner is how she deals with problems in the face of adversity.

Chapter 12

The Client Interview

A CLIENT INTERVIEW is the first meeting you will have with a prospective client. During this interview, the client will outline the event she has in mind. In turn, you will assess the event, check your calendar, and offer possibilities. The initial meeting is referred to as a client interview, but in reality this is a chance for your client to interview you to be her event planner. This chapter provides a step-by-step approach to interacting with your clients in the initial interview.

The Importance of Phone Etiquette and Manners

A prospective client will most likely make first contact with you by phone. Make your first impression a memorable one by utilizing proper phone manners. Your first interaction by phone could mean the difference between an event inquiry and a secured event. The initial conversation can set the tone for a successful event.

Before answering any calls, collect yourself. Do not answer the phone while you are eating your lunch, conversing with a colleague, or answering an e-mail. The task you are performing will come across in your voice as you greet your caller. Stress, anxiety, and disinterest can all be detected over the phone. So before you answer, take a second to focus on the task at hand and say hello.

Establish a Rapport

In event planning, the goal of a conversation is to turn the caller into a client. If you can establish a rapport over the telephone, chances are you are closer to reaching your goal. One way to establish a rapport over the telephone is to connect with your caller. Making a connection or finding something in common is a start. Inquiring about an accent, the guest list, or a client's company may start the connection.

At the very least, it will indicate to the person on the phone you are personable.

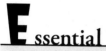

Essential

Smiling as you answer the phone sends a warmer greeting to your caller. When you smile it convinces your voice to follow. Your voice will become more upbeat, alert, and friendly. Try it the next time the phone rings.

Discovering a commonality over the phone may put the caller at ease. It may even gain you a bit of trust. Be sure to be brief in conversational dialogue. Sharing too many personal details can turn off a caller off and give the impression you are not a good listener.

Placing Calls on Hold

Ideally you should answer a call within three rings. If you are in the middle of a call, ask the first caller to hold while you ask the second caller to wait a moment. In the case of a lengthy call, take a message for the second call. Having a voice mail system, which allows a second call to be routed to a voice message, is a good investment. This is especially true when running an office without an assistant or receptionist. It is easy to engage in phone tag with callers if you are always leaving voice mails for each other. Be sure to make yourself available for a return call.

Fact

In event planning, an inquiry refers to a call or visit from a person investigating your services. An inquiry can also refer to a lead or a referral you received from a client or another event planner.

End a Phone Call with Persuasive Language

It is important to end each call with persuasive language. It will leave your caller with a lasting impression. Additionally, a positive upbeat tone in a conversation will leave your caller looking forward to your next conversation. Following are examples of positive, persuasive ways to end a conversation.

- "I will follow up with you in a few days."
- "I promise to send this information right out to you."
- "Feel free to contact me with any questions."

Alert

Never ask a caller to hold more than three times during your telephone conversation—it is not polite. Tell the client you will call him back when you can give him your undivided attention. Once you call your client, do not let any interruptions distract you.

Your Availability to Clients

One of the challenges of event planning is coordinating your schedule. Event planners frequently work nights and weekends managing events. This leaves little time for office hours in the morning or midafternoon. Create the perfect balance between administration and marketing with planning and executing events. Reviewing your office hours can point you in the right direction.

Planning Office Hours

A common schedule among event planners is to begin each day in the midafternoon and work throughout the day in the office and then go to an event in the evening. The problem with this scenario is your absence during the morning when new clients may be trying to reach you. Balancing your time between the events you have and the events you are hoping to secure can be tricky. Experimenting with different office hours will result in fewer missed calls and lost opportunities.

Question

How should I prioritize clients, inquiries, staff, and events?
A good rule of thumb is to prioritize inquiries first. Next would be to handle upcoming events. Lastly, you should address vendors, staff, and other issues. This rule of thumb applies to phone calls, meetings, and administrative duties.

In the beginning of your career, you should experiment with 9-to-5 office hours every day. These hours will allow you to take every phone call and meet with every inquiry walking through the door. This is assuming you have no receptionist or assistant who can manage your calls while you are away. For those of you fortunate enough to have an assistant, your office hours may be slightly more flexible.

Your target audience while working 9 to 5 will range from corporate planners who are using work hours to plan an event to working people who may use a lunch hour to make an inquiry to a planner. You may need to extend your office hours past five o'clock when a potential client may be getting out of work. During the first two months of this schedule, keep a log of your phone calls, meetings, and drop-in business. Then you can take inventory of your heaviest call volume, appointments, and so forth.

 ## Fact

Drop-in clients are those who may happen upon your office because they are walking by your storefront and come in without an appointment. Pop-up bookings are clients who are planning events with less than a week's notice.

Your log will be a valuable tool when it comes time to assess your office hours. If you are finding the heaviest day of the week for inquiries is on Mondays, it will be wise to maintain or lengthen your Monday hours. Perhaps Friday is a light day for inquiries, but you are using your time in the morning to prep for any weekend events. Shortening your Friday hours may be wise, especially if you find you are working weekends. Be sure to give clients two weeks advance before you alter hours.

Days Off and Holidays

Not taking days off can lead to event-planner burnout. Be selfish with your time, but take the proper measures before you take time off. Start by recording your office hours on your outgoing voice mail message. Some event planners may clear a calendar and take the day off after a late event. When you take an unscheduled day off, re-record your message to announce your absence, even if only for a day. For computer communication, program an out-of-office reply to let people know when you plan to return e-mails. Do the same on event days when you may need to cut your office hours short.

Alert

It may be tempting to give a client your cell phone number, but beware. A cell phone number in the hands of a needy client can quickly lead to cell phone abuse. It is always better practice to speak to clients in your office where you can take notes. Resist giving out your cell phone number to clients for emergencies until the day of the event.

Throughout the year there will be holidays and vacations you will want to take. Plan these far in advance and avoid scheduling events during this time unless you have another event planner covering for you. Be upfront with the client and let her know you will not be able to attend her event if it coincides with your vacation. If possible, hire a temporary employee during your holidays and vacations, perhaps an apprentice event planner. Having a live person answer the phone while you are away can put clients at ease.

The Meet and Greet

Once you are past the inquiry phone call, it is now time for you to use the basic information you have collected and brainstorm for your meet and greet. The goal after the initial phone call is to use the basic information given and elaborate on any ideas to prepare for the next interaction with the prospective client. There can be an exchange of proposed menus, a mention of house cocktails, and a summary of a floor plan. This transfer of information can be done through mail, fax, telephone, or e-mail, and it occurs before the initial meeting.

During your first meeting, you will provide a description of the event you can produce, perhaps using ideas from past events. Remember, your first meeting may not be a meeting at all. The session may be done over the phone or through e-mail. These sessions are tricky because while you want to impress the client with great images, you may not have a signed contract. Be protective of your ideas until the client has signed with you and you have secured a deposit.

A few minutes before the prospective client arrives, familiarize yourself with her material. Have a copy of all of the information you have sent on hand as well as your notes from the initial phone conversation. Draft a proposal, budget, and contract in case your inquiry is ready to take the next step and become your client during the initial meeting. For information yet to be determined, simply put "TBD" (to be determined) on the line. Your scrapbook and letters of reference should also be available.

E ssential

A meet and greet is the initial face-to-face meeting between you and a prospective client. Meeting a prospective client is an exciting and nerve-wracking experience. Taking steps to prepare yourself for the meet and greet will bring you closer to landing the client and the event.

Remember, you are hoping to host this person's event. From the time the prospective client walks through the door, show her how serious you take the host position by offering her a beverage, taking her coat, and pulling out her chair. Upon departure, ask if the client needs a recommendation for dinner, directions back to her car, or a taxi called.

What to Accomplish in the Initial Meeting

The goal of the initial meeting for the prospective client is to meet you and gather more details. The goal for you is to solidify your relationship and turn the prospective client into a paying customer. Again, be careful not to divulge too many individual style ideas until a contract is signed. However, this may be the only chance a client may have to tour the venue space, if you are a facility planner, so be thorough. Make mention of linens, table setup, and chairs and table styles. Answer any questions that come up during the meeting.

Timeline of the Event

Even though you are waiting for a signed contract to schedule a creative meeting, you can still discuss the timeline of the event. The following is a list of items you might discuss with a future client.

- **The guest arrival:** A proposed arrival and departure time of the guests may be mentioned at this time, though the time should be confirmed in the contract.
- **The guest greeting:** Ask the prospective client how he envisions his guests will be greeted. For a business meeting, a client may prefer nametags be assigned for a guest greeting. For a cocktail reception, the client may suggest his guests be greeted with a glass of champagne upon arrival.
- **The timing of courses:** Since a menu has been discussed, it is appropriate to suggest the timing of courses during the initial interview.
- **Speeches or announcements:** Inquire if the client or another host will need to make speeches during the event. If so, consider the rental of audiovisual equipment in the budget.

- **Entertainment:** A client may have a favorite band or may need a referral for a DJ. Have your price list of entertainment available for your client.
- **Decorations:** Consider the venue when discussing decorations with your client. Simple venues like community centers may require additional dressing, while swanky, bohemian nightclubs may not even need flowers to decorate for events.
- **Transportation:** Clients may be interested in transportation for their guests, especially if the event has a second location or subvenue. Limousines, hired cars, and even valet services may need to be discussed with a potential client at this time.
- **Other services:** You may provide invitations, calligraphy, or programs.

E ssential

It is traditional to have a cocktail hour prior to dinner. Once seated for dinner, a three-course meal typically follows with an appetizer, entrée, and dessert. A luncheon may have only two courses.

For party planners, one or more creative meetings will follow once the contract has been signed. For a banquet, hotel, or restaurant planner there may not need to be an additional meeting prior to the event. Most details can be handled via e-mail and telephone these days. However, you should welcome any meeting requests from clients.

Creating an Event Sheet to Gather Details

Once you have a signed contract (see Chapter 11 for more on contracts), you have officially secured a client. An event sheet is a way to conveniently organize your events on a single sheet of paper. An event sheet for a restaurant may be different from that of a banquet facility. An event sheet is also referred to as a BEO (banquet event order), resume, or function sheet. In some cases, these documents will substitute for a contract with the client signing the event sheet.

Using the Event Sheet to Communicate

Aside from organizing the details of the event, the event sheet is a line of communication between you and your staff. The event sheet will have the following information to aid the chef, the staff, and vendors in the setup of the event.

- **Reservation name.** The name of the company or last name of the individual hosting the event. Used to guide guests to the proper function in the likelihood the facility has more than one private space.
- **Contact name.** This line on the event sheet is for the person planning the event, possibly different than the person hosting the event. Include your contact's phone number, fax number, and e-mail address as well.
- **On-site contact.** This line is intended for the person who is hosting the event. This person will be present at the event while the contact person may not be present.
- **Menu choices.** This space is used to communicate to the chef and staff. The menu choices will involve courses, special requests, and allergies. The function's menu may be a limited menu with a choice of appetizers, choice of entrées, and desserts. Limited menus are also referred to as prix fixe menus and usually entail a per-person charge. A function can also have the option of passed hors d'oeuvres in the case of a cocktail party, or a stationary (food stations) menu for a banquet-style event. Another menu option is family-style dining, in which large platters of appetizers, salads, and entrées are placed on the table for guests to help themselves. This is also referred to as communal dining.
- **Beverage choices.** You can have a line item for specific beverage types (nonalcoholic beverages, wine, beer, or cocktails). Beverage billing can be based upon consumption using a cash-and-carry bar in which all guests pay for each individual

drink consumed, or the client can pay a set amount for all the drinks in an all-inclusive open bar or host bar.

- **Room setup.** All events need different table setups depending on the size of the function. An event planner may denote the size of the table with the number of chairs or simply attach a floor plan to the event sheet.
- **Notes for FOH.** The notes for the front of the house relay any communication to the servers, staff, managers, and bartenders.
- **Notes for BOH.** The notes for the back of the house relay communication to the chef, pastry chefs, and sous chefs.
- **Initials.** Initials on an event sheet will let the planner know that everyone has seen the information to order and staff the event appropriately.
- **Credit card number.** Depending on your company's policy, you may need to secure the deposit with a credit card number. Some companies may accept a deposit in the form of a check and in addition still secure a credit card number. Having a credit card number on file will secure any funds, in addition to the deposit, forfeited as a result of a cancellation or damage. For example, it is the policy of some companies to charge 25 percent of the proposal plus the deposit if the event is cancelled with less than a week's notice. The forfeited funds may go toward paying the losses of the vendors and purveyors, if any, plus any scheduled staff.
- **Form of payment.** Notes how the guest intends to pay for the event. This line should also have the notes regarding the deposit.
- **Room charge.** Many companies, hotels, banquet halls, and restaurants levy a room charge for events. In addition some establishments may impose a room charge for private and semiprivate areas. The cost of the room charge varies from business to business.
- **Service charge.** A service charge usually reflects a server fee, although occasionally this fee can refer to a management or administrative fee. A service charge can translate as an

hourly rate for servers or be charged in addition to a gratuity. For example, if a board meeting requires a server for six hours, the gratuity may be low because the sales are based upon beverages only. You will want to charge the client a service charge to pay your server additionally. In major cities, clients are charged $25 per hour for each server. Bartenders command higher rates. Be sure the client understands any service fees up front.

- **Valet charge.** The client may want to host the valet. In other words, the client would like to pay for all of her guests' valet charges. Inquire as to whether the valet company imposes an automatic gratuity to the clients' valet charges. A standard tip for a valet is $2 per car.

- **Gratuity.** Denotes a percentage of the bill to which a gratuity will be applied. As a national average, 15 percent is the standard gratuity, although in major cities the percentage is higher at 18 to 20 percent. In some cases, your commission will be deducted from this percentage, and the server will consider you a tipped employee much like a busser, bartender, or food runner. Your tipped income needs to be reported to the IRS.

  The gratuity is based upon the food and beverage total. There has been much debate on the controversy of tipping servers on the wine and alcohol portion of the bill. The IRS applies an 8 to 10 percent tax on the food and beverage sales of a server. Essentially the government is recognizing patrons tipping on a wine and beverage total. For more information on gratuities visit *www.irs.com*.

- **Tax-exemption.** Some businesses are exempt from being taxed by the government. When planning events, the contact must provide a copy of the tax-exempt letter to be considered exempt. Hospitals, universities, and government offices usually hold tax-exempt status.

- **Charge for confirmed guests.** The final number of guests is considered the confirmed guest count. This number is based upon the number of RSVPs received by the client. Depending on your company, the confirmed guest count is due two to five days prior to the event. This is the minimum number of guests the client will be charged for, and the ordering and staffing for the event will be based upon this number.

- **Billing information.** Businesses have individual billing preferences. Event-planning companies are no exception. Your company may prefer to invoice a client after an event rather than charge a credit card. Nowadays many companies will choose a check over a credit card to avoid credit card fees. Credit card companies charge 1 to 3 percent of the transaction amount. In other words, for a $20,0000 event, you will save $200 by accepting a check rather than charging the client's credit card.
- **Additional requests.** Requests can range from linens to candles to music and everything in between. List the client's special requests on this line.

Developing a Task Calendar with Your Client

Once the client has signed the contract, you may suggest drafting a task calendar together. This is especially true with larger events that take six months or more to plan. The task calendar will highlight the client's responsibilities and tasks during the planning stages.

Client Tasks

The client's tasks will depend on the services she has hired you to perform. For example, client A has secured your services for a basic event-planning package. Client A has agreed to handle the invitations and has added this service to her package. Client B has secured your services for a deluxe event-planning package in which you handle the invitations. Client A will have invitations on her task calendar where Client B would not. Below are further examples of possible client tasks.

- Send a save-the-date card six months before the event.
- Meet the vendors four to six months before the event to choose the caterer, if applicable, and the photographer, entertainment, florist, and so forth.
- Confirm the final guest count the week before the event.

Event Planner Tasks

As an event planner, your task calendar will vary depending on two variables. The first is the type of event you are planning. The second is the services secured by your client. Below is an overview of tasks you may place on your task calendar.

- Once the venue has been secured, schedule a site visit with your client and facility planner for a walk-through. You will want to create a floor plan to discuss the location of tables, bar, band, etc.
- Four to six months before, coordinate a meeting with vendors and your client. You should attend every vendor meeting.
- Four weeks before, schedule another site visit with your client. During this site visit you will want to discuss table arrangements.
- Three months prior, meet with caterer and client to taste seasonal menu options.
- Two weeks before, secure rental equipment. During busy seasons, call six weeks ahead of time.
- Two weeks before, post staffing schedule for FOH employees.

The Proposal, Budget, and Deposits

When it comes to finalizing the details, the client will be looking for your expertise to guide him through the financial process. With a signed contract, you have entered into a legally binding relationship with your client. If possible, draft a contract and event sheet for the initial meeting. It is best to review the budget, deposits, contract, and proposal in person. This way if your client has any questions you can address all issues in person.

Alert

It is wise to seek legal advice from a lawyer and have her review your contract and its contents. Your lawyer should make corrections to your contract based on the law in your area. Most events you plan will not result in a legal battle, but it is wise to make sure you are protected just in case.

The Proposal

The proposal is an estimated invoice for an event. Many clients will request a proposal prior to your initial meeting. The proposal will outline food costs, beverage estimates, room charges, taxes, and gratuities. The proposal will also outline additional services for the event; for example, flowers, rentals, and valet services.

To price out your event you will likely need the assistance of your chef or caterer. If a client is planning a cocktail party for one hundred guests, the caterer may price the event out at $25 per person. For a three-course formal dinner, the event may be priced out at $85 per person. Usually caterers and chefs will create menus with pricing formulas to simplify this aspect for you. If a formula is not yet in place, ask to sit with your chef and create menus together. You just might learn a thing or two about menu pricing.

Based upon your proposal, the client may then ask for changes to fit within her budget. She may ask that the $25 per person cocktail party be increased to $30 per person. You would then consult the chef about the additions the client could receive with the price increase. He may suggest adding a stationary artisanal cheese platter to the event. After some negotiations, you and the client will have established the budget.

The Budget

The budget is something of an abstract number when you first speak with a person inquiring about your services. For example, a prospective client may call and ask if you can plan a family reunion for one hundred and fifty guests for $10,000. The amount of $10,000 is her budget.

The definition of a budget changes a bit during your initial interview. Once you have drafted the proposal, the budget then becomes a much more concrete figure. The proposal for the family reunion, for example, is now $10,000. You are making a commitment to plan this event within the proposal figure.

Deposits

In event planning, a deposit is an amount of money to secure your services. Deposits are usually taken within ten days of signing the contract. If a deposit is not received, the signed contract becomes null and void.

The deposit amount is subtracted from the final invoice. A deposit policy varies from company to company. Some event planners require 15 percent of the budget total up front. Other event planners request a set amount, such as a $2,000 deposit to secure an event. Still others simply ask for a receipt of a credit card number. If a client cancels in this case, the credit card may be charged a cancellation fee.

Alert

Industry standard suggests proposals fall within 10 percent of the final invoice. Alert the client of any changes she makes to the event that might jeopardize the budget.

A deposit represents a commitment from the client to the event planner. In some instances, a deposit is required to begin the event process, meaning the deposit amount may be used to begin purchasing items for the event. Check with your local bank to research the proper use of deposits.

Fact

Be sure to include a cancellation policy in your contract to avoid a credit card charge back. A charge back is used when there is a dispute between the credit card company and a business or individual and results in the credit card company charging back (crediting the client) the disputed amount until the issue is resolved. Without acknowledgment in your contract, a client can file a charge-back dispute with his credit card company and claim he was unaware of the policy.

Congratulations. You have survived your first client interview. Assess your performance by jotting notes in a personal journal. Were you well prepared? How can you better prepare next time? Were you nervous or relaxed? You will also become more relaxed as you speak to more clients. As time passes in your career, you will find you are more excited and less anxious. Learning something new with each experience will better prepare you for your career in event planning.

Chapter 13

It's All in the Details

EVENT PLANNING HAS BECOME TRENDY. Everywhere you look, from magazines to Web sites to television programs, event-planning experts are offering tips on how to throw a great party. For event planners, the details are the components leading to a successful event, because even the smallest detail can make or break an event.

The Process of Securing a Venue

A venue is the location of an event. It can be a small park or a large nightclub and everything in between. An event can have more than one venue, such as a wedding. More extravagant events can have a cocktail party or an afterparty at a separate location from the main event. Following is a list of common venue sites:

- Parks and picnic areas
- Banquet halls
- Museums
- Private rooms
- Hotels and restaurants
- Private residences

Consider offbeat venues to make an event more creative. Great event planners can transform any location into an amazing event. As you begin your career in event planning, imagine hosting an event at locations in your community. Whether at a bookstore, library, or flower shop, begin envisioning different events fitting specialty locations. Examples of creative venue sites are:

- Private libraries
- Botanical hothouses

- Gardens
- Airplane hangars
- Lofts
- Rooftop gardens

 **Alert**

> Make your client part of the process when choosing which sites to visit. A venue may perfectly suit your client but be out of her budget. Be up-front about venue costs and let your client decide whether she would like to include the more expensive venues on the tour.

To give your client the best range of options for venues, it is important for you to know the venues first. As you are getting your start as an event planner, use your downtime wisely. Schedule tour appointments with facility planners in the off-season when business is slower. Visit as many facilities as possible. During your appointment collect pricing information, menus, and photos if possible. You can then add this information to your venue files for future client meetings. Your clients will appreciate having venue information to review. It will narrow down the number of site visits you take your client on if she can preview the venues ahead of time.

The Site Visit

When visiting a venue with your client, you are acting as his advisor. It is your responsibility to collect information from each facility you visit. If you are using a file you have collected, be certain the information is current and updated. Let the facility planner lead the tour, but be sure to cover essential information while your client is present.

Avoid giving the facility planner hypothetical examples. Design the ideal event and present the specifics to each facility planner you visit. In the event design you want to be sure to include:

- Ideal timing
- Length of event

- Menu
- Estimated guest count
- Bar or beverage service
- Valet and parking
- Deposits and billing

The specifics of the event may have variables affecting the budget. Costs may fluctuate according to the time of day or length of the event. Tweaking the menu or bar service may lessen the cost of the event. Ask the facility planner to suggest changes to the event design to suit the client's budget.

Room Charge

A room charge is the cost associated with securing a private event. To make a restaurant exclusive for an evening, facilities may impose a room charge. Room charges will fluctuate depending on the time of day and day of the week and will also vary depending on the special events occurring in your community. A large convention coming into town, for example, may increase a room charge. From the restaurant's perspective, the logic behind the increase is justified because the profits from the convention would increase sales.

Essential

If the idea of a room charge confuses your client, elaborate using sympathetic language. Explain that securing a private space for a hundred guests equals lost revenue to a nightclub on a Saturday night when it normally serves three hundred guests. A client may soften to the idea of a room charge if he better understands the reason behind it.

Room charges are necessary for establishments generating daily income such as restaurants, bars, and nightclubs. Closing to the public usually means lost revenue to busy venues. Some venues will forgo imposing a room charge to attract additional sales brought in by a private event. Other venues will create a food and beverage minimum and waive a room charge.

Question

As a fledgling event planner, how can I determine suitable room charges?

If your employer is asking you to research room charges and food minimums, your best resource is a comparable venue. You may be the event planner at a new restaurant, but you can research other restaurants with private rooms and inquire about room charges and costs associated with a buyout.

A hotel may have a private room for thirty guests and charge a food and beverage minimum of $75 per person with beverages based upon consumption. The client would agree to a twenty-guest minimum with tax and gratuity charged additionally. If the food and beverage minimum is not met, the balance will be billed as a room charge. The hotel will be guaranteed the revenue in either case.

Securing a Venue

During your site visits there will be a lot of information presented to your client. It is a good idea to take notes on her behalf. Once the site visit is over, ask the facility planner to send a formal written proposal based upon the specific details of your client's visit. Your client may want to meet to review all of the proposals before making her decision.

Your client will likely need to sign a contract and pay a deposit to secure a venue. As the event planner, you are an integral part of this process. Review the contract and ask for an explanation of any points you may not understand. Be aware of the cancellation policy. In some cases, cancellations will result in the forfeit of the deposit. Once the contract is signed, make a copy of the contract and deposit check for your client file.

As you begin introducing vendors to the event, schedule a site visit with each vendor. You client may want to be included in each vendor site visit. Some venues have a vendor list that authorizes only certain vendors. It is possible, for example, to request that your client's photographer be added to the vendor list. For caterers however, some facilities prefer only using one or two that have a history of working in the on-premises kitchen. Requesting the addition of a favorite caterer to this list may be a little trickier. The facility may consider the caterer if you offer to place an additional deposit to be used in case of damages.

Securing the venue is the first piece of the puzzle in planning a great event. Once the venue has been finalized, the other pieces of the puzzle begin fitting into place a little easier. For example, your client may fall in love with a Moroccan restaurant as a venue. The other details of the event, like the menu, decorations, and beverage service, will be based upon the offerings of the restaurant. Your client can then focus on this particular restaurant's menu, wine list, and décor.

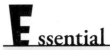

It is important in this industry to follow up with another event planner after a site visit. A quick note, phone call, or e-mail thanking the facility planner for his time will be appreciated. Avoid making the facility planner wonder if your client is going to book his venue and make the call as soon as your client makes her decision.

Working with Chefs to Develop a Menu

Designing the menu for an event can be the most enjoyable and creative detail for your client, especially if there is a menu tasting involved. Of course, not all events require a menu tasting, in which case the client will rely on your expertise and colorful language to describe the food options.

The recent popularity of gourmet cooking has brought with it a backlash against banquet-style cuisine. At functions across the country, savvy guests are left to wonder how a kitchen can simultaneously serve three hundred chickens at a fundraiser without compromising the quality of the food. At breakfast business meetings, gourmands and foodie guests alike remark as to whether the béarnaise sauce used on the poached eggs is traditional or from a box. And banquet servers are being asked if the salmon is farm-raised or wild, and if the beef is organic or grain-fed.

The public's awareness of the ingredients on their plates is inevitably raising the level of quality of cuisine. As a result, event planners have had to follow suit. The competition among event planners to serve gourmet meals has become a challenge handed down to banquet and private dining chefs.

The most important idea to remember when designing a menu with the chef is execution. A beautifully written menu means nothing if it cannot be executed. If the chef is preparing a new menu item, ask to be part of the tasting. You can disguise your apprehension about the dish by explaining to the chef your need to describe all the menu items to clients. Troubleshoot with the chef if possible by asking if the new dish can be served to a large group of people or retain heat if not served right away.

E ssential

Many event planners hired from event-planning companies will send a client an all-inclusive invoice. This invoice will not include an itemized breakdown of the costs associated with the event. In this case the client is unaware of the facility fees, and as the facility planner you may be asked not to discuss the venue prices during the site visit.

Budgeting the Menu

Budgeting a menu takes a lot of practice. In the beginning of your career, you will need to work with the chef quite a bit to solve the mystery of pricing out a menu. To a chef, budgeting a menu is second nature since she places the order and then compares the order to the invoice. A chef will also have a better understanding of labor costs and food waste. A menu budget factors in the ingredients, labor, overhead, waste, and profit.

Alert

Chefs, by reputation, are notoriously willful and may not take criticism well. When making suggestions, carefully choose your language. Using harsh remarks may offend some chefs and lead to a negative working environment.

Chefs use different formulas to price out a menu, so ask your chef for his formula to better understand the process of budgeting the menu. Prior to submitting a menu proposal to a client, consult with your chef so he may review the cost and approve the menu. Any changes should be made internally before your client makes her decision regarding the cuisine.

In your follow-up meetings with your chef or caterer, it is a good idea to run down the budget from recent events. Also request participation in budget meetings for your company. The result will give you a better understanding of the budget formula.

Beverage Service

The menu budget also needs to include the bar or beverage service. There are a few options for clients when budgeting for beverages. The first is to have an open bar and not restrict the consumption of beverages from the bar. For open bars, beverage costs are usually based upon guest consumption. In some cases, venues charge a set amount for an open bar. The price is typically very high. In fact, it is not unusual for a price tag of $10,000 or more to accompany an open bar for a large event.

The second option for bar service is to offer a cash-and-carry bar, which means each guest is responsible for paying for his or her own beverage. Cash and carry is not well received among guests and usually causes a traffic jam as servers have to handle cash transactions. To enhance the guest experience, a client may choose to host beer and wine. The client will ultimately spend less money and the guests will appreciate the gesture. A popular option these days is to offer a punch bowl or a signature cocktail in addition to beer and wine. The trendy cocktail will pair nicely with a classic wine selection, offering a bit of variety and creativity to your event.

 Fact

A client looking to save money may request that wine purchased from an outside source be served at his event. Most venues restrict outside beverages being served. No alcoholic beverages equals lost revenue. In some cases, venues will allow wine to be brought in but will charge a corkage fee. A standard corkage fee to open wine is $10 to $20 per bottle.

Venue Packages

A venue package is an all-inclusive price for an event. Some venues offer packages to simplify the planning process. For example, a banquet facility may include all vendor services in one package to avoid a client having to shop for her own vendors. A venue package may include any combination of the following:

- The menu
- The bar service
- Table settings and accessories
- Floral arrangements
- Centerpieces
- A cake or extravagant dessert
- Parking or valet service for your guests
- Limousine service
- A house photographer
- Decorations

When a client is considering a venue package, inquire about upgrades on certain services. Some venues will price an upgrade to a standard package particularly high to make a higher-priced package seem more reasonable. Venue packages also leave little room for your client's ideas and creativity. Be sure to price out a few other venues for your client. A venue package may be less of a deal than your client originally thought.

Finding Professionals Who May Enhance the Event

Clients look to event planners for creativity and ingenuity. Event planners look to other professionals for the very same inspiration. There are many detailed accessories that can complement an event. From lighting to music to art, introducing specialized details will allow your client's personality to be expressed in the event.

Just as vendors market themselves to specific events, subvendors do the same in the event-planning world. These subvendors are by no means subpar; they offer specialized services to the elite event planner. These vendors may include:

Calligraphers

Exquisite penmanship on an invitation will add Old-World style to any event. If your event is more modern and trendy, some calligraphers have added more fonts to their handwriting to keep up with trends. Avoid impersonal computer-generated labels.

Interior Decorators

Not too long ago, interior decorators were hired by only the very wealthy. Much like the increasing popularity of gourmet cooking television shows, interior design programs have also found a bit of celebrity in recent years. Interior designers are migrating outside of the habitat of the home and into event planning. As part of the creative team, interior designers work alongside the lighting, staging, and production crew. Offering advice from linen colors to stage design, an interior decorator can add a stylish element to your event.

Food Stylists

Food stylists work on commercials, television shows, and print media to enhance the appearance of edible props. Because some food products do not film well, a food stylist may work with different products to get the best shot, for example, substituting milk in a cereal commercial (a glue mixture, by the way is what you see in most cereal advertisements, not milk). A stylist may also create dozens of replicas of the same dish to be served on the set of a television program. Each dish must be exactly the same to avoid discrepancy in future shots.

When designing an elaborate buffet table or centerpiece, who better to have on your team than a food stylist? For an event where food is the main focus, enlist the expertise of a food stylist to create an art installation out of the menu.

Animal Handlers

Exotic animals have long been used as accessories at elaborate events. Whether it is white doves released into the sky or lions on leashes, animals add a wow factor some clients look to add to their events. When researching the possibility of animals at an event, contact your area's gaming commission for the laws governing the import and use of domestic and wild animals. Also check and double-check the background of the animal handler. Your chosen venue may also have regulations regarding animals on premises. Some venues require an additional insurance binder in case of damage caused by the animal.

Trapeze Artists

Broadway shows and movies featuring trapeze artists and contortionists have catapulted this ancient art form into an event entertainment extravaganza. Perfect as a background element for an event or as the main attraction, contortionists can work floor routines as well as on ropes descending from high ceilings. Again, it is a good idea to check with your venue's policies before hiring contortionists.

Musicians

With the boom in technology of recent years, many entertainers have incorporated different forms of media in their performances.

DJs of recent years have turned to plasma screen televisions with live simultaneous broadcasts of the event around the venue. Light shows, fireworks displays, and laser performances occur at events in sync with the DJ extraordinaire.

Bakers

Baking has always been something of an art form. Nowadays, cakes can be created of any image imaginable. Replicas of antique cars, 3-D images of cartoons, and life-size portraits of masterpieces can be created using flour and sugar. Local bakers have expanded their clientele with the advent of the Internet and overnight shipping.

Researching your city's greater business bureau or business alliance is a great way to find these high-end professionals. You may want to ask other event planners as well. For more obscure services, such as artist installations, get involved in the artist community or art school in your area.

Choosing Staff That Will Complement the Event

Every staff member adds a different element to each event. Aside from personalities and talents, your staff should be armed with the basic knowledge to effectively do a great job. Think of your servers and front-of-the-house employees as performers in a show. If you were the director of the show, you would set up rehearsals and give the performers a script. Even the back-of-the-house staff needs direction, just as the production crew of a play might. Event planning should be thought of in the same respect. Give your staff the tools to succeed and your event will be even more successful.

Educate Your Staff

With food allergies affecting so much of the public, education of your staff is crucial. As part of the training process, it is important to cover basic knowledge of food allergies and life-saving techniques. Explain how important it is for the servers to convey all information on guest allergies to the kitchen. An unprepared staff member can ultimately be the demise of a lot more than just the event.

Appealing to each guest's taste can be a challenge in the event-planning industry. It's not uncommon for a banquet service to serve the same course to each guest, for example, at a wedding where each guest is served a medium-rare prime rib roast beef. How does the chef know if a guest is a vegetarian or prefers his beef medium rather than medium-rare? Empower your staff to engage with the guests to determine whether the menu is suitable to their tastes. Have an easy backup dish available for a guest with dietary restrictions in these cases.

Your servers are the buffers between the guests and the kitchen. A staff should be trained to walk guests through the menu. A staff should also be knowledgeable about the ingredients on the menu if a guest would like to make a substitution. It is important your staff handles special requests graciously. Guests with special requests should not be a bother to back-of-the-house or front-of-the-house staff. This is an area where your staff can really make a positive impact on a guest's experience with your company. Exceed the expectations of your client and make guests with special requests feel special.

Staff Strengths and Weaknesses

When planning an event, it is best to keep in mind the strengths and weaknesses of your staff as final preparations are being made. An exuberant, outgoing server may be perfectly suited for a cocktail party but not a board meeting. A knowledgeable, snooty server may be perfect for a wine tasting but not a bachelorette party. A young, talented chef who is great in her own restaurant may not function well at a catered event.

Decorations

In event planning, decorations can be just as subjective as the menu. Offering understated decorations for an event is a good start. But take the client's lead if she is hoping for a more dramatic effect with decorations. Event decorations can be monumental, featuring trapeze artists and trampolines, or subtle, using delicate place-card holders and simple floral centerpieces. Avoid offensive or tacky decorations at all costs.

Choosing a spectacular venue can lessen the need for decorations. This can affect a client's budget if a venue may be a bit out of his price range. When considering a picturesque space, money from the client's decoration budget may be carried over into the venue budget to offset the additional cost. Restaurants and hotels may already commission artists to hang artwork on the walls and have floral designers bring in fresh flowers every week. To give your client a better idea of decorations, ask the facility planner on your site visits how previous clients have used the space.

Your goal for decorations is to stay in the same theme or color scheme. Researching party and festival themes has never been easier with the Internet. The following is a list of popular event themes.

- Mardi Gras
- English tea parties
- Carnival
- Religious ceremonies
- Fantasy
- Sporting

Extras an Event Planner May Provide

Event planners have been known to go above and beyond the terms of a contract to attract clients. Adding personalized touches is a way to provide specialized services and set yourself apart from your competition. For larger events, some event planners have been known to send a gift to a client after an event. Planners may also send a gift to a client for a referral.

Stationery and Invitations

Choosing invitations may be the responsibility of the event planner if so stated in the contract. If not, assisting the client in the invitation design provides a nice additional touch. Offering to have the invitations professionally addressed will also be well received by a client. Place cards and personalized menus will impress a client if the service is not offered by the facility. Lastly, event planners have taken on the RSVP list as an extra service for some events.

Dry Cleaning

Dropping off dry cleaning is a chore that is easy to forget, and picking up dry cleaning for an event can be a monumental task in the hectic days before an event. Having an event planner arrange for dry cleaning will leave your client grinning from ear to ear.

Remember to leave yourself ample time for the dry-cleaning process. Picking up garments from the cleaner at least two days ahead of time is advised in case of mistakes and emergencies. This will also give your client time for a final fitting. Keep this offer open to the men in the event and extend the invitation to include tuxedos as well.

Car Service

Some event facilities have transportation available on their premises. Check the regulations regarding client use. In some cases, a car service is solely for airport transit. If not, offer the car to a client to make event-related errands in the area or send the car the day of the event to pick up the host.

The client may also be unfamiliar with an area, making it convenient to utilize a car service. If your event facility does not use a car service, offer to take the client to meet vendors and similar errands. Private drivers may also reduce rates to repeat clients, so make sure you develop a rapport with drivers you use on a repeat basis.

Reminders

In the beginning of your career it may not be possible to offer extra services. Certainly during busy times of the year it will be next to impossible for you to fit in extras at an event. Do not offer extra services if it means you are spreading yourself too thin. If it will compromise the event or increase your stress, do not take on extra responsibilities. Sometimes just a reminder call to your client in regards to dry cleaning will be helpful and appreciated. Ask the client what other tasks need to be completed before the event. When you can pitch in, let your client know. At the very least, your efforts will be rewarded when you phone with a reminder.

Details are subjective. One client may be perfectly fine with the thought of a detail going awry, while another client will be devastated. Consider each detail surrounding an event as being important to a client. And when things do not go as planned in the details, have solutions that will appease your client.

Chapter 14

Confirming Details with Your Client and Vendors

CONFIRMING THE DETAILS with your client and vendors is an important part of the process of event planning, as it gives you a chance to freshen the details in the minds of all involved. The details also need to be confirmed to avoid confusion between the client and vendor. As the event planner, you are the link between the client and the vendors.

The Final Count

The final count is the number of guests used to base the costs of an event. A client will determine the final count based upon RSVPs she has received from her guests. In some cases, the event planner will receive the RSVPs on behalf of the client. Before submitting the final count to a vendor, it is a good idea to confirm the number with the client, especially when you are receiving the RSVPs. The final count will determine staffing and products purchased for the event.

Since the final count is what the vendors use to purchase products, the minimum number charged to the client the night of the event equals the final count. For example, a client may call on Thursday with the final count of one hundred guests for her event on Saturday. The menu price has been set at $45 per person. The minimum number you would charge for the event is 100 guests × $45, or $4,500. If the actual count is 120 guests, then you would charge the client $5,400 (120 × $45).

A Risk to Keep in Mind

When confirming the final numbers with the client, you should take into consideration any undecided guests. Vendors such as caterers might base their product purchasing and staffing on the final count plus 10 percent. If your client has thirty undecided guests out of one hundred, your client is running the risk of not having enough food and beverage to feed her guests. When submitting the final count, ask your client if she has a response from all of her guests. It is OK to convey the consequences to the client for underestimating guest costs.

Check your company's policy for when a client does not meet his final guest count. Normally the per-person price is charged to the food sales of the company, just as wine sales are charged to wine cost. Instead of allotting the sales to the food costs, some companies charge the balance as a room charge. The room charge will be allotted to the profit, whereas food sales subtract losses such as labor, food costs, equipment, and so forth. Since the company is making a straight profit from the guests who cancelled, the balance may go to a room charge.

E ssential

Before charging the final count balance to a room charge, check with the chef and other members of your team. If products have been ordered from the kitchen, a portion of the room charge should be given to food sales. This way the kitchen will not have lost revenue from expected guests not showing up.

Weather Permitting

The weather in some parts of the country may play a large part in guest attendance, especially around the holiday season. Most contracts have specific terminology regarding inclement weather and cancellation of events. Check your company's policy regarding weather cancellations. Some banquet facilities will allow the client to reschedule the event without penalties. With other companies, the client will assume all losses associated with weather cancellations, or the client may forfeit the room charge and a percentage of the total cost of the event. In this case, a 25 percent forfeit of the total is an industry standard.

Food and Beverage Minimums

A food and beverage minimum is a monetary amount a guest must spend in order to secure a private space. Some hotels and restaurants offer a food and beverage minimum to waive any room charges. If a food and beverage minimum is not met, the difference may be charged as a room charge.

When confirming the details with the client a week before the event, refer back to the contract to revisit the food and beverage minimum. Confirm with your client how a food and beverage minimum may affect the room charge. Your client should have a firm understanding of the penalties of not meeting the food and beverage minimum. It is best to avoid having this conversation the night of the event.

The room charge for not meeting the food and beverage minimum may be set at a certain price rather than charging the difference. For example, if a food and beverage minimum is $85 per person, the minimum number of guests for a private room may be thirty guests, creating a food and beverage minimum of $2,550. If only twenty guests RSVP, then the room charge will be $850, which is very high. As an event planner you may allow a set room charge to be implemented. A set room charge is a monetary price of a lesser amount than the penalty charge. In the above example, rather than charging $850 for the room charge, you may agree to a $500 room charge. The $500 room charge would be in effect if the event produced ten less guests or twenty less guests.

Businesses these days need to be very particular about how a receipt or invoice reads to its accounting department. Even though a room charge may be imposed, it may need to be listed as a separate cost on a receipt or invoice.

For example, you are charging a business a $200 room charge for the use of a private room. You are also requiring ten guests as the minimum number in attendance. The per-person amount for each guest is $45 for the menu. If only eight guests attend, you are charging an additional $90 for the two missing guests. Rather than charging $290 as the room charge, many businesses will ask the $90 be charged as a cancellation fee. This way a person in the accounting office will more easily understand the charge.

Itemize All Charges

Confirming the details includes verifying the costs of the event with your client. When you began planning the event, there may have been certain unknown variables such as rentals and centerpieces. As the event draws closer, these unknown costs will become actual costs. All of the invoices and receipts you have been collecting will allow you to itemize all charges and discuss them with your client prior to the event.

E ssential

As details are being solidified throughout the event, send your client e-mail confirmation of items you have discussed in person or over the phone. These e-mails will act as a reference for you to review the event. To refresh your memory, you can also refer to these e-mails before drafting an updated invoice.

The Importance of Confirming Charges

It is a good idea to touch base with your client and confirm all charges prior to the event. You have likely been in solid communication with your client for every decision, such as rental prices, entertainment costs, decoration costs, and so forth. In a perfect scenario, these charges have all been approved by the client and are within the client's budget. For a client, it is helpful to be able to see all of the charges listed on an updated invoice. Upon re-evaluation of her budget, the client may scale back on certain details or add money to the budget for other details.

Presenting an updated invoice also prevents any miscommunication that may have occurred during the planning stages. For example, the floral designer may have submitted a preliminary invoice for centerpieces. You listed the line item for flowers on your updated invoice. The client realizes she gave you the wrong figure for flowers under her budget. The figure should have been $200 less. You are then able to contact the floral designer and ask her to scale back on her centerpieces before the event.

Updated Invoice

Before signing a contract with the client, you most likely drafted a preliminary invoice. This invoice shows the client the costs involved regarding room charges, menu, and the beverage formula. As time goes on you will develop a better understanding of actual costs and not just use estimates on the invoice. Presenting an updated invoice to the client is wise when you are confirming details.

Actual Costs on the Updated Invoice

Since the planning stages you have been collecting receipts related to the event. Before confirming the details with the client, you will need to get the receipts organized and draft an updated invoice. For information such as beverage totals, place a TBD (to be determined) instead of a price, since the beverage may be based upon consumption. You can also use an estimated amount on the updated invoice, but be sure to signify this is an estimated cost, preferably next to the line item.

 Fact

The updated invoice is not a legal document. However, it is a good idea to have your client initial the invoice. This will prevent any discrepancy arising at a later date. E-mailing a copy of the invoice is also a good way to prove your client has seen the latest figures.

Developing a Timeline

An event timeline charts the progression of the tasks leading up to the event. Things that need to be tracked include the staff's arrival time, the production team's arrival time, and prep time for the kitchen. The event timeline can also refer to the sequence of events during the event itself. This would include the arrival time for guests, the timing of the courses, and the entertainment's start time.

 Fact

Buffing a table is an industry term referring to polishing silver and glassware. Buffing is usually done once the table is set up to avoid fingerprints and to ensure all items are free of debris.

Timeline of Occurrences Before the Event

As the event planner you may decide to draft two timelines, one for setup, one for the event itself. Following is an example of a timeline for an event setup.

- 1 P.M.—BOH to arrive for setup of kitchen. BOH begins prepping menu.
- 4 P.M.—Rental dropoff.
- 4:30 P.M.—Stage and lighting team arrive.
- 4:45 P.M.—FOH staff arrives. Servers 1 and 2: table setup. Servers 3 and 4: linen setup. Severs 4 and 5: glasses and flatware. Bartenders to set up bar. All servers buff tables upon setup.
- 5 P.M.—Band arrives.
- 5:30 P.M.—Florist arrives with centerpieces.
- 5:45 P.M.—Baker arrives with cake.
- 6 P.M.—Band rehearsal.
- 6 P.M.—Completion of production. Room is completely set.
- 6:15 P.M.—Staff meeting.
- 7 P.M.—Guests arrive.

Event Timeline

The event timeline is an itinerary of the event itself. A copy of the event timeline should be discussed in advance with the client in case she would like to make changes. The event timeline should be drafted and confirmed at least one week prior to the event.

- 7 P.M.—Guests arrive. Servers greet guests with champagne. Band is playing.
- 7:15 P.M.—Hors d'oeuvres are passed.
- 8 P.M.—Guests are seated for dinner.
- 8:15 P.M.—First course is served.
- 8:45 P.M.—Entrée is served.
- 9:15 P.M.—Dessert buffet is set for self service.
- 9:30 P.M.—Dancing begins.
- 9:45 P.M.—Tables are cleared. Rentals are organized for next day pickup.
- 10:30 P.M.—Host needs microphone for toast.
- 11:30 P.M.—Favor bags are brought out and passed around.
- Midnight—Band stops playing. Event ends.

By drafting a timeline for the event, you are organizing the arrival times of all your vendors. Staggering vendor arrival times organizes the use of the loading zone and relieves any parking pressure. This is especially true when working in the city where parking can be problematic.

Alert

List all vendors and staff cell phone numbers on the setup timeline. This way you will have each person's phone number in case someone is running late. Have one person be solely responsible for checking in vendors and staff if you cannot be present. This person can be an event assistant or a member of the staff.

Having a timeline allows you to keep track of when your vendors and staff arrive. The timeline will ensure all staff knows each assigned job and when tasks need to be completed. Lastly, a timeline will cue each department, from the lighting technician to the chef, as to when the next occurrence will happen in the event. This allows each department to be on mark a few minutes ahead of schedule.

Confirming the Menu with Caterer or Client

At the start of the event-planning process, you may have proposed a menu with your client. Chances are you and the chef designed a menu and pricing regarding the menu items. If the planning process is longer than two months, it is a good idea to meet with the chef and verify the menu as the event draws closer.

When the Menu Changes

Many factors can affect a change in the menu. Ingredients can become unavailable. Inclement weather may have affected a crop of vegetables. A health concern can change the public's opinion on a food-related item. Prices of meat and seafood can rise, which can blow up your client's budget. When planning an event with a client, these issues should be raised as you discuss the proposed menu. As long as a suitable substitution can be made, your client should be understanding.

Essential

Changes you make to a client's menu should still stay within his budget. If you and the chef did not price out the menu properly, you should consider offering the same menu at the client's original budget. The client should not be penalized for any mistakes made by your staff.

Confirming Menu Details

The best reason to confirm all details is to avoid any mistakes made in the proposal. Details, including the menu, change from the start of planning the event to the day of the event. Confirmation is the best way to make sure the event details are current and up to date.

Essential

For example, the client planning a birthday party for her mother may have changed the dessert selection. She has asked to include blueberries, her mother's favorite, as one of the ingredients. The client made the request via a phone call a month beforehand just as you were headed out to another event. You forgot to update the event sheet and alert the pastry chef of the new request. Upon confirmation of the menu, your client notices the dessert does not include blueberries and points out the discrepancy. You are now able to correct the oversight before the event.

Meeting with your chef once a week is a good habit to develop. During the meeting you can discuss any upcoming events, design menus for potential clients, and change any out-of-season ingredients. During this meeting you can also confirm the menus of upcoming events. The chef may call her purveyors and check the availability of ingredients and prices before signing off on the final menu. The chef may also inquire about guest counts during these meetings so she may staff properly. Of course, you won't have the final guest count until one week before the event, but you will have a good idea of the guest count a few weeks prior.

If you cannot meet with the chef, schedule a meeting specifically to confirm the menu of your events. To be safe, schedule this meeting two weeks before the event. Have all documented changes to the menu available as well as an updated event sheet. It is also a good idea to have a draft of the menu for the chef to review.

Fact

A menu header is a personalized message a client places at the top of a menu. The date of the event usually follows underneath. A client may choose to write "Happy Birthday" or "Congratulations" with the person's name following. It is also becoming popular to include a logo at the top of a menu for corporate events.

Once the chef has signed off on the final menu, contact your client to verify the menu. It is absolutely necessary to point out any changes or substitutions. The client should approve all menu changes prior to the event. You should also have a copy of the menu for your client to review and initial. Confirm any menu headings with the client at this time.

Handling Menu Discrepancies

Menu discrepancies with clients should be handled gingerly. Hopefully you have prepared the client for any changes that happen along the way. First, be apologetic. You could be changing the one dish the client was looking forward to ordering. Next, if a menu change will be disastrous to your client, check back with the chef. Sometimes you can find another purveyor to obtain certain ingredients, though the cost may be affected. In this case it is appropriate to offer the client the ingredient and adjust the cost. Lastly, avoid changing the menu completely. If possible, certain ingredients of the menu can change without a complete menu overhaul. Subtle changes are much more appealing to a client than an entire new menu.

Listing Miscellaneous Information

Miscellaneous information is anything that doesn't fit under the standard event headings. Miscellaneous information can include the sequences of service and affect only the front of the house. Any special requests should be listed under miscellaneous information. Because this information can affect any department, correct placing is very important. Even though it is considered miscellaneous information, it is still integral to the event and should not be missed.

Times

The different staging of tasks can be considered miscellaneous information. If the host is due to arrive at noon to set up company materials but the board meeting does not start until 1 P.M., this should be listed on the event sheet. The kitchen may be ready to serve lunch at noon if you list the host's arrival time as the start time. The servers may not have the room set up until 1 P.M. if you list the board meeting's time as the start time. The same is true for surprise parties or dinners beginning with a cocktail hour. Be sure the separate arrival times are listed on the event sheet where both the kitchen and staff will see the information.

Allergies and Special Requests

Allergies and special food requests also have a header under miscellaneous information. Food allergies are severe for some guests, and this information should be written on the event sheet and also verbalized to the kitchen and staff. Highlight the information if possible.

Less severe, but important nonetheless, are special requests. A special request can be from a vegetarian guest, a guest on a special diet, or from a guest requesting a special menu item. For example, the client may have requested beef Wellington for the guest of honor. Due to the high cost of the dish, the client was not able to serve all of the guests beef Wellington. The chef made an exception and offered to make a single beef Wellington for the guest of honor. This miscellaneous information needs to be conveyed not only to the rest of the kitchen staff but to the servers as well.

Elaborating on Miscellaneous Information

Miscellaneous information may need more explaining than an event sheet allows. For lengthy explanations, type the information on a separate sheet of paper. You can also attach any e-mail correspondences between you and your client explaining the miscellaneous information in better detail. As a final option, you can make quick notes to contact you if the need arises. This way, if you are not attending this event, your event manager will know it is appropriate to phone you for the details.

E ssential

Remember, your event sheets need to be interpreted by your staff and the kitchen. For this reason each sheet should be easy to read. More importantly, you should make the event sheets easily readable in case you have an emergency and cannot attend the event in person.

Troubleshooting

Troubleshooting the event is the act of imagining certain details of the event going wrong. By imagining certain details going wrong, you can envision solutions or put a backup plan into effect. Confirming the details is the ideal time to troubleshoot the details of the event.

An apprehensive client may need a bit of reassuring as the event gets closer. It may not be enough to simply reassure your client with dialogue. An apprehensive or negative client will find ways to criticize the event if everything does not go according to plan. There are different steps you can take to be proactive and troubleshoot the event with your client.

Chances are the venue you are working with will be having an event prior to yours. Ask the facility planner if you can arrange a site visit prior to the start time of another event. Seeing the venue set with linens, flatware, and centerpieces can put your client at ease and trigger different ideas for his event. Viewing the venue with your client may also jog your imagination as well. Either way, you cannot lose. The client will have a firm understanding as to how her event will be set up.

A menu tasting before an event is popular for large functions, but it does make you wonder how a chef can cook a tasting menu in December for an event occurring in July. Produce availability changes with the seasons, as will the availability of meats and shellfish, not to mention the cost of ingredients fluctuating. It may be a good idea to invite a client to a menu tasting a few weeks before the event rather than a few months before. Tasting the menu is one way to troubleshoot the availability of the ingredients.

Troubleshooting Your Vendors

Much like the venue setup, you can offer to troubleshoot your vendors with your client. When the floral designer is arranging flowers for an event similar to your client's, ask her for an appointment. Your client can view the flower arrangements and troubleshoot any aspects of the arrangements he would like to change. An especially nice touch is sending your client a similar floral arrangement to her home.

In the past, clients were invited to other events to preview entertainment as well. The hosts of these events now frown upon this practice. Musicians now send a sampling of shows through compact discs and videos.

Alert

In the initial phase of the planning process, you might have written "pending" or "to be determined" for certain details such as the wine selections or rental inventory. When confirming the details with your client, acknowledge all pending details. Work with your client to finalize these details.

Troubleshooting with Your Staff

Visiting the venue and vendors might not be worth the time for a small meeting or casual dinner. Still, it is a good idea to troubleshoot each event with a staff member. Together you can decide which details need to be elaborated and which details may not work as well. Any concerns can be brought to the attention of the client before the event.

Checking items off of your list has its advantages. You are beginning final preparations on the event you have worked so hard to plan. Hopefully your organization is paying off at this time and you have breezed through your confirmations with your client and vendors. With the event now days away, being organized is critical. The result is confidence in yourself and a stress-free event.

Chapter 15

Final Preparations

THE FINAL PREPARATIONS begin after the confirmations have been made with the client and vendors. These are the final stages of the event-planning process. With all of your dedication and organization, the next five days should be an extension of your potential as an event planner. The next five days will be a reinforcement of all of your planning thus far.

Five Days Ahead

You should have the final count into the chef and all of your vendors at this time. Some tough work still lies ahead of you. By staying organized, you will prepare yourself and your staff for a successful event.

Draft Both Timelines

Five days prior to the event, go over your event sheet, notes, and e-mail correspondence and look for any discrepancies. Your event sheet should be up-to-date. Any discrepancies or questions should be reconfirmed with your client and brought to the attention of the chef. Carefully build the itinerary for the setup and the event itself. Once both timelines are complete, e-mail the event timeline and menu to your client for review.

In these final days, it is wise to create a crate or tote bag you will be taking with you on the day of the event. This on-site bag will be in addition to your travel bag and should hold any items relevant to the event. Timelines, client files, e-mails, and so forth should all be placed in your on-site bag.

Determine Staff Responsibilities

In your setup itinerary, list your service staff with their corresponding responsibilities. By delegating responsibilities at the start of the event, you lessen the risk of staff wandering and looking for direction from you. It is also a good idea to list on the setup itinerary a particular zone or station each staff member will be working.

List any tools your staff may need ahead of time. Wine keys, crumbers, pens, notepads, lighters, and uniforms are all essentials, and your staff should be notified ahead of time in an e-mail what is required of them. Also list any ingredients your bartenders may need to prepare as well. Lime juice, simple syrup, and lemon twists, for example, should be listed in the server packet for the bartenders so he or she can begin prepping the bar upon arrival.

 Fact

A crumber is a tool used to sweep crumbs off of table linens. A crumber is used between courses but especially before the dessert course when all dishes should be removed from the table. To crumb a surface without linen, a neatly rolled linen or bar cloth works nicely.

Consider Your Outfit

Dressing appropriately is not just a concern of the guests. The manner in which you dress speaks volumes about you as an event planner. Dressing fashionably is suitable for some events, but keep your attire professional. Remember to pack an extra set of clothes for emergencies. Event planners have been known to pitch in with heavy lifting and prep work. The possibility of a torn hem or butter-stained tie warrants having a backup outfit.

Drop your outfit at the cleaners five days ahead of time. Prepare to pick up your dry cleaning two days prior to an event. This will leave you ample time to try on your outfits one last time before the event. Having to race to the cleaners on your way to the event will cause unnecessary stress. Avoid catastrophes and ask your dry cleaner if he expects to keep the same hours for the next week. If time off due to holidays or vacations prevents you from picking up your dry cleaning, use another service.

Confirm Rental Orders

The rental order should be the last item confirmed. At the beginning stages of planning the event, you most likely called in a large rental order based upon the client's initial guest count, but the order may need to be adjusted because of dropoffs in the final guest count. Now is the time to call in your final order to the rental company. Usually the rental company does not penalize for decreased orders. But it is best to check the policy before placing your original order.

Double-check the rental checklist before confirming the order to ensure you have not missed an item. Most rental companies have a catalog, but be sure to call for this ahead of time. Oversights such as linens for the kitchen staff or staff aprons can leave you scrambling at the last minute for replacements.

Finalize Printed Materials

All printed materials should be completed five days prior to the event. Copies of the menu should be ready to be placed in the server packets. If you are handling place cards, nametags, or table numbers, set aside some time to coordinate these. Any cards describing stationary cuisine or a cheese plate should also be completed on this day.

Use a computer so printed materials have a professional appearance. Of course, a handwritten script will look beautiful on printed materials and add a personal touch, but it may not be suitable for a business event. Once the printed materials have been taken care of, place each in a manila envelope and label the materials. Save any information on your computer and do not erase until the event is over. Be sure to place the envelopes in your on-site tote.

E ssential

A good practice is e-mailing the information to yourself in case of mishaps. It is also wise to back up any computer information on a USB drive. You will be able to access the e-mail (if using a Web-based e-mail account such as Google or Yahoo) or USB from another office and print materials. Keep extra printing paper and your USB drive in your travel kit.

Three Days Ahead

Three days before the event you are entering the home stretch. If you are organized and up-to-date, you may feel like taking a personal day or working from home. However, with the event so close, it is best to remain available by phone at your office. In the next few days, you will be flooded by calls with last-minute questions from your client and vendors. Guests of the event may also contact you asking for directions or lodging recommendations. With only three days to go before the event, it is a good idea to remain close to the phone.

Organize Files

Three days before the event is a good time to organize any remaining paperwork. Your client file should be current and organized with up-to-date receipts and invoices. Draft a final invoice to your client and request final invoices from your vendors. If your client needs to write checks for other vendors, send her a list of vendors with amounts due. Offer to pass out the vendors' checks upon receipt if their services have been rendered.

Prepare Server Packets

A server packet includes all information pertinent to the front of the house. The server packet should include the event sheet, both timelines, table settings, and a floor plan of the space. These packets will serve your staff well for basic information and instructions. Any questions from your staff can be addressed at the staff meeting an hour before event time.

 Fact

A floor plan is an aerial-view drawing of the event space. Table arrangements should be included in the floor plan as well as the number of chairs allowed at each table. Buffet tables should also be drawn in place. Seat numbers are the positions of guests around a table; these allow servers to place dishes in front of guests subtly and without calling out each dish and waiting for each guest to respond.

A server packet should also include a copy of the menu with menu descriptions. Wine offerings with a paragraph description about the varietals will arm your staff with specific information about the night's offerings. Adding signature cocktails with additional information regarding the spirits offered will elevate the staff's service.

Update Your Travel Kit

As an event planner, part of your role is to arrive prepared. Different event planners need to be prepared in different ways. For large events, your client will appreciate you being as prepared as a boy scout. Placing an emergency toiletries kit in each bathroom is thoughtful but can get expensive if you are providing this for each event. A better, more efficient means of providing emergency items is placing a basket of mints in the restroom with a note stating: "Toiletries items available on request. Please see a member of the staff." Other items you'll want to include:

- **Headache and allergy medicine.** Check with your local pharmacist regarding dispensing over-the-counter medication. If there is some discrepancy about this issue, instruct your client to keep these items in her purse in case of emergency.
- **Sewing kit.** Buttons are famous for popping off during special occasions. A small sewing kit can come in handy in these situations.
- **Nail file.** A torn nail is not just unsightly but can snag fabrics.
- **Variety of nylons.** Getting a run in a pair of stockings will happen more times than not.
- **Toothbrushes, toothpaste, and dental floss.** These are an after-dinner must.
- **Concealer.** Comes in handy, especially if pictures will be taken.
- **Feminine hygiene products.** Most bathrooms are equipped with a machine, but be prepared just in case there isn't one.
- **Scotch tape.** Scotch tape can remove some makeup and flower dust from fabric.

- **Clear nail polish and nail polish remover.** Clear nail polish can stop a run from getting larger. Nail polish remover can remove strong adhesives and tags from surfaces such as mirrors or glass. Be sure to do a surface test first.
- **Stain remover stick.** Certain brands can even remove red wine and blood from fabrics.
- **Hairspray.**
- **First-aid kit.**
- **USB drive and copy paper.** Being able to print event materials from another office or printer will come in handy.

All vendors have tricks of the trade. Ask the advice of your vendors and collect the best tips from the professionals. For example, a matchbook works in a pinch as a nail file, and to remove a fishy smell from your hands, wash them with lemon and a metal spoon.

One Day Ahead

Last-minute crises often surface the day before an event, so be at your office to solve any problems that may arise. With one day to go, a final check of your supplies should occur before you leave the office.

Check in with the Chef

By now the chef will have ordered and most likely prepped the products for tomorrow. Simply checking in with the chef is crucial on the day before an event. Last-minute changes or substitutions may happen at this point. Consider the weight of the changes before contacting your client. For example, if one type of mushroom needs to be substituted for another, it is probably not necessary to call your client. If the white wine she chose suddenly becomes unavailable, you should alert her of the change.

Check in with Your Client

The menu and itinerary have been approved. You have sent an e-mail to your client listing her financial responsibilities with the vendors for the event. An hour before you are ready to leave the office for the day, phone your client for one last check-in. Leave with your client your schedule for tomorrow, as well as a number where you can be reached in case anything comes up.

Alert

The client should approve most last-minute menu substitutions or changes. Always call with a recommendation and reassurance that the change is a positive one. Be honest with your client during the event if a detail has to change. It is, after all, his event.

Make a Checklist

Before leaving your office for the day, make a checklist of items you should have in your on-site bag. If you are not planning on returning to your office the day of the event, you should make sure you have all of your supplies. Also keep a notebook by you for any details you might think about in the hours before the event.

Your on-site bag should include:

- Menus
- Nametags or place cards
- Table numbers and cards for stationary items
- Server packets complete with event sheet, menu, menu descriptions, beverage descriptions, the floor plan, and both timelines
- Client files with notes and e-mail correspondences
- The event file, complete with invoices, receipts, and vendor payout information
- A clipboard including a server packet for yourself with vendor and staff phone numbers

Pack Your Car

Packing your car the night before will save you time the day of the event. Keeping your materials in your car is risky if you do not have a reliable car alarm. It is also not worth the risk if you have a hatchback car with no trunk. Whenever you choose to pack your car, before you head to the venue, be sure you have the following packed:

- Your on-site bag
- Travel kit
- Two outfits, shoes, and accessories

E ssential

Leave an outgoing message on your voice mail to let other clients know you will be out of the office on the day of an event. If you have an associate who can be reached in case of emergencies, leave his contact number on the message as well. It is also a good idea to leave a vacation message on your e-mail.

Five to Seven Hours Prior

This is it: event day! All of your hard work and planning is about to pay off. Your organizational skills have ensured a stress-free morning. Hopefully you have had a restful night's sleep and you are mentally prepared for the long day ahead.

Catch Up

Devote some time to catch up on any details not completed thus far. This time can be dedicated to certain items that may need extra attention. As an event planner, you may use this time in the morning to meet your floral designer at the flower market. A last trip to the hardware store or party supply store may also be warranted.

Exercise

Event days can be long and stressful. If possible, fit exercise into your day. It will help relieve any tension or anxiety you may be feeling. Eating properly throughout the day can also be beneficial on an event day. Pack a sandwich and some healthy snacks to avoid low blood sugar.

Provide a Staff Meal

In your plans with the chef, it has most likely been decided who will provide the staff meal. The back of the house usually handles staff meals, but on some occasions it may be necessary for you to make the arrangements. Deli sandwiches, pasta, or pizza make great staff meals. Call ahead to place the order for pickup. Do not forget paper products and drinks.

Three to Five Hours Prior

Ideally you should be heading over to the venue at this time. It is a good idea to let the facility coordinator know your arrival time. You should coordinate your arrival with that of the rental company. If by chance another staff member is checking in rentals, call the venue for a progress report. Let someone at the venue know if you are running late, and give instructions for vendor check-in.

Staff Arrival and Setup

If it was not necessary for you to be at the venue to check in the rentals, it is mandatory you are there for staff arrival. Remember, you have the server packets and instructions. Station yourself or another staff member to greet staff as they enter the venue. Most front-of-the-house staff will arrive in street clothes. Give verbal instructions on when to be dressed and when staff meals will be served.

As you are greeting the arrival of staff and vendors, keep an eye on the time. Be mindful of any vendors who are running behind schedule. Do not hesitate to phone a vendor for his arrival time.

Finally, your staff has been equipped with instructions and all of your vendors have checked in. Now is the time you should be pitching in to help any team members falling behind schedule. Do not get too focused on one task. Pull yourself away every fifteen minutes or so to oversee the rest of the production team.

Bar Setup

The bar setup may need to be managed by a veteran bartender or yourself. A poorly set bar can leave the bartenders working inefficiently. The bar can be a busy spot in the venue, so avoid traffic jams here at all costs. A satellite bar can be created in lieu of a traditional bar. Most restaurants will have a traditional bar, but for a cocktail party you may want to set up a satellite bar to relieve pressure from the main bar. Following are instructions for setting up a satellite bar:

- The bar should be set up on a long table. Place all wine glasses and bottles of wine and beer on one side of the bar. Instruct the bartenders to chill the white wine and beer upon arrival.
- All martini glasses should be placed at another section of the bar along with shakers, ice, and spirits.
- The next section of the bar can hold the spirits for mixed drinks, ice, and highballs and other glasses to make mixed drinks.
- Use a long tablecloth for the bar and store glass racks, ice, and dump buckets underneath the table. Extra wine, spirits, and beer can also be stored underneath out of sight of the guests.
- When setting up a bar, avoid stacking glasses. Use a table behind the bartenders to create more surface space for glasses.

With this arrangement, three bartenders can work three separate stations efficiently. If you have only two bartenders scheduled for the event, you can easily station yourself behind the wine station until the bar traffic eases up.

One to Two Hours Prior

The majority of the setup should be completed by now. The venue should be taking shape following the vision you created with your client. Your busy staff should place the finishing touches on the venue and prepare for the staff meeting. Before the staff meeting, you should change into your event outfit and be ready in case your client arrives ahead of schedule.

The staff meeting is a great way for the staff to meet and address any questions. Serving a staff meal during the meeting helps encourage a community feeling between the front and back of house. If each member of the team has done his job efficiently, this time should be a small reward for working so hard thus far. Allow staff members a few minutes to eat and socialize before jumping in with the event details. When speaking with staff before an event, be sure to address the following concerns:

- Proper procedure for intoxicated guests
- Restroom location
- Fire exits in case of emergencies
- Smoke breaks and cell phone use

Before the meeting breaks, thank the staff for their hard work. Go over any last-minute touches that may need finishing, such as lighting candles, buffing the tables, and adjusting lighting. Ask each staff member if she is ready for a successful event. If the kitchen is running behind, send servers to help.

 Fact

Delegate a staff member to cut stamens off of any open flowers to avoid staining. The Scotch tape in your on-site tote will aid in removing stamen stains from clothing. The trick is to tape the pollen off and not rub it into your skin or clothing. This also works with some makeup.

The moment has arrived. All of your planning has led up to the first guests walking through the door. Once the guests have arrived, the planning process has officially ended. You have now transformed into an event manager overseeing all the details you have painstakingly organized. There is a saying on Broadway that holds true to this moment: "It's show time!"

Chapter 16

The Event Itself

THE TABLES ARE SET, the candles are lit, and the centerpieces look lovely. Everything is in place, including your staff. The venue is set and your staff is ready to begin greeting guests. The client will likely arrive before the first guests. Take a minute for one final walk-through before your client arrives.

Your Role with the Client

A client may arrive at an event with grace and confidence and you barely need to spend a minute with her. Another client may arrive at an event a bundle of nerves. With this client you will probably spend the better part of the evening as a personal supporter. Whichever type of client you may be dealing with, be the perfect host and check in with the client throughout the evening.

Make the client feel comfortable upon arrival. Offer to hang her coat or take an umbrella. Let her know where her personal belongings will be kept in case she needs to access anything. If applicable, have her parking validated at the beginning of the evening to ensure a smooth exit. Finally, offer your client a glass of wine to calm her nerves.

Your client may arrive with a bit of prep work that she needs to finish. Perhaps the favor bags need to be transported into the venue. If your client has arranged for the place cards, she may need assistance arranging each one in alphabetical order. Enlist the help of a staff member to finish any last-minute details your client may have.

It is acceptable to settle any outstanding payments before the guests arrive unless prior arrangements have been made. After your client has been situated but before the guests arrive, offer to take this time to collect checks for the vendors.

As the host of the event, your client should be served second, after the guest of honor is served. Alert your staff who is the host of the event. By keeping hors d'oeuvres flowing past your client, you are establishing she is being taken care of. You are also establishing the quantity of food at the event. If your client is not taking food in order to socialize with his guests, make a plate of food and keep it in the kitchen. Escort him into the kitchen under the pretense of business talk and he may just stay for a bite.

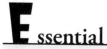

Ideally the room should be set up upon client arrival. Vendor equipment should not be in sight when the client arrives. Production crews should secure any loose wires under a runner or with duct tape.

Stationing Staff

The staff at an event becomes the first line of defense between the kitchen and guests. Your staff should be capable, professional individuals with experience. It is customary to require at least two years experience from a server or bartender to be qualified for a position. Bussers, hosts, and food runners are considered entry-level positions and are not required to have experience before being hired.

Servers

Choosing your servers for particular events can be challenging. Servers should be able to read guests and adjust service accordingly. Unfortunately, this does not always occur. When designing your server stations, keep in mind server strengths and weaknesses. For example, a more exuberant server should be stationed to interact with the guests at a wine station. A quieter, more reserved server would do well as the lead server for dinner. A shy server with less experience may exceed as a back server with less responsibilities and out of the spotlight.

Question

An industry formula calls for one server for every twenty guests. The guest-per-server ratio can increase a bit for a cocktail party. For a coursed dinner, you may consider more support staff depending on the expectation of the level of service. A five-course fine dining menu for forty guests may require a back server and busser.

Designing an efficient server station can be a bit of a juggling act. To set up an efficient operation, station servers at different places at different times in the event. For example, server A can be stationed to pass cocktails at the beginning of the event and switch to a lead server when the guests are seated for dinner. Server B can assist with coat check at the beginning and end of the event and switch to a back server when the first course is served.

Fact

Bartenders

Bartenders are known for their robust personalities. The bartenders on your staff should be no exception. In addition to a winning personality, a bartender should also be quick, talented, and experienced. Much like a server, a bartender should know how to read a guest. Bartenders also have the challenge of making small talk with guests. Knowing when to make a quick exit from a lengthy conversation to serve another guest can also be a challenge for a bartender.

When hiring bartenders for an event, an industry standard suggests three to five years experience for cocktail service. The standard fluctuates slightly for wine and beer only service. In event planning, some staff members cross over from servers to bartenders for simple mixed-drink service.

 **Alert**

When serving alcohol at an event, arm your entire staff with the procedures for handling intoxicated guests. Offer water or a nonalcoholic beverage first. Alert the manager on duty before cutting off a guest. Attempt to put the guest in a cab or nearby hotel. Call the valet and security if the guest attempts to retrieve his car.

Upon checking into the event, the designated bartenders should stay behind the bar for most of the evening. One bartender may float on the floor to help serve meals. But for the most part, bartenders should be a constant face behind the bar in one station. The reasons for this are to maintain a high level of service and to keep track of the number of drinks guests are being served.

Additional Support Staff

Depending on the type of event you have planned, you may need to employ additional support staff to support the servers and bartenders. Because support staff positions do not require previous experience, the pay tends to be less. An industry standard is half of the salary of a server and bartender.

- **Coat check personnel:** Checks the coats of each guest. A standard system of coat check is giving each guest a ticket to claim his coat at the end of the evening. A coat check employee may make an hourly wage and additionally collect tips from each guest. A coat check employee may not share in the gratuity from the event.
- **Valet:** Usually a private licensed company provides employees. Valet companies carry additional insurance and screen the driving records of each employee. Valet employees are usually tipped separately by the guests and are not part of the tip pool for the event.
- **Host:** Greets the guests at an event. May manage the venue's phone calls as well as take reservations if the venue is a restaurant. The host is usually paid hourly and does not get a portion of the gratuity from the event.
- **Busser:** This employee clears tables at an event. Bussers make an hourly wage and are tipped employees.
- **Food runner:** The main objective for a food runner is to serve, or run, dishes to guests. A food runner may also support the servers by pouring water and clearing dishes during downtime. A food runner is paid by the hour and is entitled to a percentage of the event's gratuities.
- **Bar back:** This employee supports the bartenders. Some of his duties may include getting ice, stocking the bar, and washing glassware. Bar backs are paid hourly and share in an event's gratuities.

Essential

The pay structure for your company may determine how your staff is paid. Some events may pay a straight hourly salary. Some events may pay hourly plus gratuities. Other events may pay minimum wage plus gratuities. Check with your company's personnel department to determine the pay scale for your company. Double-check this information with your area's labor commission.

Greeting Guests

How a guest is greeted at the beginning of an event leaves a lasting impression. A theory in the industry is that the greeting and farewell are the most memorable aspects of a guest's visit. Walking into a venue can be intimidating for some. Put your guests at ease with a warm welcome from you and your staff.

In cooler months, the first step to making a guest feel welcome is offering to take her coat. In rainy weather, be prepared to check in umbrellas as well. The first few moments of coat check can be hectic, so instruct as many staff members as possible to take a guest's coat. Unless the event is being held in the middle of summer, have a coat check area prepared.

E ssential

Provide a twist on the traditional coat check and offer shawls to guests on breezy nights. Collect umbrellas to give away to guests leaving in inclement weather. And for fall or winter functions, a warmed blanket on an outside veranda will make a guest feel extra cozy.

You and your client most likely designed a plan of attack for when guests begin filtering into the venue. Greeting each guest with a glass of champagne has always held a high-society touch. With the recent revival of the cocktail, miniature signature drinks are much in fashion. You might also consider having a server offer punch from a stylish punch bowl.

Avoid having guests wait in line for ten minutes at the bar. Whatever your means of attack, a good host will make certain her guests want for nothing. Placing a beverage in the hand of each guest upon arrival is a good start.

The next phase of the attack should be food-related. If guests are not immediately sitting for dinner, plan for hors d'oeuvres to be passed. A less expensive alternative to passed hors d'oeuvres are stationary items such as cheese plates or antipastos. Do not forget your table markers identifying each stationary cuisine. Be sure to keep this course light to avoid the guests' filling up before dinner. For a cocktail party, the first rounds of hors d'oeuvres should be light followed by heavier more substantial fare.

Taking Precautions

As the event planner you can take certain precautions to avoid mishaps. You also have a responsibility to provide a safe working environment for your staff as well as a safe facility environment for your guests. Contact your local health department for more information on food handling safety.

Sanitary Work Environment

With your staff clearing plates and serving food, you need to provide a hand-washing sink close to the kitchen area. This hand-washing sink needs to be separate from a kitchen prep sink where fruits and vegetables may be washed. All hand-washing sinks must be equipped with soap and paper towels. All employee restrooms should have signs posted instructing your staff to wash hands before returning to work. If your employees will be sharing the same restroom with guests, give each staff member verbal instructions on washing hands.

 Fact

In cases where only one hand-washing sink may be available to your staff, provide bottles of hand sanitizers in workstations around the venue. Hand sanitizers do not require soap and work in a pinch when there's no sink nearby. Also teach your staff to wash hands frequently to prevent the spread of germs, especially during the cold and flu season.

Safety Measures

When serving food and beverages, floors can become quite slippery due to spills. Your staff should be properly outfitted in skid-resistant shoes to avoid slips. Instruct your staff to clean spills and broken glass immediately to protect guests and other staff members from getting injured. For complete instructions on safe work environments, contact your local OSHA chapter.

Alert

During inclement weather, be prepared with mats and floor runners for entryways. Industrial mats can absorb some moisture and prevent hard surfaces from becoming slick. Mats are available through rental companies or linen services. If guests are traveling in severe weather, having a staff member appointed to show guests to the restrooms to freshen up is an added touch.

Overserving

As much as you want to make guests feel welcome with a glass of wine or a cocktail, it is important to be a responsible host. Take precautions with alcohol consumption and make water readily available. Switch passed cocktails to rounds of nonalcoholic beverages or sparkling water. If possible, try passing rounds of espresso shots, a classier option to coffee service.

After the initial cocktail, encourage guests to sip wine, which slows down alcohol consumption. Wine also tends to have a lower alcohol content than spirits. Before the event, train your staff on a proper wine pour. A guest will drink less wine if her glass is half full rather than three-quarters full. Pouring four ounces of wine is also proper service.

Getting Your Staff Home Safely

In the event-planning industry, late nights are part of the package. As an event planner, you have a responsibility to see that your staff gets home safe. Trains and buses are not a wise choice after a certain time of night. Arrange for transportation for your staff through carpools or taxis. Be sure employees are escorted to cars, especially if parked in parking garages or alleys.

Putting out Fires

The best event planners are experts at putting out fires (a term for averting minor catastrophes). A fire can be anything from identifying an unhappy guest to dealing with a complaint from a client. Putting out fires takes some practice, but by thinking on your feet at each event you will pick up the skill in no time.

Complaints

Working in this business you will be presented with complaints of all varieties. Some of these complaints will be legitimate and others will be trivial. Guests will complain about the food, the host may complain about the service staff, your staff will have complaints about guests, and so on. Treat each complaint as if it has merit. Most people who complain simply want to be heard.

Take the time to listen to a person's complaint, but do so in private away from other guests and staff members. When the person is done speaking ask, "What can I do at this moment to improve your experience?" You can then take a few minutes and consider the request. Fulfill the requests that you can, but compromise with the requests you cannot honor. Avoid engaging the other person in a heated argument. For larger problems, give the person your business card and ask him to contact you the next day. This will give you the opportunity to ask the advice of a colleague. The best recommendation is to remain calm and detached from the complaint but offer an apology. Always thank the other person for bringing the problem to your attention.

For large events, carry a cell phone on your person at all times. If emergency response personnel, like the fire department, needs to be called, you will not be wasting time looking for a phone. Keep the numbers to the local fire and police departments programmed into your phone. For serious emergencies call 911. Always have your phone charged and make sure you get phone reception for off-site locations. A cordless phone or walkie-talkies can substitute for large outdoor events where phone reception may not be adequate.

Vendor Problems

It is hard to imagine your vendors not coming through on an event day, but life is full of surprises and you should be prepared for this nevertheless. Ask your photographer whom he will rely on if he has an emergency the day of a wedding. Your photographer should have an assistant or another professional photographer's name in case of emergency. Request the phone numbers of his assistant and recommendation to have as backup.

If the idea of a baker transporting a $10,000 cake makes you nervous, you are not alone. Inquire how the bakery will handle any accidents that may happen during transport. Keeping the phone number of a neighborhood bakery in your cell phone is also not a bad idea.

Thinking on Your Feet

In event planning, situations will arise without a moment's notice. You need to be able to solve problems quickly. There are no situational scripts to refer to when problems take place. So you need to be prepared and manage each conflict quickly and safely without compromising other guests.

Emergency Situations

Before you begin your career as an event planner, it is wise to obtain CPR certification. Once you have your staff in place, schedule a CPR class to certify as many staff members as possible. The fee is about $75 per person, but the peace of mind you will have entering events will be worth the added cost. Inquire about the Good Samaritan law in your state. Contact your local Red Cross for more information.

Some events have a need to hire an on-site medical team. If you are planning a marathon, road race, or organized walk, be sure you have medical staff at certain points along the route. Large outside events, like a concert taking place in the warmer weather, will also warrant medical personnel on site.

All-Women Events

Unfortunately, public events attracting mostly women have also attracted a negative element. When planning large fundraisers or booking events drawing a large female audience, take extra precautions. Convince your client to hire security. Alert your local law enforcement. The police may dispatch a car to patrol the parking lot when the event is finishing.

Allergies

With the heightened awareness to food allergies in recent years, the event-planning industry has made some slight adjustments. Event planners should seek the advice of chefs to provide meals that won't induce allergic reactions. The probability of serving a guest with an allergy is high. Guests' allergies may include nuts, wheat, gluten, and shellfish. Since a large number of medical personnel have developed latex allergies, restaurants have switched from using latex to rubber gloves.

Security Issues

Local laws may require you to hire a security detail for large events. For adequate crowd control, you may need a security detail for each one hundred guests. High-profile or celebrity events may also warrant hiring a security detail. Check with your police department for more information and pricing. Your area may also have a private security company that can be hired for events.

Check Restrooms

Have staff members periodically check the restrooms during an event. The staff can keep the restrooms tidy and also alert you to any incidents. Sometimes arguments occur in restrooms, as does drug use. An intoxicated guest may also find his way into a restroom. Equip the staff member with a walkie-talkie before entering the restroom or have your staff check the restrooms in pairs.

Conflict Resolution

Before an event begins, appoint a member of your management team to be a mediator for arguments. The team member should have a calm demeanor and know how to effectively talk with people. Imagine a hostage negotiator, only for social situations.

Guest of Honor

For events featuring a guest speaker, it is a good idea to send a car to pick up your guest. This way you will not have to worry about your guest getting lost or running late. Have the car return at the close of the event to take your guest to a nearby hotel.

Party Crashers

Highly publicized events will always attract a few party crashers. Help alleviate the situation by having a registration table or guest list located outside the venue. Having a security guard stationed outside the entrances and exits will also deter unwanted guests.

Lost or Stolen Property

Employing coat check personnel is not a foolproof plan. Mistakes and theft can and will happen. When a guest is missing property, enter her name and phone number in a lost-and-found log. Most restaurants, hotels, and nightclubs are not responsible for lost or stolen property, but this is no consolation to your guest leaving without her coat. The fact is, she trusted your facility with her personal belongings. Make it right by replacing missing items.

The band has played its last song. The tired staff is breaking down the tables and chairs. The production crew is bringing down the lights and staging. The event has come to an end and all of the planning and organization has paid off with a successful event. Your client was thrilled with all of the details you organized. But before leaving the venue for the evening, make note of the positive and negative aspects of the event. These notes will come in handy with your follow-up call.

Chapter 17

The Follow-Up

AH, THE EVENT IS OVER. Even if you hit a few bumps in the road, you should still be feeling tremendous satisfaction. A few fires might have needed to be put out, but every event should be considered a learning experience, a way for you to improve your skills for each subsequent event that you book. You might think your work on this particular event is completed. However, you still have a bit more to do before filing this event away.

Calling Your Client

A few days after the event, you will want to phone your client directly to follow up on the event. Avoid calling the very next day. Allow your client time to get feedback from her guests and decompress from the event. You should also get feedback from your staff and vendors you might have missed at the event. You will want to complete your notes before phoning your client.

After exchanging initial phone pleasantries, let your client know how much you enjoyed working with him. Explain to your client you were calling for any feedback he may have for you. Have your notes ready and be prepared to take notes from your client as well. Remember, you are calling for your client's feedback. Do your best to listen rather than talk.

Just asking if your client was happy with the event is not enough. Ask open-ended questions such as the following:

- Have you heard from any of your guests regarding the menu?
- From our end all aspects of the event went really well. How did things look from your end?
- Were you happy with the flow of traffic through the venue?

- Did it seem as though the kitchen kept up with all of your hungry guests?
- Did you have any positive or negative interactions with the staff? Overall, were you happy with the event?

By asking one or two of these questions, you may get your client to open up a bit and elaborate on the event. By now you will know your client's personality. The more vocal clients will give you the most feedback. Occasionally you will have a reserved client, in which case you should not push for feedback. Sometimes hearing that everything was fine will be enough.

Alert

Serious concerns warrant a follow-up call the next day. If something major happened at the event the night before, do not hesitate to call your client. You should address any emergencies that needed police or medical attention at the event first thing in the morning.

Take Notes

When taking notes over the phone, try to get specifics from your vendors as well. You are still in the unique position of being the main line of communication between the client and your vendors. Offer to follow up directly with any vendors. With e-mail follow-ups to your vendors, copy your client on all correspondences.

Include all positive remarks from the client; however, anything negative should be addressed with your vendors over the phone or in person. If you have followed up with your client through e-mail, pass that along to your vendor as well. If the incident is minor, suggest that the vendor write an apologetic note or e-mail. With major occurrences, request a meeting with your vendor to discuss ways to make it up to the client.

Apologize for Any Mistakes

There will be events in which details will be missed and things will go wrong. When this happens, identify the problems with your client. Try not to make excuses for any mistakes and take responsibility for your actions. Assure the client you will take any issues to the vendors and find a solution to any problems.

 Fact

The cc (carbon copy) feature on e-mails is useful in the follow-up with vendors. The cc feature allows the recipient to view the exact e-mail conversation from your client. A bcc (blind carbon copy) allows your vendor to view remarks from the client without the client seeing the vendor's e-mail address.

Acknowledge any incidents that may have happened within your staff. If you can give your account of the situation, proceed gingerly with an apology but do not make excuses. In large events, mistakes may have occurred that your client may not be aware of yet. Take responsibility and be honest about mistakes that may have happened. The client will appreciate hearing from you first rather than a guest.

Thank Your Client for Feedback

The dialogue between you and your client will most likely be positive. When you address any mistakes and promise to address the negative experiences, your client will be impressed with your willingness to solve problems.

Let your client know you are thankful for the opportunity to host her recent event. Communicate to your client you are excited about the prospect of hosting future events for her. Be sure to express your appreciation for any referrals.

E ssential

Thank-You Notes to Vendors

With client notes in hand, this will be an opportunity for you to sit and write each vendor a thank-you note. Include specific compliments to each vendor in the note. Any specific, positive comments from the client should also be included. Negative client comments should be handled over the phone. A handwritten thank-you note may only take a few moments of your time, but it is a testament of your commitment to your vendors.

The biggest compliment you can send to a vendor is repeat business. Continuing to work with the same vendor on subsequent events is the beginning of building a solid relationship. The same can be said of vendor referrals. Be sure your vendor knows when you send her referrals. You want to make certain this new client gets treated extra special. Ask the potential client if you can pass along her name to your vendor. Or let the potential client know it is okay to use your name when contacting the vendor.

For events taking six months or more to plan, a vendor gift may be something worth considering. You may also contemplate a vendor gift if the event was particularly stressful. Vendors often work miracles at the last minute, and when they do they should be rewarded with a gift. Planning an event can be very stressful for all involved. Sending a thoughtful gift will not only show your appreciation, but it will also strengthen your relationship with your vendors.

In lieu of a formal gift, get in the habit of sending your vendors a compact disc of the photos from the event. Pictures on a compact disc are great for vendors to add photos to a Web site, brochure, or scrapbook. Ask the photographer ahead of time to chronicle all vendor-related services and products. These services include:

- The cuisine, with photos of plates, buffet tables, and the kitchen staff in action
- The cake
- The flowers
- The bar setup, especially if the bar features wines and spirits related to a specific vendor
- Staging and lighting design

Of course, you will need to get creative and think of a different gift for your photographer. A gift certificate to a restaurant is always appreciated.

Following the event, you may at some point receive a note of thanks from your client. Take a moment and make a copy of client notes to send to each of your vendors. This is good practice even if each vendor was not specifically named. You had assistance planning a great event, and your vendors deserve to share in all of the praise. Your client may have also written a note to each of your vendors, but do not take any chances; send a copy of the original note.

Checking Back with the Venue Manager

Chances are you have established a strong working relationship with the venue manager or facility planner. At some point in the days following the event, you should make a point to check back with her to follow up. This conversation should happen before your client phone call. You have likely spent quite a few hours planning the event with the venue manager. A phone call is appropriate, followed by a note of thanks.

Retrieving Lost Items

Many staff members, guests, and vendors spent time at the venue the day of the event. The likelihood of a few items being left behind is high. Check your lost-and-found log and ask the venue manager if those specific items were recovered. Pass along the name and number of the guest in case the lost item surfaces. Also inquire if any items were left behind, especially in the kitchen area, coat-check room, and employee changing area.

Ensuring Proper Cleanup

Part of your responsibility to the venue is ensuring a proper cleanup. Unless previous arrangements have been made, the staff should break down the venue and organize the rentals. In some cases, the venue may charge a cleaning fee to have the event broken down. In other cases, the venue may penalize your company if the event was not broken down properly. Check with the venue ahead of time for its cleanup policy.

 Fact

Organizing the rentals from the event may not be something you leave to a cleaning crew. Have your staff rack all of the glassware, stack plates, and deposit silverware in proper bins. Most rental companies allow dishes and plates to be returned dirty as long as they have been cleared of food.

Ask the venue manager if the venue was left in pristine shape. There will be some occasions where you might leave the event early and entrust the breakdown to the staff. You want to be sure your staff left the venue in great shape.

Ask for Details on Incidents

With large events, it is impossible for you to be everywhere at the same time. You will need to rely on your staff and others to relay details to you. The facility planner or venue manager will also be a good source of event information. Request that the manager divulge any details from the event you might not have heard about. Let the planner know he can be candid.

E ssential

Finally, ask the planner for any feedback he may have regarding the event. The facility planner, though he worked the same event, will have a different perspective. His recollection of guest interaction and interaction with your staff might be entirely different from your experience.

Gratitude and Appreciation

As with all of your vendors and clients, express thanks to the facility planner for a job well done. Even if the event had a few mishaps, the planner also worked very hard to plan this event. The facility planner will appreciate a thank-you note with a gift. Have your photographer make a compact disc that has the photos from the event or create a scrapbook as a gift.

Going above and Beyond

Event-planning and catering clients can be loyal creatures. Attracting a new client away from his existing caterer or venue might prove to be difficult. If the opportunity presents itself, you may want to consider offering a few extras to entice a new client your way. Of course, the event itself will need to be flawless.

Discounting your services can be risky because your services may be seen as lesser quality than those of other event planners. Avoid taking a certain percentage off of your fee or company's profits. Still, there are some extras you may throw in to persuade a new client into hosting his next event.

Waiving the Room Charge

A room charge is usually a straight profit for your company. Waiving or discounting the room charge can be an easy extra to include. The new business you bring in will likely make your company a profit with the food and beverage sales.

Gift Card to a Restaurant

Offering this extra is beneficial especially if you are the event planner at a restaurant. The potential client can use the gift card or gift certificate to experience your cuisine. You can make an impression on the client by preparing a special dish or sending out an amuse to the table. If you are not a restaurant event planner, trade or barter a gift card and extend the complimentary dinner to your client.

 Fact

Amuse is an industry slang term referring to a taste from the kitchen. Amuses are sent to VIPs or regulars in a restaurant setting. Some chefs also add an amuse course to an event that the client has not ordered. An amuse bouche, which translates from the French as "fun for the mouth," is a bite-sized dish served before the first course or hors d'oeuvres.

Complimentary Valet

When you are in good standing with your valet company, you may be able to receive complimentary valet services as an extra. Some valet companies offer event facilities a certain number of comp tickets per year. If your valet company cannot offer complimentary services as an extra, perhaps you can negotiate a discounted price.

Cater a Luncheon

Offering to cater a luncheon to attract a new company is a useful device to secure a prospective event. With this measure the company will be able to preview your chef's cuisine. Be sure to add some signature dishes to the menu. If you are a facility event planner, offer to cater a company lunch at the venue's site rather than the company's office.

Calendar of Future Events

As the host of an event, you become privy to many social affairs in your area. You will get invitations to events throughout the year. A secret in event planning is becoming involved at the planning stages rather the stage when you receive an invitation. As you become introduced to guests at events, make note of any upcoming events that might be mentioned in casual conversation and mark each one on your calendar.

Your client is a great avenue through which you can make additional contacts. At the end of your follow-up call with your client, assuming the event went well, ask your client to pass along your contact information. Refer to specific conversations you may have had with her guests. Mention your interest in specific events in the conversation. Accept a guest's contact information only if your client offers.

When an upcoming event is mentioned by guests, politely ask for additional details but do not pry. Picking up on certain details such as the company or organization hosting the event might be enough to get your foot in the door. Once the event is over, contact the organization to market your services for the upcoming event. If planning stages have already begun, ask your contact to keep your information for next year and mark the event on your calendar.

During the event, you may collect quite a few business cards. After the event, use these new contacts to market your company. Your contact may lead you to a person in charge of booking events. Be sure you send a thank-you note to your new contact if new business results.

Acknowledge Your Client for Any New Business

When a client refers new business to you, it is important to thank her with a gift or a note. A referral is when a client recommends your services to a friend, family member, or colleague. Referrals are a compliment to you as an event planner, so send a thank-you to reciprocate the goodwill.

Too many times in this industry clients are not recognized for referrals. Repeat clientele and referrals can turn your event-planning company into a success. One way to show you appreciate your client's efforts to send you new business is to send a small gift. For ideas, think of events you have planned together in the past. A bottle of his favorite wine or a teapot he remarked on would make a thoughtful gift. A gift certificate to a new restaurant in town with a nice note attached would be an easy gift to send by mail.

Some event planners save their appreciation and send gifts around the holidays. For gift ideas, try recreating your client's event centerpiece. Send it to her home if you know she is entertaining guests for a special occasion. Another thoughtful holiday gift would be to send a framed photograph of your client at her event. The photo will evoke the festive memories from her event.

A gift is not always the best way to send thanks. If you are not involved in your clients' charities already, send a note offering your services for the next event. You can also make a donation directly to his charity. In your thank-you note, you might simply offer to attend his next fundraiser as a guest.

The follow-up is an important instrument in the event-planning process. It allows for proper closure to your client relationship. The follow-up also allows you to extend your gratitude to your vendors, and it is a great way to attract new business. The most important lesson from the follow-up call is allowing your client to critique your performance as an event planner. How you use this criticism for future events is up to you.

Chapter 18

The Wedding

WEDDINGS RUN THE GAMUT from the intimate to the grand. You will be hard-pressed to find an event with more variety than a wedding. Couples try hard to make their weddings individual and creative. As a wedding planner, you will embark on this journey with the bride and groom. This chapter covers every step of a wedding plan, from choosing and securing the venue to the personal touches and details that make the event truly special.

The Venue

A wedding venue can range from a cozy affair to a grandiose celebration. From a small country inn to an extravagant castle, any venue can host a wedding with the right amount of imagination. Venues can be simple, needing only a fair amount of decorating. Other venues have every detail a wedding needs under one roof. Securing the location is the first step in designing the event. All other details will fall into place.

The Wedding Planner Versus the Facility Planner

With the average cost of a wedding these days around $30,000, some planners specialize only in weddings. A wedding coordinator, wedding specialist, and wedding consultant are other names that wedding planners go by. A wedding planner may market herself as a cost-effective way to plan and execute a wedding. A planner can do this by offering to save the couple money and stay within their budget.

Staying within a couple's budget is not an easy task and is a tremendous responsibility. With more and more wedding planners advertising over the Internet (check out *www.theknot.com*), competition is at an all-time high. When first starting out, fledgling planners may consider quoting a slightly lower salary percentage than the competition to attract clients. The typical wedding planner charges 10 to 20 percent of the total wedding cost.

Venues specializing in holding weddings usually employ an on-site events coordinator. Smaller venues may have a manager in charge of coordinating events. A facility wedding planner's responsibilities differ dramatically from a hired wedding planner. While both jobs navigate wedding-planning territory, a facility planner is simply responsible for the arrangements that are outlined in a contract or are promised by the facility. The responsibilities include:

- Presenting menu selections
- Pairing food and wine
- Hiring staff
- Coordinating rentals
- Pricing all costs related to the facility
- Recommending vendors

The facility planner may recommend and coordinate vendor services, while a wedding planner will assist the couple in shopping for necessary vendors. Wedding planner responsibilities include some of the following:

- Staying within a budget
- Setting up site visits for venues
- Arranging for the rentals and staff if the caterer has not
- Invitations and managing the RSVP list
- Recommending a calligrapher
- Coordinating accommodations for the bride and groom and out-of-town guests
- Setting up appointments for vendors, such as florists, photographers, musicians, and videographers
- Suggesting wedding favors
- Counsel couple on wedding insurance and obtain any permits needed for the wedding
- Outlining marriage license procedures

- Managing the event itself
- Publishing the wedding announcement

A wedding planner, with her tremendous to-do list, will see a couple from the beginning of the journey to the very end. A facility planner tends to work only with the couple in reference to the venue. Wedding planners often work in conjunction with a catering manager or facility planner on an event.

 ## Fact

Many facilities do not allow an outside caterer, which can pose a dilemma for couples who love a venue but are not excited about the menu. Some venues may allow kosher meals to be brought in and served for Jewish ceremonies.

Banquet Facilities

With weddings generating five billion dollars a year, it is no wonder that facilities are built with one event in mind. Banquet facilities and ballrooms cater to weddings and other large events. These venues will have the equipment for a wedding built into the space. Tables, chairs, table settings, an outside gazebo, a dance floor, and perhaps a stage are available at these venues.

Banquet facilities usually have wedding packages in which all costs associated with the wedding are built into a budget. A standard wedding package may include:

- A two-course menu with passed hors d'oeuvres
- Centerpieces
- A champagne toast
- A wedding cake
- Place cards

Upgrading from these packages can alter the cost significantly. Being forced to select the in-house catering can occasionally mean compromising the quality of the menu. Be sure to arrange a tasting to preview the menu.

Dressing a Venue

A simple venue can be a couple's dream, but the cost of decorations can price this dream out of their budget. Couples want their wedding site to be original. Whether a beach or a bowling alley, venues outside of banquet halls may need a fair amount of decorating to be transformed into a wedding reception. Before considering a specialized venue, the couple may need to budget for the following extras:

- Rentals
- Caterer
- Bar service
- Flowers
- Bakers
- Additional decorations
- Dance floor
- Gazebos or plant rentals

Securing the Venue

In the United States, wedding venues usually book out a year in advance. For spring weddings, some venues book two years in advance. Outside the United States, wedding planners may secure a venue and plan a wedding in less than six months. The same is true for untraditional reception sites. When a couple hires you to plan their wedding, there are three details to discuss before setting up site visits.

The Date

Couples usually have an approximate date in mind soon after the engagement. For couples looking to save money or get married quickly, ask if the date is flexible. Weddings held on Sunday afternoons or Thursday evenings tend to be less expensive. Days of the week other than a Friday or Saturday night are less popular and can be available with less than a year notice. Couples choosing to marry on a parent's wedding anniversary or a relative's birthday may not be open to the idea of changing the date.

E ssential

Some venues are fully equipped with bridal quarters where the bride and her party can change and relax prior to the wedding. Bridal quarters are usually intended for use before and during the wedding. A honeymoon suite is a room in the venue where the couple can stay overnight after the reception.

Budget

Before planning the wedding, couples usually have a good sense of the budget. If applicable, ask if a parent or family member intends to contribute to the wedding. The cost of a wedding may start at $60 per person. Advise the couple to include everything from the cost of favors to the cost of the honeymoon in their budget. If a couple intends to charge the wedding to a credit card, it may help to include the interest into the budget as well.

Ceremony Site

Some couples may have a ceremony site chosen. Traditions, religion, and family history may endear the couple to a particular place of worship and official. If the ceremony site will be different from the reception site, consider keeping a short travel distance between the two venues. Having guests travel more than a half hour from the ceremony to the reception is quite a distance. Additionally, keeping a short time frame between the two events is ideal. The time from the end of the wedding ceremony to the start of the reception should not exceed an hour.

Determining these details will allow you to begin scheduling site visits. If the venues are in close proximity, schedule three to five site visits a day. By scheduling a site visit on a weekend, the couple may get a sneak peek at the setup of another wedding. Chronicle each site visit by collecting the bridal package, contracts, menus, and information on bar service. Take photographs of the space, inside and out. Also ask the facility planner about deposits and payment schedules. Because the site visits may span a few weeks, having all of this information for the couple will make their decision easier.

 Fact

Venues frequently ask for deposits to secure a wedding date. Venues will also require a percentage of the balance due a few months before the wedding date. For example, after the initial deposit a venue may want 50 percent of the balance to be paid thirty days before the wedding.

Couple's Assignments

The wedding planner may be hired to perform most of the wedding duties, but the couple has quite a bit to contribute as well. The couple will need your guidance to complete any tasks not in your contract. These duties might include:

- Choose the wedding attire. This includes the bride's dress, groom's tuxedo, and wedding bands.
- Choose the ceremony site and officiant.
- Choose traveling outfits.
- Arrange for the attire of the bridal party.
- Write wedding vows.
- Arrange for hair and makeup.
- Organize wedding rehearsal one to two days prior.
- Obtain the marriage license.
- Register for gifts.
- Write thank-you cards for gifts.
- Plan the honeymoon.
- Plan any prewedding activities for the bridal party.

E ssential

For a bride who has been imagining her wedding since she was a child, making her wishes come true can be an impossible task. As a wedding planner, you must dream as big as the bride. You should make every attempt to fulfill a bride's wishes. If a request is just not possible, offer alternate solutions.

Keeping with Tradition

In today's era of weddings, the wedding ceremony is often an innovative expression of diversity. Combining Old World tradition with New World style, couples are putting an imaginative slant on ceremonies. It is not unusual to see brides wearing full gowns in colors other than white. Family heirlooms containing pearls, rubies, or sapphires are now replacing diamond engagement rings. But with all of the changes, some traditions remain the same. As a wedding event planner, familiarizing yourself with traditional ceremonies will help you plan memorable affairs.

Planning Traditional Ceremonies

Traditional ceremonies differ from culture to culture, although some ethnicities share some of the same traditional details. In this country, immigrants have brought wedding traditions from various cultures and religions, the result being ceremonies that have been passed down from generation to generation

As you begin your career in event planning, it would be informative to visit local churches and synagogues. Request an appointment with each officiant. Make inquiries regarding the traditional aspects of each religion. For example, a wedding procession from a Christian ceremony differs from that of a Jewish ceremony.

Combining Traditions

Traditions can vary not only from a religious and cultural aspect but also from a familial aspect as well. Tradition dictates the bride should be walked down the aisle by her father. But what about a stepfather? A shift in family dynamics has left couples to be creative during ceremonies. This creativity highlights the special connection between all people close to the couple, not just blood relatives. The best approach for you to take is to be accepting and sensitive to the couple's needs.

Ceremony Details

Because the ceremony is an individual symbol of the couple, event planners are often focused on the details of the reception only. Couples in some cases may request the planner be present to oversee the ceremony. Ceremonies occurring at the same venue as the wedding may also request the presence of the event planner. Even though the event planner's main involvement may be the reception, couples may still need guidance on the various ceremony details. These details include:

- **Wedding programs:** Ceremonies often include a program to list all members of the bridal party. The program also details the music selection. A ceremony dedication is often printed on the program as well.
- **Position of the bride and groom:** Most traditions call for the bride to be on the left of the officiant, with the groom on the right. Family and friends are seated behind the respective side of the bride and groom. The couple can choose to stand facing the audience, each other, or the officiant.
- **Decorating the ceremony site:** Pew markers can be a bundle of flowers or ribbon positioned at the end of each pew. A floral designer can adorn the altar with large plants or flower arrangements. Flower boxes can also be placed in each windowsill. And do not forget the flower girl and her basket of petals.
- **Receiving line:** A receiving line is a chance for guests to wish the newly married couple and parents well after the cer-

emony. A receiving line can take place at the ceremony site or upon arrival at the reception site.

- **Music:** The music program will include melodies as the guests enter, a song for the bridal procession, and a song for the bride to walk down the aisle. The traditional "Here Comes the Bride" bridal march tune has been replaced in recent years. Also, the couple will need a song to return down the aisle to after the ceremony. Organs, violins, and harps are popular live music choices for a ceremony.

When meeting with the couple for the first time, be sure to outline any ceremony details you are able to add to your services with the additional costs. Even if the couple decides not to hire you to oversee the ceremony in the original agreement, it will be comforting to know it may be an option in the future.

The Personal Touch Couples Look For

Couples will look to you to place a personal touch on their wedding day. You will have to utilize your event-planning skills to make this couple's day special. After the initial meeting, ask the couple a few questions to determine pastimes and hobbies. You can then begin designing a wedding specific to the couple. A few specialized details can make a wedding a truly unique affair.

Place Cards and Holders

Place cards indicate a table setting to a guest. In larger weddings, place cards are located on a large table upon entrance to the reception. You might suggest the couple bring their creativity to this detail. For example, place cards can be beautifully handwritten on card stock. Suspend the place cards from the ceiling using ribbon for a dramatic effect. Be sure the place cards are hung low enough and in alphabetical order for easy locating.

You can also suggest creating a scene using a patch of grass and adorning small printed place cards onto miniature houses to resemble a town. Or use sand with the small printed place cards on miniature cocktail umbrellas to resemble a beach.

The Venue

Decorating the venue is another way the couple can get creative. You can suggest the couple transform the venue into a photo gallery. Ask the venue to set up smaller tables around the space. Have the parents bring in framed photographs of the couple growing up, along with any childhood memorabilia. The parents should also bring in any old family wedding photos. Imagine the effect of the photographs decorating the venue along with the bride's tattered teddy bear or the groom's old train set.

Transforming even a large venue into a cozy museum will make the guests feel closer to the couple. Adorn the guests' tables with favorite poems. In addition to floral arrangements, creative centerpieces can be a reflection of the couple's hobbies, careers, or interests. Centerpieces can also fall in line with the theme of a wedding.

The Favors

Favors of the past have been almond candies wrapped with tulle and a ribbon, but favors have graduated over the last generation. A favor should be a keepsake, not a throwaway. Since favors have also increased in price, suggest favors that will have some longevity. Play with the couple's last name for creative favors. Does the couple share a name with a liqueur? Wrap a small bottle in tulle as a favor. Perhaps the bride shares her first name with a famous author. Give a paperback of the author as a favor. If the couple enjoys sipping mint juleps, give a julep cup as a favor with a recipe rolled inside.

Details of Planning a Wedding

Based upon an engagement lasting a year, most experts follow a formula to plan a wedding. Completing the details of the wedding in a certain time frame will keep you current in the planning process. Personalizing some details may add some time to the formula.

Ten to Twelve Months Before

Ideally the couple will have decided on a budget, a proposed date, and the guest list. These details will allow you to begin narrowing down the search for a venue. The site of the wedding ceremony should be chosen at this time as well. The couple may be open to the idea of having the ceremony at the same location as the reception. If so, add this to your site requirements.

Eight to Ten Months Before

With any luck, the ceremony and reception sites have been chosen and deposits secured. A second site visit to both locations should be scheduled with all vendors. The floral designer will better estimate the cost of the flowers if he is present for a walk-through. Some vendors, such as the baker, may not need a site visit the reception, however, as the bridal couple most likely will visit the bakery for a tasting. Other vendors, such as the photographer, may have worked at the ceremony and reception site in the past and may also not need a walk-through.

Begin interviewing different entertainment options for the couple at this time. Similar to venues, popular entertainers get booked far in advance.

E ssential

Instruct the couple to view other wedding portfolios from the photographer. Write a list of must-have photos the couple would like the photographer to take throughout the wedding. The couple should also instruct the videographer on the look and feel of the video.

Four to Six Months Before

Collect stationery samples for the couple. Save-the-date cards (designed to let guests know the date of the wedding before the invitation arrives), should be ordered at this time along with the invitations and monogrammed stationery. Send the save-the-date cards closer to the six-month mark rather than four months prior to the wedding.

Two to Four Months

Once the invitations arrive, begin to shop for a calligrapher. The calligrapher should have her materials one month before the invitations are sent out. Order ten extra envelopes per hundred invitations to allow for mistakes. Be sure to include directions as well as lodging recommendations in the invitations. For a wedding, the couple will usually set aside a block of rooms for out-of town guests at a nearby hotel.

 Fact

Encourage all couples to purchase wedding insurance. In case of damage to the venue, wedding insurance will cover any money the bridal couple puts down to secure the venue. Because deposits are often given a year in advance, wedding insurance will cover your losses if any vendors go out of business.

Invitations should be sent six to eight weeks before the wedding date. Keep this in mind when deciding on an RSVP deadline on the invitation. At this time you should also:

- Recommend rehearsal dinner sites
- Secure any rentals
- Arrange for wedding day transportation
- Recommend accommodations for the couple and out-of-town guests
- Order the favors

One Month Before

The planning stages are almost coming to an end with the wedding a month away. Schedule a meeting with the couple to finalize the last details. During the meeting you will want to run the couple through the sequence of events of the wedding. The sequence of events will include all of the details from the receiving line to the first dance to the cutting of the cake.

You will also want to discuss publishing the wedding announcement in the local papers. The wedding program will also need to be designed at this time as well as the seating chart and place cards. For the seating chart, you will need the final count from the RSVP list. The caterer or facility planner will require the final count one to two weeks before the wedding.

Making Guests Feel Welcome

Weddings bring together many family and friends to celebrate the couple's union. With some guests traveling great distances to attend the wedding, there are certain measures you can take to make everyone feel welcome before and after the ceremony. In lieu of a traditional rehearsal dinner with only the bridal party, suggest the couple host a welcome reception to all guests the day before the wedding. A short cocktail party allows the couple to spend more time with their guests.

Also arrange for a welcome basket to be placed in all the guests' hotel rooms. A welcome basket can be a cookie basket, a bottle of wine with glasses, or an assortment of mixed nuts and local beer. Include an invitation to the welcome reception in the basket.

Planning for a farewell brunch on the morning following the wedding will give the guests a little more time with the couple and a chance to say a good farewell.

Planning a Wedding in Less than Six Months

When you are presented with the opportunity to plan a wedding in less than six months, do not shy away from the challenge. Most decisions will need to be made right away, but with the key details in place, like the venue and vendors, the other details can be planned using the formula outlined previously only compressed into six months.

Being a wedding planner is not an easy job. A wedding is a very stressful time for a couple. It is likely you were hired to shoulder some of this stress. While planning the event, keep in mind the individual tastes of the couple. The reward you feel once the journey has ended is the creation of a memorable wedding two people will remember for a lifetime.

Last-Minute Venues

The large banquet-style wedding palaces may have been booked for months, but with a little creativity you can still find fantastic locations for your couple. Suggest the following venues for last-minute nuptials:

- Restaurants or upscale bars
- Nightclubs
- Private dining rooms (for smaller weddings)
- Museums or galleries
- State parks or beaches

Wedding-Planning Shortcuts

When the planning needs to be cut short, these tips can help you get a head start on the event:

- **Choose an alternate date.** If a couple has a specific popular venue in mind, consider an alternate date if the venue has been booked. Thursday and Friday evening weddings are becoming increasingly popular, as well as Sunday afternoon receptions.
- **Skip the ceremony.** The couple may consider having a small civil ceremony with close friends and family instead of a religious wedding. This will lift the obligation from guests who may not be able to make it to the ceremony and reception.
- **Suggest an abbreviated event.** Rather than an all-day weekend affair, your couple may decide to shorten the duration of the wedding. A cocktail reception will pair well with a Thursday evening wedding.
- **Keep it small.** A wedding with forty guests has many more options than a wedding with two hundred. Weigh the options with your couple to determine if a large guest list can be shortened to fit a smaller venue.
- **Get a jump on rentals.** Many events require a planner to secure rentals two weeks prior, but a wedding is an exception. Weddings with shorter planning time require more persistence with rental companies, especially if tents or gazebos are on the list.

Chapter 19

The Gala

WHOEVER COINED THE PHRASE an "affair to remember" must have been referring to a gala. As an event planner, having a backstage pass to a gala is like having a sneak peek into the eye of a hurricane. Galas tend to involve at least a few hundred guests and depend on a production team. Galas can be extremely formal and sophisticated or have a high-energy party atmosphere. Whichever the case, when the time comes for your guests to leave and they are thanking you for a lovely evening, all of your planning will be well worth it.

What Makes an Event a Gala?

Gala events come in all different shapes, but for the most part these events are equal in size. A gala usually refers to a few hundred guests in a formal setting or cocktail party. Galas can be an annual fundraiser or have a celebrity aspect such as an award ceremony. Galas tend to involve formal attire, feature additional entertainment, and have a ticket price charged if the event is benefiting a cause. People will also host galas for milestone events such as fiftieth birthdays, twenty-fifth wedding anniversaries, or an annual yachting event.

A gala event needs momentum to be successful. A large e-mail/ mailing list, a number of supporters, and a respectable sponsor are all ways to create buzz around your event and gain momentum. For this reason, the common goal of a gala is to become an annual or semiannual event. As an event planner working on an annual event, you will have some advantages and disadvantages. One advantage is obtaining last year's event sheet script, detailing vital specifics of past planning. A disadvantage is the underutilization of your creativity compared to your past events.

Types of Event Planners for a Gala

When you are presented with the opportunity to plan an annual gala, you could be faced with a few different scenarios concerning your involvement. The client can be a business looking to hold a charity event, and you could work in their event department. You could work for a fundraising company that is hired by different companies and organizations to host a gala. You could also work in the events department of an organization that hosts an annual public event like a marathon, walk, concert, or regatta and is looking to plan a large gala around their major annual event. Working for a restaurant, hotel, and party planning company may also allow you to take part in annual gala events.

 Fact

In event planning, the production team is responsible for building the event, or setting the stage, so to speak. The team will coordinate the linens, plate ware, flatware, glassware, and table decorations. The team will also inventory the rentals at the venue and orchestrate the setup and breakdown of the event. For smaller events, the front-of-the-house staff often doubles as the production team.

Party Planner

For the party planner, hosting the gala will often mean taking on the event from start to finish, including everything from securing the venue to overseeing the event itself. The party planner will secure a venue if one hasn't been chosen. The party planner will also oversee the creative department, production team, and staffing for the event, apart from the catering or banquet staff.

If the client has started this gala as an annual event, the planner needs to follow the guidelines put in place from the previous year's event, such as the budget, the venue, and the theme.

Facilities Planner

As with weddings, the hired planner may secure a venue that may have its own planner employed to book events. Also much like with weddings, certain venues, such as ballrooms or banquet halls, are more conducive to holding galas. These venues hire planners to specifically oversee the events on premises. Again, the planners should collaborate with the client and share key information, like the facility's contract, so details do not get missed. The lead planner (in this case he would be the planner hired by the client) would take the point and act alongside or in lieu of the client. The lead should confirm the particulars of the venue such as load-in time, event time, and final guest count. In the early planning stages you should try and meet with any planners who worked on the event in the past.

Fundraising Planner

A planner from a fundraising company may also team up with a facility planner to collaborate on a gala. Organizations sometimes hire specialty fundraising companies that employ a team of event planners. One of these event planners will be the point person on a fundraising committee or foundation. With fundraisers, planners work for the foundation or nonprofit fundraising company whose sole purpose is to plan an annual gala or a calendar of events to raise money throughout the year.

The fundraising company will likely have several galas booked throughout the year, spring being the most popular season. Some gala benefits are annual events that occur in the same venue year after year.

E ssential

It is important to choose a suitable venue for a large crowd. Remember that it's easier to accommodate more guests at a cocktail-style party than a sit-down dinner. Some popular venues for galas are restaurants, nightclubs, art galleries, museums, and large open spaces such as private residences and lofts.

With such a large volume of people involved, you may be in close contact with other event planners. You might be a facility planner, a fundraising planner, or a planner in charge of production, creativity, or development. Galas are great ways to collaborate with other event planners, and every effort should be made to create a team atmosphere in which everyone works together.

As a facility planner, you, along with the catering manager, will be in charge of creating the menu, selecting wines and cocktails, and overseeing the front- and back-of-the-house staff. As a fundraising or company planner, you might be in charge of collaborating with the facility planner and acting as a liaison between the other production teams and planners. You may also be responsible for booking the entertainment and overseeing the lighting, sound, and staging team. If you work at an event company, your involvement might take place in the creative and production development. You would be in charge of choosing the décor and the design, and you would order the equipment rental and decoration. The production planning may also fall into your job description, in which case you would organize the setup and breakdown of the lighting, staging, rentals, and other decorations with the companies that are providing them.

 Fact

The setup of an event is the time devoted to preparing the venue on the day of the event. You should allow three hours of setup time for a large gala. The breakdown is the time after the event is over used to dismantle stations, return rentals to crates, and do general cleaning.

For recurring annual events, the major elements, like the venue, date, and time, have been decided. These are the first details that should be verified between the facility planner and the company planner and sponsors. Once this has been decided upon, if you are the facility planner or catering manager, you will send the company planner a proposal of the food and beverage program as well as staffing for the event. If you happen to be the company planner, you will take the lead in securing your production team outside of the facility planner's duties.

Creating New Aspects of Annual Events

Creating an event from scratch poses additional challenges but will allow you to be more creatively involved in the production. It is exciting to think about how the decisions you make now will be reincarnated year after year. During your first experience as a lead in planning a gala, don't take any risks during the planning stages. Over-communicate with your chef, production planners, and the rest of your team. Formulate the entire crew's responsibilities. Keep everyone on the same e-mail list so you can more efficiently refer back to all communications.

Changing Details

Creating new aspects of a pre-existing event may also mean simply changing out a few details from previous years. Again, a meeting with last year's planners is always a good idea. Before reinventing the wheel and changing the entire event, you should consider making minor changes.

For example, the company you are working with might be looking to increase ticket sales. They are thinking of moving the event from a hotel where it has been in the past to a larger establishment that will hold more guests. Moving the venue is risky in this case because the fundraiser has depended on attendance from the hotel's regulars and supporters. The hotel has also given a generous discount to guests attending the event that are looking to spend the night. Because this is a cocktail event sponsored by a popular vodka, it has been a well thought out decision having the hotel as a supporter.

In this case, rather than changing the venue you might suggest raising the ticket price a few dollars. Because of this increased cost, your guests will be expecting a new addition to the program. Having a guest speaker, celebrity chef, or hired band might be ways of justifying the higher ticket cost.

Logistical Changes

A hair salon that hosts a yearly fashion show may be looking for a new venue. The marketing coordinator of the salon will be acting as the lead planner on the event, and he has asked you, as the event planner of a hotel, for a proposal. Before submitting the proposal, ask him for a meeting and ask for specific comments and opinions on last year's event. Some details you might not be able to change, for example:

- The sponsors
- The donated products
- The entertainment
- The celebrity host
- The charity

Details you can suggest and use your creativity:

- The menu
- The cocktail list
- The floor setup
- The featured wine list

The logistics often come together coherent when all planners are involved. For this reason, you need to meet with all department heads prior to the event. Plan a walk-through with the lighting and audio-visual contacts. Do the same for the entertainment services, such as the DJ or the band. The goal of the meeting is to walk the perimeter of the venue and discuss the layout. Once the layout is visualized, the staging crew will know where to set up, the audio technician will know where to place the speakers, the lighting technician will know how many feet of extension cords he will need, and so forth.

 Fact

A walk-through is a meeting at the venue to go over the layout and logistics prior to the event. Collaborating event planners may arrange a walk-through before the gala. A soon-to-be bride may schedule a walk-through with her vendors prior to her wedding to discuss the floor plan, centerpieces, and the location of the dance floor.

Product Donations

The facility planner is usually responsible for acquiring all food and beverage donations. Getting product donations will help the bottom line of your facility as well as the company or organization sponsoring the event. When products are donated for a fundraiser, the event costs less. This means most, if not all, of the proceeds can go directly to the charity. If a beer company agrees to donate product to a charity event at a fundraiser with a sporting theme, the beer company then uses the event as a tax exemption. An added benefit for the beer company is greater product exposure. Perhaps their logo gets printed on the invitation and on programs at the event.

A sport beverage company may donate its new flavored water for a marathon. In turn, thousands of spectators and runners will taste the new product and see the water advertised on various banners along the marathon route. In this situation, the water company can consider the product donation as a pure marketing investment.

Philanthropy and event planning have a long history together. Whether you are asking for donations, volunteering your time, or donating your resources, the objective is to bring your craft or product into the public's eye. Whether on an invitation, banner, program, or advertisements, visibility is one main reason companies get involved in charities. Remember this as you begin planning your gala: Your participants offering donations must be well represented. (See Appendix A for a sample donor letter.) From the rental company to the event company to the product vendors, you are responsible for how the participants are represented throughout the event. Show your appreciation by giving thanks when and where appropriate.

Company or Brand Sponsorships

Company and brand sponsorships are influential in charity galas. A sponsorship differs from a donation in that in exchange for the sponsorship the company may be considered a partner in the gala and be held in a more prestigious position. A company should make an additional investment beyond its donation to be considered for a sponsorship.

Look to match sponsors with appropriate events in which there may be added benefits. You would not, for example, approach a cigarette company to sponsor a gala benefiting lung cancer research. Who would you approach to sponsor a marathon, a sneaker company or a fashionable boutique? The sneaker company would be the best choice since promoting sneakers would benefit both the marathon and the company selling the sneakers.

A brand sponsor is similar to a company sponsor with one exception. A brand sponsor may or may not have a product to sell. The brand sponsor may be offering a service or promoting a Web site. A health-care facility might be approached to be the brand sponsor for a gala benefiting asthma. An online dating service might partner with a nightclub on a singles night event. More examples of brand sponsors include:

- Investment companies
- Sports teams
- Magazines and newspapers
- Political offices
- Personal foundations

Approaching a Company

Once you have decided who you would like to approach as your product or brand sponsor, you must then decide the best way to propose your event. You first must outline the event in a letter on your letterhead. Next, you will need the name of the person in charge of marketing or charitable causes. Calling the company to ask is perfectly acceptable. If the company is in your area, ask to meet with the person directly. Be sure to bring your letter and business card to leave with your contact. If the company is not within traveling distance, ask your contact if you may send a letter with the event's details. Check back in a week for a followup. Since it may take some time to secure a company or brand sponsor, factor a few additional months into the planning schedule. Approaching a company for a product donation can begin a month before the event. When the event is over, use the same idea for your product donation contacts. Convey in a message that the successful event was a result of their efforts and products. Ask that your event be placed on the calendar for the same time next year. Six months before next year's event, you can make contact again with a letter about the event, their previous year's donation, and the event's tax ID number

Signing Contracts

It is customary to sign a contract when a company is donating products to an event. The contents of the contract outline the amount of product donated, instructions for any extra product, and exclusiveness to the event.

Alert

Company interests might not always be apparent to the public. Be sure to add all of your sponsors to your donation letter. There may be connections between a company and its affiliates. The soda company offering the donation may own a water company. If you have secured a donation from a different water company, you will create a conflict of interest for the soda company.

While you may approach a wine company for a donation to a gala, feel free to approach a gin company for a donation as well. Once your gin company contact agrees to donate product, she may require an exclusive right to the event for liquor product. The contract may state no other liquor, outside of beer and wine, to be served at the event. Or the contract might mention that the gin will be the only hosted or complimentary liquor served. The guests will pay for all other liquor beverages. The contract may also require the venue's alcohol license and insurance papers to be produced before delivering the gin.

Favor Bags

Traditionally, favors are given for gala events as a thank-you to your guests for attending the event. Favor bags or boxes should be creative and individualized for the event. Favors are also a great way for participating companies to market products. A company may donate sample products or gift certificates for placement in the favors. Favor bags should also contain literature on the charity if applicable.

Ideas for Favor Bags

The container for the favor bag itself should showcase the charity or participating company. Ask your brand sponsor if a bag or container with a logo is an item that might be donated. If not, use your theme to create a possible container for the favors. You might suggest a Chinese takeout box for an event celebrating Chinese New Year, a lunchbox for an event benefiting a children's charity, or a popcorn bucket for a movie premiere.

Next, fill the bag with at least five items related to the event. Items in the favor bags may have longevity in your guests' home. For this reason, company placement should be offered first to the businesses involved in your gala and mentioned in your donation letter. Again, give yourself ample time to secure your favors. Approach outside companies for donations to your favor bags if necessary. Be sure the company is not in direct competition with your sponsors or donors. Be sure to research each company if you are not sure.

E ssential

The gala has ended, and for some reason you are left with extra favor bags. You will likely want to show some appreciation to the staff working alongside you during the event. Giving each member of your staff a favor bag is a great token of appreciation. Extend this to members of the production teams and all of your vendors.

Delivery and Assembly of Favors

Once the favors have been determined, establish delivery with your contact. Ask your contact to place a tracking number on the packages if the product is being shipped. Give specific instructions as to the date and location of the delivery. If you will not be at the location to receive the product, be sure to alert your contact. Set up arrangements for the products to be delivered a week ahead of time to allow for any delays.

Assemble the favors ahead of time. Two days before is ideal to ensure a stress-free assembly. You will want to assemble at the venue to avoid transporting the bags. The favors should be carried out by staff members toward the end of the event for your guests to receive as they leave. Guests may feel obligated to take a favor bag if they are placed in the entryway at the start of the event. You will also run the risk of the favor bags being pillaged.

Entertainment Ideas

Entertainment is part of the draw at gala events. If finding entertainment is on your to-do list as an event planner, you will want to book the best entertainment for your gala. Determine your target audience based on your guest list, charity, and venue. The entertainment can be musical, art-related, fashion-focused, or celebrity-inspired.

A gala concluding a golf tournament might attract a golf professional who has recently published a book. A gala at a nightclub may feature local bands. An orchestra gala may feature a concert with a famous pianist. A hair salon may host an annual fashion show as its form of entertainment.

The first step in booking entertainment for your gala is to assess the needs of the talent you are approaching. If it is a band, will they need a stage, equipment, speakers, and so forth? How will you provide the band with equipment? Can this expense be taken out of the ticket price or will it be a donated item? If the gala is in a nightclub setting, the nightclub may provide some of the equipment; if not, it should be considered an expense. Once you weigh your costs, devise a schedule of the evening's events. Following is an example of a schedule for a gala:

- 3–5 P.M.—Setup
- 5–5:30 P.M.—Staff meeting
- 6 P.M.—Guest arrival
- 6:15 P.M.—Begin passing hors d'oeuvres and cocktails
- 8–10 P.M.—Entertainment
- 10–11 P.M.—Favors and general cleanup
- 11 P.M.—Event closes and breakdown begins

You will draft a more detailed schedule in the days prior to the event, but for entertainment purposes, you are trying to give the talent a general sense of performance time.

Next, a letter should be drafted. This letter should be slightly different than the donation letter you have written. Like the donation letter, general information should be included about the event and the charity. The letter should then specify why you have chosen this type of entertainment for the gala and, more specifically, why you chose the band, violinist, or DJ. Mention whether you are asking the talent to volunteer their time or if you have a budget to compensate the talent. Also mention any hotel, flight, and meal accommodations in addition to equipment you plan on providing.

The next step to securing the entertainment is to get the letter in the hands of the right person. If you are trying to book a DJ, you may be able to call the DJ directly. If you are trying to book a band, the right person may be the band's publicist. If you were holding your gala at a nightclub, the booking agent for the nightclub would be a useful resource to contact. Also consider a publicist or a public relations firm that may have ties to your organization or sponsor companies. Be creative with your resources.

 Fact

A publicist also works in fundraising. Public relations firms are involved in the planning of clients' philanthropic efforts. From providing a guest list to soliciting donations for auction items to securing a sponsor, a client's public relations company aids in event plans. On some occasions, the public relations company will be the catalyst for introducing a client to a venue or a brand that they represent.

Congratulations! Your desired entertainment has been secured for your gala. Standard practice dictates signing a contract with the performers, even if they are volunteering. The contract should outline the specifics such as the date and time of the event, as well as the time and length of the performance. The contract should also include which party is responsible for the equipment. Necessary arrangements in case of a cancellation or emergency should also be stated on the contract.

Chapter 20

Large Casual Events

FAMILY REUNIONS, COMPANY PICNICS, alternative weddings, and less formal rehearsals and bridal luncheons all fall under the category of large casual events. Moreover, these types of events encompass the most diverse group of guests, where sometimes the age group and social spectrum of the guests vary quite a bit. Large events such as these may incorporate children as well as friends from the workplace and grandparents. They take place more in a relaxed setting like parks, vineyards, restaurants, or a large private residence and less in the formal setting of a ballroom or banquet hall.

Finding Suitable Venues for Families

Large-scale events are also differentiated by the time of day that they take place. A Saturday or Sunday afternoon is not an unlikely time to see on an invitation for these functions. For this reason, outdoor venues or an outdoor activity, such as ice-skating on a pond, are perfect for events for all age groups.

Parks

A park can be a beautiful setting to host a casual event. Picture a band playing under an old-fashioned gazebo, guests rowing canoes down a stream, or nature hikes scheduled throughout the afternoon. From a hillside park to a state park on a river, picturesque parks are an ideal spot to gather family and friends. Before considering that perfect park, consider the following factors:

- Are there clean public restrooms available?
- Is there a natural cover in case of rain, or will you have to rent a tent?

- Are there other activities like horseback riding to add to the event?
- Are there any fire pits or barbecues to use?
- Are there any permits needed or reservations needed for the space?

Beach Resort

An event at a beach resort can be enjoyable for people of all ages. With the many activities for guests to partake in at a beach resort, the event could be extended into a weekend getaway. When shopping for venues, look for resorts with event facilities. Some resorts will have a cabana, clubhouse, or game room to secure as a venue to make your event private. Beach resorts tend to book in advance. Consider off-peak season or midweek periods to expedite planning times.

When consulting with the client on the invitation, be sure to add a dress code, if any. Guests may be uncertain how to pack if the recommended attire is not listed. Also be sure to include any extra activities being offered. Guests can pack swimsuits, hiking boots, or skis if told ahead of time.

Private Rooms or Small Restaurants

Depending on the size of the event, arrange site visits to private rooms and restaurants. Most restaurants can be made private with a buyout, especially for an afternoon. Although these venues can be slightly more formal for a casual event, attempt to find a venue with an outdoor space or garden for the entertainment.

These venues are perfect for a bridal luncheon. Although there may not be much need for an outside space, such as a garden, for entertainment, it can be used by guests to enjoy a welcome respite from planned activities. A soothing instrument being played, such as a harp or violin, will be quiet enough without interrupting conversation. Invite a storyteller to entertain children who may be present.

Inns or Lakeside Cabins

There are many recreational activities that guests can enjoy at a country inn or a lakeside cabin. Before and after the event, guests can meander the grounds and enjoy the relaxed setting. Guests may undertake a game of bocce on the lawn, or a fierce chess competition may ensue.

Vineyards

Vineyards often are equipped with beautiful picnic grounds. Meeting the winemaker at a wine tasting is always a nice way to spend an afternoon. Consider arranging overnight accommodations for a group of wine tasters. By the end of an afternoon spent tasting wine, the guests will appreciate the thought.

Creating a Theme

Tying all of the details into a theme allows the event to have continuity from the menu to decorations to entertainment. After choosing the venue, the theme is the next to follow. Pull natural elements from the venue's surrounding area to create a theme. If the event location is in a historic city, arrange for a trolley as group transportation. Arrange for an impromptu tour around the city before the trolley ends at the event site.

Seasonal Themes

Suggest creating an event around an outdoor activity. The great winter escape will excite snowboarders to snowshoers. Having an activity is a great way for guests to spend an afternoon. The image of serving hot chocolate to chilly skaters or cross-country skiers in the winter around a cozy fire will surely warm up your client. Again, be sure to secure a venue with some indoor relief. A rented cabin will work as a venue in the snow.

An autumn event comes complete with natural decorations of turning leaves and bountiful produce. Chilly weather will have guests snuggling up under blankets. Your client will want to take advantage of all fall has to offer. With a farm as the venue, guests could pick apples, visit a pumpkin patch, and enjoy a hayride.

The long days of summer can be a backdrop to any celebration. Pig roasts and luaus translate well into casual events. Begin the event in the afternoon to savor as many hours of sunlight as possible. Again, a rented cabin or community center will make a great bathhouse for those who want to take a dip in a nearby pool or ocean. Have the twinkle lights ready to carry the party into the twilight hours.

E ssential

For any venues where weather may be a factor, have a backup plan. Renting a tent may protect against rain, but if it has been raining for three days prior to the event, there will be no protection against the mud. Check with your rental company for flooring as well as tent options.

Celebration of Family or Company

For family reunions, create a theme of celebration and unity. Work with your client and graphic artist to design a family tree. Hire a photographer to take a group photo and attach to copies of the family tree. Let elders take turns telling family stories. Take this time to swap family recipes.

This theme can also be modified for a company outing. Have your client create a history of the company for employees. The client will create a sense of employee pride by sharing the company's beginnings. Perhaps the client can design a company jacket for an employee appreciation gift.

Medieval Fair

Once a client is sold on the idea of a medieval fair, the enjoyment begins. Renting costumes and falling into character will be an added benefit to planning a fair. All family members will be animated at the idea of a medieval fair. This theme also translates well to a company outing and even a wedding. Guests love the idea of dressing up. A costume ball can succeed as a casual affair.

Creating a Fun, Approachable Menu

Depending on the level of casualness, the client may also entertain the idea of having family-style or buffet fare. With these events, planners may be encouraged by the client to be innovative and have fun with the menu. The catering manager should avoid an adventurous menu, and the beverages should be suitable for a warm afternoon outside. A martini bar, for example, may not be a good idea.

Food Service

The level of service changes slightly with casual events. Where a formal event may require one server for every twenty guests, a casual occasion may require one server for every forty guests. In family-style meals, guests sit at communal tables and pass large platters of food. In buffet style, guests help themselves along one long buffet table. Meals are rarely coursed out; courses are served simultaneously.

 Alert

If alcoholic beverages are being served, advise your client to employ a bartender. A bartender will manage the beverage table as well as beverage consumption. Offer punches for the adults and nonalcoholic smoothies for the children to make it fun.

Use the Theme to Create a Menu

The theme plays a big part in the menu. As always, choose produce that is in season and possibly native to the local area. For a fall harvest, serve butternut squash soup in sugar pumpkins and add cider donuts for the children. At a country inn, offer a hearty country brunch. A luau or a pig roast complements any summer event. And you can involve your guests with a Southern barbecue. For a family reunion, add a touch of nostalgia and ask each guest to make a dish from the family recipe box.

Catered Affair

More often than not, your client will request a catered event. When you secure a nontraditional venue, the caterer or facility's chef will be your next stop. Schedule a caterer's tasting with your client. Give the caterer specific information as to the type of cuisine your client might prefer for his event. Complicated dishes may not have a place at this event. Food that is simply prepared with bright flavors should be on the menu.

Keep the Audience in Mind

In your discussions with your client, try and get a feel for the type of guests she will be expecting. Package the event with everyone in mind. Events with a large group of children may offer only grilled cheese and hot dogs, but an event at an oceanside seafood shack might offer a raw bar.

Take into account that some adults are unadventurous eaters. Your client may think nothing of offering venison as an entrée for everyone, but this may turn off some adults. A simple menu does not have to be unrefined. Grilled pizzas with fresh produce or grilled chicken with a housemade salsa make friendly meals.

Caterers should be prepared with adequate refrigeration when cooking outside. Before the event, arrange for a walk-through for the caterer. Equipment may need to be rented if the kitchen capabilities at the venue are not adequate. Also inquire about the cooking methods the caterer will be using if serving the meal outside.

Children love being involved in the cooking process. You can get children involved in cooking by arranging for a kids' cooking seminar at the beginning of the event, out of the way of the caterer of course. Children can volunteer for different jobs throughout the meal, especially dessert. Have kids make cookies, cakes, lollipops, or even ice cream. The children will be excited to show off their creations on the dessert table.

Choosing Diverse Entertainment

The entertainment for a casual event can include music, specialty acts, or performers. Often more than one type of entertainment is chosen for a casual event. This can break the guests into smaller groups without compromising the event. Also consider types of entertainment that will appeal to all guests.

A DJ or live band can work very well at casual events. To ensure a friendly playlist, meet with the musical group ahead of time. Outline a music set with your audience in mind. Be careful of risky lyrics with young children present.

If children will be present, the planner may suggest entertainment or performers specifically for children in addition to a music act. The children's entertainment can be separated from the distractions of the day's main activities. Performers such as contortionists, mimes, and jugglers will be sure to grab young minds.

Consider a mystery theater or a treasure hunt to entertain older imaginations. A caricaturist, trapeze artist, and storyteller will capture the attention of children of all ages, and perhaps some adults as well. Most other children's services—such as balloon artists, face painters, and moonwalks—should be saved for birthday parties.

As an added bonus for the parents, hire a few qualified babysitters for the event. Most parents will love the idea of having a few moments to themselves while a sitter keeps the young ones occupied. Use a professional service when researching babysitters.

In some cases, the guests at a casual event may not be familiar with each other socially. A company outing is a great example. Your client may look to you for tricks to break the ice. Recommend alternative activities to encourage interaction.

- Rent a trampoline and have an instructor give lessons.
- Incorporate spa services at the event to relax the guests.
- Build an obstacle course or play a game of laser tag.

 Fact

Just as you and your staff should be certified in CPR, make certain the babysitter service requires child CPR certification for all its employees. Ask the service how many sitters are required for the number of children attending the event. Hire only from services that perform background checks on their employees.

Outdoor Activities

Plan an event that lasts all day. Utilize the venue's surroundings and arrange for outside activities around the event. Whatever the weather, guests can make the most of the outdoors. Just be sure to include extra activities on the invitation so guests can be prepared. Outdoor activities can include:

- Ice skating
- Skiing
- Snowshoeing
- Hayrides
- Apple picking
- Swimming
- Canoeing
- White-water rafting
- Horseback riding

Juggling the Needs of Different Guests

When planning a large event, you may need to be more involved with the guest list. Elderly guests may need handicapped-accessible restrooms or elevators. Parents of young children may need changing facilities and would take pleasure in the idea of babysitting services. Singles and couples alike may need a break from the festivities and enjoy more grownup activities like a wine tasting. Juggling the needs of different guests can be challenging, but it's worth the effort when you see the guests enjoying themselves.

When planning a large casual event, avoid a venue located out in the middle of nowhere. Make sure there is a town nearby in case of an emergency. A guest may forget shaving cream or medicine and need a pharmacy within a short distance. When planning for activities with horses or trampolines, check if there is a hospital within a few miles.

For weekend events, recommend accommodations a short ride from shopping areas and restaurants. Having to search for these services can make a relaxing weekend not so relaxing after all.

Part of the event may involve taking the guests out of their element and on a weekend getaway. As the event planner, you can arrange a group itinerary where the guests can gather for meals, hikes, or tours. On the itinerary, also list additional recreational activities, local museums, and points of interest. Be sure to include phone numbers and hours of operation. Place an itinerary in each guest's room or in a welcome basket.

Not all of the guests will be able to keep up with the itinerary you have planned. For groups that include a large number of children, elderly guests, or guests in wheelchairs, design an alternate itinerary. In addition to the weekend itinerary, include an itinerary for families. List activities like miniature golf, children's museums, and aquariums. Be sure the sitter service's number is listed on the itinerary if the parents are looking for a night out.

If the group is partaking in a strenuous activity, planning alternate activities for the elderly or handicapped guests would be a nice idea. Note activities and museums in the area that are handicapped accessible. A guided tour may be a lovely alternative to a hike for older guests. For groups that have a small number of children or elderly guests, find activities that everyone can enjoy.

An event held in a beautiful setting can relax the guests and put the focus on the celebration. Creating a simple, friendly menu and approachable entertainment shows you have the needs of all of the guests in mind. When you consider the diversity of your guest list before planning large casual events, your endeavors will result in a successful event.

Chapter 21

Corporate Events and Dinners

LARGE CORPORATIONS, UNIVERSITIES, and hospitals have event planners on staff, often within different departments. Typically these planners secure the details for the host or guest speaker and do not attend the event themselves. This position is often referred to as a corporate event planner. A corporate event planner's responsibilities include securing the venue, establishing the budget, choosing the menu, arranging audiovisual equipment, and organizing transportation and lodging.

Securing a Restaurant or Hotel

A corporate event planner should know which hotels and restaurants in his area have conference rooms and private rooms. As a result, he or she will usually establish a good working relationship with the on-site event planners at these facilities. Not all corporate functions require a private or conference room, but most will.

The corporate event planner makes arrangements for a department, the company in its entirety, a guest speaker, or department head. The corporate planner works with a contact attending the event. This person is called the on-site contact or event host.

Working with the On-site Contact or Host

Depending on the needs of the host or on-site contact, the corporate planner will handle all of the details leading up to the event. Guests of the event will contact the corporate planner for directions, special dietary requests, or transportation. On the day of the event, the corporate planner will hand the host or on-site contact a copy of the BEO (banquet event order) and resume. The BEO provides the details of the event. The resume provides details of the attending guests and lodging and transportation accommodations if applicable.

Working with a Facility Planner

The facility planner is the corporate event planner's contact on the venue side. All of the details are arranged between the two planners ahead of time. On occasion, the on-site contact will call the facility planner to confirm the details of the event. This call will usually take place when the on-site contact receives the BEO, the day before the event. The on-site contact will then manage any last-minute details or requests with the facility planner.

The facility planner will want to set up a meet and greet with the on-site contact. The pair may quickly outline the evening's program, menu, and payment. The on-site contact usually arrives before any guests to perform a walk-through. The on-site contact may use this time to set up any printed materials, equipment, or place cards in the private room.

In some cases, the event will incorporate a guest speaker or guest of honor. As the corporate planner, it is advisable to arrange for the guest speaker's transportation to the event. This will lessen the risk of the guest speaker getting lost or running late. When the speaker arrives at the venue, the on-site contact will brief him on the evening's program.

In a hotel or restaurant setting, a planner's schedule will vary from company to company. Expectations regarding her presence at events are arranged in advance with the owner or manager of the facility. When a facility event planner books events, a client may assume she will be present for the event. The facility planner should alert clients whose events she may not attend.

Often at corporate events the on-site contact will request a contact person at the venue. If the facility event planner cannot attend, she should convey this to the corporate event planner in the early stages. The facility planner's replacement should be listed on the BEO.

Fact

A facility planner may start his day early taking calls and organizing events and may not attend all the events at his facility. He may begin the evening with the host and leave the event, passing the responsibility to servers and managers. His assistant or partner may come in to manage the event until the end.

Differences Between Private Rooms and Conference Rooms

The needs of corporate events differ for each function. An event may require a projector and screen for presentations or a Polycom box for a conference call. Function rooms often have specialty capabilities. For a corporate planner, it is important to know the differences between the types of function rooms.

Conference Room

Conference rooms are located in hotels and other establishments designed for a business purpose. The room may hold a boardroom-style table to encourage table discussions. The room may also have a separate telephone system for a Polycom box, as well as Internet capabilities. Newer conference rooms often have wireless Internet connection, or Wi-Fi.

A conference room's main objective is to accommodate meetings. As a result, a conference room may hold or be connected to a business center or business office. A business office is equipped with computers, fax machines, and copiers and can be used as a satellite office. A conference room is used for function rather than flair. The furniture may also be rearranged to accommodate a classroom setting.

Private Room

Private rooms are located primarily in restaurants and are designed for entertainment purposes. Corporate planners tend to look for private rooms to host a function around a meal, such as a breakfast meeting, luncheon, or business dinner. While a large table in the dining room may cause distraction for attendees, a private room provides a quiet setting for discussions and presentations.

Policies on private rooms vary. Some private rooms require a food and beverage minimum in lieu of a room charge. Others impose a room charge without considering a food and beverage minimum. Check with your facility planner for the restaurant's or hotel's policy. Be sure to confirm the cancellation policy as well.

Private rooms are not exclusive to corporate clientele. Private rooms are in high demand for casual social functions such as family celebrations, bridal showers, and birthdays. Private rooms range in size, but they can usually hold from ten to eighty guests. Larger private rooms are often referred to as ballrooms or function rooms.

Securing a Room for a Corporate Event

When booking a room for a corporate event, ask the facility planner specific questions regarding the room, such as:

- What is the capacity of the room?
- How is the room set up?
- What is the capacity of a boardroom-style setup and classroom-style setup?
- What capabilities does the room have?

To secure a room for a corporate function, the venue may request a contract or credit card deposit. As a corporate event planner, you may need to arrange payment for the dinner in advance. A corporation may prefer to be billed for its events. Your facility planner will know if the venue offers billing. If not, you may have to arrange for credit card payment.

 Fact

If your on-site contact does not have a corporate credit card, you will need to arrange for credit card payment in advance. In addition to the BEO and resume, you may also have to provide a credit card authorization form. The credit card authorization form will have the signature of the cardholder and a copy of the credit card, front and back.

Familiarize yourself with conference rooms and private rooms in your area. Schedule appointments with facility planners to take pictures and collect information on menus, pricing, and beverage programs for your files. Having this information will help you when it comes time to decide on a venue.

Booking Lodging and Transportation

Part of a corporate event planner's responsibility may include arranging for lodging and transportation for guests attending the event. This may include purchasing airplane tickets, securing transportation to and from the airport, booking hotel rooms, reserving rental cars, and organizing the guests to ensure everyone attends the event on time with no delays.

Hotel

A corporate event planner may have to book just one room for an employee or several hundred rooms for an entire company. Your company may already have a preferred membership with a local or chain hotel. Preferred members usually receive a flat rate for rooms as well as complimentary upgrades. Some hotels employ a car service or shuttle for airport pickup.

If your company has not established itself as a preferred member, visit local hotels in your area for the best rate. Corporate event planners are often invited to hotel functions a few times a year to view the hotel's services. A member of the hotel sales team can discuss rate options, billing options, and amenities for your company.

Airlines

More often than not, corporate employees book individual airline tickets themselves and are later reimbursed. Occasionally the task will befall the corporate planner, especially for conferences. Booking airline tickets can be tricky for a large group of employees. You should be considerate of busy schedules and prior commitments. Send a preliminary itinerary via e-mail months before the event. An employee may look at the flight plans and decide to book his own flight.

Car Service

To keep employees on schedule and prevent them from getting lost, it is wise to arrange a private car service for transportation to and from the airport. A car service is also advised for travel to and from any scheduled events or conferences. For large groups, a chartered shuttle is recommended. For groups expected to do a bit of traveling, you may suggest rental cars.

Reserving Supplies and Equipment

For business meetings, corporate planners often have to arrange for supplies and rent audiovisual equipment. Your on-site contact will inform you which equipment the event requires. Ask your audiovisual company for a catalog of equipment.

Audiovisual Equipment

Purchasing and maintaining audiovisual equipment is costly, and transporting the equipment runs the risk of damaging it. For these reasons your company will rent equipment as needed. It is likely you will develop a vendor relationship with an A/V company. Coordinate the equipment delivery with the facility planner.

Before reserving any A/V equipment, ask your facility planner what the capabilities of the conference room are. Even if you have booked the venue in the past, it is still a good idea to confirm the use of the equipment with the facility planner. The venue may have another company who requested the equipment. Or the equipment might be under repair and therefore not available.

Supplies

In addition to equipment, a business meeting may also need supplies for an event. The supplies may include pens and legal pads for taking notes. An easel, large-format paper, and dry-erase board may be needed for presentations. Conference rooms also tend to keep complimentary supplies on site for business meetings. Your company may prefer to use logo stationery and pens for business meetings. If this is not the case, check with your facility planner before ordering supplies.

Collateral Materials

Occasionally a business event may require collateral from the guest speaker or your company. Your on-site contact should inform you if materials are needed. When materials are needed, it may be your responsibility to order the collateral. For smaller events, your on-site contact may be able to carry the materials to the event. In instances where it is necessary for the on-site contact to travel, the collateral may need to be shipped in advance.

Be sure to track the packages in which the collateral is sent. The facility planner should be listed as the contact person to receive the package and alerted prior to the shipment. Ask the facility planner to confirm the package's arrival.

Guest Speakers

In the academic and medical fields, guest speakers are often involved in events. A guest speaker may be invited to give a presentation, teach a seminar, or give a lecture.

A guest speaker's schedule may include more than one seminar or lecture during her visit. As the corporate planner, you may be responsible for securing the travel and lodging as well as arranging the itinerary of the guest speaker.

Itinerary

The head of the department, dean of students, or chairperson may have input into the speaker's timeline of events and help you organize a guest speaker's schedule. To get the most value from a guest speaker, a company will pack his schedule, leaving little downtime. It is important to be efficient when planning the schedule of the speaker. If someone other than you arranged the itinerary, look carefully for overlapping events in his schedule. Give the speaker adequate breaks and time for meals.

Transportation

With a guest speaker on a tight schedule, transportation is a very import detail of her schedule. If the speaker is from out of town, suggest arranging for a car service to chauffeur the speaker back and forth to events. This will avoid the speaker running late because she couldn't get a taxi or got lost on the subway. Check the company's budget to determine the length of time a car service can be rented.

Lodging

For convenience, book the speaker at the same hotel as the event, or research surrounding areas to find a nearby hotel for the speaker. Again, confirm with your accounting department to ensure you are booking within the company's budget for hotel accommodations. As an added measure, list nearby restaurants, shops, and points of interest on the speaker's itinerary.

Expense Account

Your company's accounting department may also include instructions for the speaker's expense account. Give these details to the speaker on the itinerary or in an e-mail in advance of the event. Be sure the speaker knows who is responsible for long-distance calls and room service orders.

Event BEO and Resume

In corporate event planning, the event planner organizes the event and the on-site contact manages the function. As a result, the communication between the planner and her contact needs to be flawless. The on-site contact may not have the opportunity to call the planner with questions, especially for after-hour events. The communication between the two occurs in mostly one form: the banquet event order (BEO).

BEO

An event's BEO is a form outlining all of the event's details, including instructions for the evening and the menu and wine choices. The BEO is printed by the corporate event planner. The corporate event planner will then use the BEO to confirm the details with the facility planner. Finally, within a few days of the event, the corporate event planner will pass the BEO along to the on-site contact to review all of the details. Any questionable information will be worked out between the corporate planner and on-site contact. The on-site contact may touch base with the facility planner to review all the details from the venue's side.

Resume

In event planning, a resume is a printed document describing a staff's hotel assignments when traveling. A resume comes in handy when a large number of staff members are traveling to a conference.

A hotel may also print a resume to keep track of a company's staff. The resume is distributed to all departments in the hotel and is useful to determine in-room charges, the length of stay, and VIP staff. The accounting department will also be given a resume.

Event planners often use computer software specifically designed for organizing events. The software can be used to create a BEO and a resume, as well as create a template for tracking other information and details. Most software can run on both Mac and PC operating systems. See Appendix B for a list of event-planning software.

The BEO and resume are great tools for confirming event information. In corporate event planning, the details are passed mainly between three people: the corporate planner, the on-site contact, and the facility planner. In some cases, a facility event planner may replace her own event sheet with the corporate planner's BEO. Since so many people rely on this information, it's critical that everyone be on the same page.

Corporate events require a different type of event planner. A corporate event planner is the nucleus of a corporation's events—all details and communication flow through her. Since corporate event planners often do not attend events they plan, they must rely on feedback from the on-site coordinator. The corporate planner can utilize this criticism when planning future events.

Chapter 22

An Intimate Dinner

THERE ARE MANY CELEBRATIONS at the center of an intimate dinner—birthdays, anniversaries, and promotions, just to name a few. Sometimes no celebration at all is needed to gather with friends, family, or colleagues. Business dinners and presentations involving a smaller group of people can also follow the guidelines of an intimate dinner.

The Destination and Details

There may not be an invitation more intimate than dinner at a friend's home. Translating that intimacy to a large restaurant can be a challenge. But with more and more private rooms popping up, an intimate dinner at a restaurant can be quite enjoyable.

The destination for an intimate dinner can also be creative. A picturesque winery would be a spectacular setting for an intimate dinner, as would a terrace overlooking the ocean or a handsome farm.

An intimate dinner can be formal or informal depending on the occasion. Three to five courses are traditionally on the menu, and wine is frequently paired with each course. The planner should adhere to a formal table setting unless otherwise directed by the host. Servers hired for the event should be well versed in the etiquette of fine dining, even if the client is not. There is bound to be someone at the table who will appreciate proper service. Intimate dinners tend to have less than thirty guests.

A beautifully set table can also be the measure of an intimate dinner. Add soft lighting, quiet music, and lots of candles to add to the ambiance.

Two popular opportunities may present themselves to an event planner to plan an intimate dinner. As the event manager at a catering company, a client will hire you to cater a dinner at an off-site location. Catering event managers are also referred to as event planners. The second opportunity is as a private events coordinator at a restaurant. Hotels also have private rooms small enough to hold an intimate dinner, which would be catered by the hotel's restaurant.

Creating a Three-Plus Course Menu

A triumphant intimate dinner is one that has the guests dreaming about the menu long after the event. To achieve this, first sit with the client and ask her for ideas she has for the menu. Next, meet with the chef and design a menu specifically for your client, or suggest a menu to your client based on the chef's specialties.

In the initial meeting with the client, you may want to ask for some suggestions regarding the menu. Ask your client if he had any specific dishes in mind for the menu. You may also ask him about dinner parties he has hosted in the past. Perhaps he attended a dinner and fell in love with a dish. Tapping your client for his likes and dislikes will result in a menu with all of his favorite foods.

It is entirely possible your client will not want to design the menu. She may rely on the chef's expertise and imagination. Before you sit with the chef, collect some information from your client. Your client may not have any recommendations for dishes, but she may prefer a vegetarian first course, a seafood entrée, and a chocolate dessert. These specifics will give the chef a base from which to work.

After the chef has designed the menu, send it to your client for a review. List ingredients, if needed, to make the menu easier to decipher.

Before pricing an intimate dinner, you must take into account the availability of kitchen equipment. Restaurants, of course, will have equipment on-site, especially for a small dinner party. With remote destinations, a catering company may require certain equipment that is not available on the premises. You must decide to charge the equipment rental to the client or build the rental cost into the per-person price.

A client may decide to plan an intimate dinner around or on a holiday. For these events, classic menus may be the only option. Think turkey at Thanksgiving or lamb on Easter. A client may request the chef prepare a family recipe. It is a good idea to double-check with the chef before taking such requests.

 **Alert**

Be sure to have your client inquire about any guest allergies before the event day. The invitation is the best place to ask about this detail so it is sure not to be missed. For such a small group of guests, it would be a shame to alienate someone because of an allergy. To be safe, your chef may choose to prepare a few allergy-free meals just in case.

An intimate dinner is another opportunity to learn about pricing out a menu. In the beginning of your career, defer to the chef before guaranteeing any prices to the client.

As you gain experience you can price out your own menus. Following is a basic rundown on how to price out a menu:

- Figure out the quantity of main ingredients, such as protein and produce, that are needed for each menu item.
- Using a purveyor's pricing list, multiply the prices of the main ingredients by the quantity you determined you needed.
- Figure out the quantity of secondary ingredients such as olive oil, cream, and tomato paste and price the secondary ingredients.
- Estimate the amount of seasonings you will need.
- Divide the seasonings used by the cost of the bulk package.
- Figure out the BOH labor costs by adding the total amount of BOH employee's hours and multiplying hours by the pay rate.
- Add up all of the costs of the main and secondary ingredients, seasonings, and back-of-the-house labor to get the total for your food costs.
- Multiply the food costs by the percentage of markup (usually 25 percent) to get your profit margin.

- Add your profit margin to your total food costs.
- Divide that total by the number of guests attending the event. This is your per-person cost.

Wine Pairings

Pairing wine with food is an art form. For food and wine lovers, a perfectly prepared meal with a perfectly paired wine is quite satisfying. Intimate dinners often feature courses that are paired with wine. Some pairings are quite simple while others require a refined palate. With a little knowledge, you too can create perfect wine pairings for your intimate dinners.

When designing a menu, certainly your chef can offer suggestions and assistance. But if you are not a master sommelier and have to pair your own wines, there are some simple measures you can take to be on your way.

Get Help

If you are lucky enough to have a wine director on staff, ask him to teach you the basics of wine varietals and regions. Wine pairings have quite a bit to do with their country of origin.

A wine class may be a good beginning for a novice. Wine classes are frequently taught at culinary centers, adult education classes, and community centers. Check with the instructor about the subject material before signing up for the class. Tell the instructor exactly what you hope to learn from her class. An extensive class about Oregon pinot noir probably will not benefit you if you are just starting out.

If taking a class is too daunting at this stage in your career, become your own instructor. Invest in a few good wine books. Ask for recommendations from colleagues in the industry. Utilize the Internet for research. Some wine Web sites offer food pairings as well as wine descriptions.

Sometimes asking your chef about a wine pairing is all you need. Even if the chef has no interest in wine, she may still be knowledgeable about the subject. Chefs are trained to pair wines with cuisine in culinary school. If the chef studied abroad, chances are she picked up some information along her travels.

Regional Pairings

Wine is typically matched to the cuisine after the menu has been decided. Occasionally you may have a client who would like to feature a few special bottles from his wine cellar. In this case, ask the chef to pair the cuisine to the wine. Depending on the type of menu the chef is serving, you may get some clues to a wine pairing.

Question

What if my client requests a wine that does not pair with the menu?
Not all wine pairs easily with food. New World wines (wines from Australia, United States, and South America that don't have as long a history as wines from Europe) do not pair as easily with their Old World counterparts in cuisine. If the California cabernet matched up with the filet mignon isn't to a guest's liking, offer to pour a French Bordeaux alongside.

Wines pair easily with cuisine from the same region. This is because the grapes grow in the same soil as the produce. For example, oyster shells fossilized in the soil of Chablis, France, make this white wine a perfect combination with oysters.

Place Cards

A place card indicates to a guest where the host would prefer he sit for dinner. The host may like to use place cards for other reasons, such as to introduce one guest to another or to keep certain guests away from one another. The most common seating arrangements alternate male and female guests.

For a small dinner setting, a place card will simply have the guest's name written on the card. The place card would then be arranged at a designated place setting. The most common placement for the cards is on the plate or at the twelve o'clock position of the plate.

At larger functions such as weddings and fundraisers, place cards are used to guide guests to a designated table. The place card will not only list the guest's name but also the table number at which he is to be seated. Once at the table, the guest is free to sit where he likes.

Place Card Holders

To dress up a table, the client may request place card holders. A place card holder can be a small stand or statue with a slit for the place card. You can rent place card holders from your rental company. Most home furnishings stores sell place card holders as well. A folded piece of card stock works well in lieu of a place card holder.

Place card holders are often given as favors. To avoid the guests mistakenly taking the rented place card holder as a favor, ask the server to pull the holders once all of the guests have taken their seats. This way a guest cannot mistake the place card holder for a gift from the host.

The Place Card Backlash

There may have always been controversy about the use of a place card, but perhaps years ago guests were too polite to mention it. Nowadays you may find clients strongly opposed to place cards. Some hosts now believe a guest should have the freedom to sit where she likes.

Table Settings

A table setting or place setting refers to the items needed to set a table for dinner. Table settings differ with formal and informal settings. Table settings can use proper high-end silver or flatware, or a less expensive trendy version. You can use plate ware or fine china, stemware or crystal glasses, and everything in between to design a beautiful table setting. Tablecloths, napkins, and table runners can also be used to dress a lovely table.

The Basics

A basic table setting includes:

- An entrée plate or charger
- A salad fork and dinner fork to the left of the plate
- A bread and butter (B&B) plate, with a butter knife, to the left of the forks
- A dinner knife to the right of the entrée plate
- A steak knife and soup spoon to the right of the dinner plate, if applicable
- A teaspoon to the right of the knife
- A water glass above the dinner knife
- A red wine glass to the right of the water glass
- A white wine glass to the right of the red wine glass
- A champagne flute in the two o'clock position
- A napkin—proper placement and fold varies, but if in doubt, fold it and place it on the entrée plate or charger

Formal settings may include more silverware, such as a seafood fork, a seafood knife, and claw crackers for shellfish. A mother-of-pearl spoon for caviar may be included in the place setting, as well as utensils for escargot.

In a restaurant environment, the table setting may include simply a dinner fork, knife, napkin, and water glass. The server will then bring the necessary utensils as the meal progresses. This way the table will not get overcrowded during the course of the meal.

 Fact

Caviar is a delicacy that comes from fish eggs (also called roe) harvested from sturgeon and other types of fish. Caviar spoons are traditionally made from mother-of-pearl or wood. Avoid using any metal when serving caviar. The metal clashes with the taste of the caviar, making the caviar taste tinny and metallic.

Rentals

In a restaurant setting, a client may have specific requests that might require you to rent china, flatware, or glassware. For example, your client may request Riesling, a white wine varietal from Germany, to be poured in a proper Riesling glass. In this case, you may need to rent the glassware. Your restaurant, for the most part, should be equipped with the proper table settings.

 Fact

In the service industry, positions of a clock are often used to determine placements for table settings and even food on plates. The top of a plate is considered twelve o'clock. If a plate has a logo or monogram, it should be positioned at twelve o'clock.

In the catering world, rentals are a large part of the planning process. Some event-planning and catering companies have large warehouses to stock basic plate ware and glassware. Smaller companies rely on rental companies for events.

Rentals for table settings are usually built into the per-person price. An exception to this rule is when a client desires a high-end item. For example, if your client must have lead crystal champagne flutes, the difference in price ($10) from a basic champagne flute would be passed on to the client.

 **Alert**

For events taking place in a private home, it is always a good idea to take stock of flatware, plate ware, and glassware. One of the vendors you'll use most frequently is your rental supply company. To cover against breakage, always add to the count of rentals needed.

Table Etiquette

Unless requested by the client, the servers should use proper table etiquette. Table etiquette refers more to the style of service than a guest's table etiquette. Proper table etiquette ensures that each guest has what he or she needs for each course. Table etiquette also replaces awkward or clumsy service.

Mise en Place

Mise en place, often shortened to just *mise,* is a French term that means "everything in its place." For servers the term describes their setup for the next course. For example, the correct mise for a soup course is a soup spoon placed to the right of the butter knife. All mises should be carried out on a mise tray or small platter.

Fine Dining Tips

Fine dining establishments utilize proper table etiquette as a service style. Some fine dining restaurants are famous for using over-the-top tools to impress guests with high-quality service. For example, a server may walk a female guest to the restroom so she does not get lost en route.

Before an event, it is wise to give your servers a quick lesson on table etiquette. Better yet, if a member of your staff is well versed in fine dining service, let her give the lesson. Here are some fine dining tips to pass on to servers:

- Serve from the left and clear from the right.
- Silver should be replaced between each course, unless the silver has been preset in a formal setting. Then the silver should be pulled from the table only if it is dirty.
- The server should wait for the entire table to finish with a course before clearing.
- Refold a napkin for guests who get out of their seat during the dinner.
- When serving coffee, the handle of the cup should point to four o'clock.

It is cleanup time. The guests have cleared the morsels of dessert from the plates. The client and guests are still raving about the entrée. The last sips of wine are lingering in the glass. A cleared plate is a sure sign of guest satisfaction. Sometimes you do not have to wait until the follow-up call to know you planned a successful event.

The Cocktail Party

COCKTAIL PARTIES, OFTEN featuring martinis, were all the rage in the fifties, but the cocktail party is making a comeback. Perhaps it has something to do with the revitalization of the cocktail or the rate of tapas eateries popping up in each city. Whatever the reason, planning a cocktail party should be in the playbook of every event planner in town.

Defining a Cocktail Party

Cocktail parties traditionally are held at 5 or 6 P.M. and last for two hours. They can be a precursor to dinner or hold their own with the right menu. In addition to cocktails, cocktail parties also serve beer and wine. Appetizers, tapas, or hors d'oeuvres are the main event on a cocktail party menu.

Predinner cocktail parties feature lighter fare with less variety, typically two or three types of passed hors d'oeuvres with one stationary item. The stationary item serves as a stable food supply while the hors d'oeuvres are being plated. An example of a stationary item may be an artisanal cheese board or charcuterie plate. The food selections are light so as to not fill the guests before dinner. Guests are encouraged to nibble, therefore the plates of hors d'oeuvres are not heavily passed.

A cocktail party in lieu of dinner may begin at 7 P.M. rather than the usual 5 P.M. starting time. The menu would include at least six types of passed hors d'oeuvres with two or three stationary items. The passed menu will start off with light flavors and then graduate to more substantial savory items. Guests are encouraged to eat heartily so the hors d'oeuvres are passed with more regularity.

Cocktail parties in recent years have gained acceptance as casual events in private homes and more formal affairs taking place at galas and weddings. Cocktail parties take place at restaurants, hotels, and nightclubs. An event planner may get involved in a cocktail party a number of different ways.

- A client may hire an event planner from an event planning company to host a cocktail party.
- The event planner may plan a cocktail party in which a client chooses a restaurant as the venue.
- The event planner of a catering company may also have the opportunity to plan a cocktail party.

Setting the Atmosphere

The atmosphere at a cocktail party can reflect a lot on the host, but more so on the event planner. Plan the atmosphere in advance with your client. Deliberate carefully your lighting and music selections. Does your client want a mellow jazz atmosphere or a dance-the-night-away setting? Have a strategy with your client and make adjustments accordingly.

Theme

As with other events, choosing a theme will tie all of the details together. Themes can be based on a season, a region, or a holiday. Imagine a winter solstice theme, a Moroccan theme, or a Cinco de Mayo cocktail party theme. To create a theme, decide on one key element and revolve the party around it. For example, if your client is hosting a small cocktail party on her veranda, a taste of Tuscany as a theme might transform the event out of the ordinary and into the superlative.

Decorations

Once the theme has been decided, work the decorations into the theme. Use color, texture, lighting, and flowers for decorations. For a cocktail party, simple accents such as a collection of votive candleholders lit in the space can be sufficient. A large bouquet of flowers on the buffet table is another simple touch. Hang twinkle lights or paper lanterns at an outdoor venue.

Music

Music is essential in keeping the tempo of the event in full swing. Lazy lounge tunes set a cool, mellow atmosphere. Upbeat, high-energy tunes can keep everyone dancing in between bites. Progress the music from low- to high-tempo tunes. The music should be friendly and not aggressive. The volume of music should be just low enough so people can carry on a conversation.

Alert

If a DJ or band is not needed for a cocktail party, have the music arranged on compact discs or an MP3 player. Having a guest take charge of the music in the middle of a party can bring an event to a screeching halt. Appoint one of your staff to control the music.

Seating

Seating at a cocktail party should be limited. Guests usually begin in the kitchen, close to the food and drinks, before the party progresses to a sitting room. Arrange to have some seating, but encourage guests to stand and mingle. To spread guests out, set stationary items away from the kitchen.

Imaginative Plate Ware and Flatware

Using fun, imaginative plate ware is a way to get creative with a cocktail party. Bold ceramics can really bring the colors of some dishes alive. Consider using plate ware that falls in line with the theme. The plate ware should make just as much of an impression as the other details.

Plates

With small servings of food, entrée plates have no business at a cocktail party. Use dessert plates, which are usually eight inches or smaller. You can also use B&B plates, which tend to be five inches or smaller. A set of small ramekins or colorful prep containers, both two inches or smaller, can be used as petite hors d'oeuvre plates.

Flatware

Since the menu will be in bite-size form, forks and knives won't be needed. Still, raid the utensil drawer to unearth treasures acceptable for use at a cocktail party. Fun chopsticks, seafood forks, and demitasse spoons all make great accessories at a cocktail party. Create a little container of metal and glass bar picks for easy, bite-size shish kebabs.

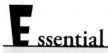
E ssential

Never underestimate the use of a utensil as a serving vessel. For example, a soup spoon can function as a bite-size portion platform. A soup spoon makes a great vehicle for pâtés, foie gras, or braised meats.

Dress up stationary items, like the cheese board and charcuterie plate, with fancy cheese knives. Check your local home goods store for great additions such as mustard spoons, oyster forks, and spreaders.

Glassware as Plate Ware

Little things come in small packages. Guests will delight in the presentation of bite-size appetizers in miniature dishes. Transform funky glassware into petite plate ware. Try shot glasses to serve shooters of soup instead of spirits. Guests will surely gobble salmon tartar if it is served in port glasses with demitasse spoons.

Cocktail Napkins

It is possible to service an entire cocktail party without utensils and plates. Cocktail napkins are versatile and easy. Avoid using cloth cocktail napkins when tomato-based products are served. A nicely monogrammed paper cocktail napkin would go over well at a large cocktail party.

Platters

When platters are filled with a beautiful presentation of hors d'oeuvres, guests will notice the food. When a platter has been ravished of most of the food, guests will notice the platter. A platter for passing should be beautiful and complement the colors of the cuisine and theme. Be creative when looking for platters for passing. Classic, high-end cocktail parties can benefit from silver platters. A cuisine inspired by Provence would best make use of gold and maroon colored platters.

Seasonal Aspects

As with all events, look to the seasons for inspiration. The seasonal aspects you can bring to a cocktail party can make guests cool in the summer and warm in the winter.

With the menu, beverages, and decorations, create your cocktail party to reflect the moment. Let the thermometer be your guide.

Spring

Spring invokes images of cool rain, fresh flowers, and pastel colors. Gathering friends to welcome in the spring may be just what your client has in mind when planning her spring cocktail party. Fill the space with fresh tulips. Create a menu with a variety of vegetables and fresh herbs—tarragon and rosemary smell of spring. Make a signature cocktail with one of the fresh herbs in the menu. Summer may be just around the corner, but guests will be savoring the showers of spring.

Alert

As an event planner, you will be working in close contact with food. You do not want to pollute the cuisine's aroma by wearing perfume. Perfume interrupts a guest's ability to smell the food and may stimulate an allergic reaction. The same is true of pungent floral arrangements and scented candles. Leave the candles in the bathroom and save the perfume for social occasions.

Summer

Give guests a respite from the heat with a cool menu. Serve a beautiful, ice-cold rosé with a tomato–mozzarella salad with mint. Save some mint for muddling to make the Cuban-inspired mojito. A summer party is not complete without a bucket of ice-cold beer. Take advantage of the abundance of produce and offer melon wrapped with prosciutto, cucumber sandwiches, and a watermelon punch. Imbibers take a beating in the heat, so provide your guests with plenty of water.

Autumn

With the coolness of autumn fast approaching, warm your guests with toasty bites right from the oven. Roasted spaghetti squash with melted feta will melt in your guests' mouths. Decorate the buffet table with leaves and fondue pots. With whiffs of the apple-cinnamon tart wafting from the kitchen, dessert cannot come fast enough for your guests.

Winter

Holiday spices are everywhere—in the air, in the beer, and in the cooking. Brew a homemade cider and place it in a coffee urn to pleasantly tingle the senses of guests as they walk through the door. Braised meats on spoons and petite casseroles in ramekins are hearty winter fare and will make your guests forget all about the cold outside.

Appetizers, Hors d'oeuvres, and Tapas

Appetizers are stationary or passed bite-size morsels. The term *hors d'oeuvre* is French in origin and translates as "dishes outside the meal." Hors d'oeuvres can be served cold or hot. *Tapa* is a Spanish word that means "little plate." A tapa can be simply a plate of olives or a Mediterranean-style potato salad. At a cocktail party, all of these translate to tasty bite-size treats. What cocktail fare lacks in size, it makes up for in taste. Since the servings are small, cocktail party cuisine should be bursting with strong flavors.

Lightweight

For predinner cocktail parties, the menu should be light but the flavors should be bold. A teaspoon-size appetizer is just the right size for a predinner event. Smoked salmon on cucumber slices is perfect as a lightweight hors d'oeuvre.

Essential

Servers should politely infiltrate small groups of guests at a cocktail party. With a warm greeting and promises of a yummy bite, guests will welcome the interruption. Servers should give a brief description when offering food. Instruct your servers to return to the kitchen when the hors d'oeuvre plate has only one or two items left.

For dinner-hour cocktail parties, the first round of passed plates should also be lightweight fare. Lightweight morsels are also truly one bite. Larger hors d'oeuvres requiring two bites should be served toward the end.

Medium Weight

Medium-weight hors d'oeuvres have a bit more heaviness in flavors and texture. Figs with melted blue cheese are a perfect example. This course of items should be passed with more frequency. A guest should be offered something new from the kitchen every couple of minutes.

Essential

Create a theme with the menu but do not compromise variety. A theme should not stop you from adding cheeseburger sliders to a Caribbean-themed cocktail party. Guests will appreciate a menu's variety if it means they can try new dishes. It is also acceptable to be adventurous in the variety of menu items.

Heavyweight

The last course of hors d'oeuvres is the heaviest and richest in flavor. Miniature cheeseburgers and petite fish tacos will shine as the main event. It is not inappropriate for the heavyweight appetizers to be two bite-size morsels. Be sure servers are equipped with cocktail napkins for this round.

After all this rich food, guests will be craving a little sweetness. A variety of truffles or petite pastries will assuage the craving. Be sure to switch to coffee service toward the end of the party.

Stationary Plates

Stationary items can balance the passed plates coming from the kitchen so there isn't a dropoff in service. Secure an appropriately sized table for the number of guests and refill with finger food items. Appetizers should be easily manageable and self contained. Little tapas should be individual and accompanied with an appropriate utensil. For a little dish, do not use an entrée-size fork.

Enlist one or two servers to manage the stationary table. These servers should contact the chef when the table becomes depleted and needs refilling. If you are serving cheese, have a backup cheese board in the kitchen as refilling the existing cheese board will take time.

E ssential

Have one or two cold dishes that are ready to eat as guests arrive. These dishes can be laid out as stationary items or passed. Also, have a plan for a variety of stationary dishes to be exchanged throughout the night. Do not just have a cheese board set out for the night. Change it up with another stationary food.

Specialty Cocktails

Gone is the day of the simple martini. It is the drink of choice of many, but these days you may find liquids of all colors and flavors in a martini glass. Bars and nightclubs around the country are looking for the next "it" cocktail. Not too long ago it was a Cosmopolitan, made with vodka, cranberry juice, and lime. There have been a few since then (anyone want an apple martini or mojito?), but the search for the new cocktail has bartenders looking toward the past.

Mastering the Art of Cocktails

With the cocktail renaissance of recent years, liquor companies are racing to create new products and flavors. Some bartenders have jumped on this train, while others decidedly have not. Once upon a time, a cocktail was something that was prepared and took time, much like a meal.

Thankfully, a revolution has begun and classic cocktails are making a comeback. Aviations, Whiskey Smashes, and Mint Juleps are beverages you might see at cocktail parties these days.

A Signature Cocktail

With so many choices for cocktails, how can anyone choose? As an event planner, you may suggest offering a signature cocktail, especially for an off-site location. This means you only need to bring preparations for one cocktail rather than thirty, which will also allow you to better estimate the supplies you'll need to order. You may want to have enough staples on hand to prepare commonly requested drinks such as a gin and tonic or vodka and cranberry juice.

The signature cocktail should be paired with the menu. Use an ingredient from the kitchen for your creation, like mint or even basil. Being adventurous is acceptable if there are staples like wine and beer for guests to fall back on. Write up some fun literature for the guests as a conversation piece.

Bartender Extraordinaire

For smaller cocktail parties, hire one bartender. Suggest setting up a second bar with self-serve beverages such as wine, beer, and punch so the host doesn't have to get involved with the service. As with all events that serve alcohol, give your bartender instructions for intoxicated guests. For larger parties with more than forty guests hire two or more bartenders.

Alert

Lend a hand in creating a responsible host. Post a taxi number near the exit. Some hosts have even gone so far as having guests leave car keys in a dish on the way into the party. A guest can only retrieve his keys if he is able to perform a sobriety test of the host's choice. It adds a little fun to a very serious matter.

Trendy Glassware

With all of these miniature dishes, it is hard to imagine your guests carrying around a twelve-ounce martini glass. Use fun, trendy glassware to highlight the signature drink. Glassware comes in all shapes and sizes. Petite glasses will complement the petite fare and look great while being passed by the servers. Petite glassware will also keep the liquor consumption slightly under control. Your client, the responsible host, will appreciate this effort.

Wines and Punches

A cocktail party can serve more than just cocktails. There is also room for wine, punch, and even beer at this soiree. Give the guests variety when spicing up the beverage list. Do not forget the water to keep the party hydrated.

Wine

When choosing the wine, remember the theme. If the theme is based upon a holiday or country, try some different wines from these traditions or regions to tie in with the theme. Chances are if the cuisine is based upon a region, the wine will add a nice complement. For tapas dishes, experiment with a white albarino, red tempranillo, and a sparkling cava—all wines from Spain.

Punch

The choice beverage at high school dances has become more sophisticated. As with cocktails, punches are also experiencing a resurgence. Ice molds laden with fruit and flowers adorn beautiful antique punch bowls and make stunning centerpieces on any bar.

Beer

A bucket of ice-cold beer can make some guests forget about cocktails altogether. Again, aim to have the beer selection fall in line with the theme. If that seems like a stretch, attempting to pair beer with certain foods might work easier. For example, some cheeses complement Belgian ale very well. For a variety, mix up the selection with local ales and lagers.

Nonalcoholic Beverages

Since cocktail parties occur in the evening, you might not expect children at these events. You should expect to find guests who are not of the legal age to drink. Assume also that there might be guests who simply do not drink. For these guests, take the emphasis off of the cocktail and offer a fun nonalcoholic beverage instead. Try sparkling juice cocktails made with sparkling water and juice. Serve the nonalcoholic cocktail in champagne flutes so young guests and non-drinkers can still feel festive. Be sure to use a juice different in color than your signature drink to avoid confusion.

Simplifying Labor for the Host

Labor in this case does not refer to staff labor. In this case, labor refers to the actual work the host needs to finish long after the staff has gone home. When catering an event in a private home, you want to lighten the workload for the host as much as possible. Leaving her with a lot of gritty housework could leave a bad taste in her mouth.

Rentals

For off-site events, the rentals may arrive before your staff does, so have a staff member confirm the rental order upon arrival. Set aside an area as a bus station. All dirty plate ware and glassware should be brought to the bus station for prebussing. Prebussing is clearing and stacking dirty plates back into crates for the rental company to pick up. The same is done for glassware.

Cleanup

If your staff will leave before the party ends, leave the host with only the last guests' glasses to prebus. In regards to the catering, all other cleanup should be completed before the staff leaves. Provide your client with instructions on rental procedures and pickup as well. If you are the point of contact, have the rental company send the invoice directly to you. This way you can follow up with your client and staff to solve any discrepancies concerning breakages or missing items.

For large cocktail parties with one hundred or more guests, consider hiring a cleanup crew. Some facilities employ on-site cleaning crews with the fee built into the cost of the venue. For all other venues, quote the cost of cleanup in your initial meeting with your client. Hiring a cleaning company on your own will prevent your client from being charged later by the venue.

Checking in the Following Day

If possible, schedule a follow-up meeting with the client the next day at the venue. Meeting with the facility planner for a walk-through is a good idea in the aftermath of a large event. Any extra cleaning fees or maintenance charges can be taken care of at that time. If you are not available, arrange for a member of your staff to manage the walk-through in your place.

Sample Event-Planning Documents

Contract

Contact: _____

Company: _____

Address: _____

_____

Telephone: _____

Function Date: _____

Setup Time: _____

Event Time: _____

Number of Guests: _____

Menu
Soda, tonic, juice, and water available

Passed food: 6:00 P.M. – 7:30 P.M.

Two food stations: 6:00 P.M. – 8:30 P.M.

(will need to be replenished)

Coffee & tea setup: 8:30 P.M. – 9:00 P.M.

Basic; a Sweet Optional

Setup
Flowers

Tables: Food stations, silent auction tables,

DJ table, tall cocktail tables

Chairs

Linens

Serving utensils and silverware

Plates and napkins

Glassware: Beer, wine, and martini glasses

Staff
Bartender

Servers

Setup and breakdown

BEO

Date _____

Time _____

Room _____

Function _____

Setup _____

Rental _____

Subject to change without notice.
A guaranteed count must be received by 12 noon EST, 3 business days prior to the event. If no guarantee is received, the expected number of guests indicated on the private event order will be charged. Please sign the Banquet Event Order below to agree to all the details provided. Any changes or amendments will not be in effect until approved by your company.

TIMING INSTRUCTIONS

7–8 A.M.: breakfast

10–10:30 A.M.: morning break

12–1 P.M.: lunch

2:45–3:15 P.M.: afternoon break

5:15 P.M.: adjourn

MENU

Serve: 7:30 A.M. – 5:15 P.M.

BEVERAGE

Serve: 7:30 A.M. – 5:15 P.M.

   Daytime Beverage Menu
   45 assorted sodas @ $4.00
   43 mineral water @ $6.00 each
   18 coffee station @ $4.00
   Juice @ $4.00 each

Full beverage station set, refreshed throughout day as necessary

Beverages charged on consumption

SETUP INSTRUCTIONS

U-Shape for 22 pp, table set for LCD

Pens/notepads/candy/water pitchers at table

2 waste baskets in room

Buffet setup/3 rounds of 6

AUDIOVISUAL

Event:

2 Post-it style flipcharts @ $52.17 each

1 conference phone

Speakers for computer

Wireless Internet setup

MISCELLANEOUS

7:00 A.M. – 5:15 P.M

Hosted valet @ $12.00 per car

2 servers @ $300.00 per server

Subject to change without notice.
A guaranteed count must be received by 12 noon EST, 3 business days prior to the event. If no guarantee is received, the expected number of guests indicated on the private event order will be charged. Please sign the Banquet Event Order below to agree to all the details provided. Any changes or amendments will not be in effect until approved by your company.

BILLING

Direct Billing

Subject to change without notice.
A guaranteed count must be received by 12 noon EST, 3 business days prior to the event. If no guarantee is received, the expected number of guests indicated on the private event order will be charged. Please sign the Banquet Event Order below to agree to all the details provided. Any changes or amendments will not be in effect until approved by your company.

Event Intake Form

Day: _____

Date: _____**Time:** _____**a.m./p.m.**

Reservation Name: _____**Count:** _____

Location (circle) Mezzanine / Stage / Dining room / Private Dining Room

Buyout _____

Contact Name: _____

Phone Number: _____

On-site Contact: _____

Additional Phone Number: _____

Event: _____

E-mail: _____

Ordering Off-Menu? Y N

Prix Fixe Menu Y N

Price $_____ per person

Includes: Menu Wine Beer N/A BEV _____

Prix Fixe Selections and Special Requests

Apps

stationary / passed / family-style / choice of / individual:

_____   _____

_____   _____

2nd course

stationary / passed / family-style / choice of / individual:

_____   _____

_____   _____

3rd course

stationary / passed / family-style / choice of / individual:

_____   _____

_____   _____

vegetarian option Y   N _____

Desserts

stationary / passed / family-style / choice of / individual:

_____   _____

Beverages

Beer: _____ * _____ * _____ * _____ *

Wine: pre-selected   tbd before arrival   tbd upon arrival

_____ * _____ * _____ - _____ *

wine notes: _____

Bar: no restrictions cash & carry

Room/Table setup: _____

FOH notes: _____

BOH notes: _____

FOH date: _____   BOH initial & date _____

Date posted _____   Pastry initial & date _____

Payment

CC#: _____ exp: _____ to be charged: yes / no / tbd

Posting master number Y   N

Group name: _____

Room charge: Y   N $ _____

Service charge: Y N $ _____

Valet charge: Y N $ _____

Auto grat: Y N % _____ Tax exempt: Y N # _____ ES will bill: Y N _____

Charge for all confirmed guests: Y N

_____

Billing info: _____

Fax receipt Y N: Attn: _____

Fax number: _____

Open food $ _____ Open wine $ _____ Open beer $ _____

Open liquor $ _____ Open misc. $ _____

Cake: Ordered   Bringing in   Date posted: _____

Cutting fee: _____

Instructions: _____

_____

Audiovisual Y N: Instructions:

_____

Additional notes: _____

_____

_____

Sample Sponsorship Letter

Date
Name
Company
Address
Address

Dear NAME,

We are thrilled that COMPANY has chosen to be a sponsor in the first annual EVENT NAME to be held EVENT DATE. We expect more than XX PEOPLE to join us in raising critical funds to support the innovative research and extraordinary patient care for children and adults that has become the hallmark of the Charity Institute.

Thank you for your generous commitment of ENTER GIFT AMOUNT and for being a part of this important fundraising effort. Your continued generosity and commitment to our efforts is the foundation upon which the institute's goal of conquering major forms of cancer within the next decade can and will be achieved.

The details and benefits of your sponsorship of the EVENT NAME and the Charity include the following:

EXAMPLE:

TANGIBLE BENEFITS – CORPORATE IDENTIFICATION AND RECOGNITION:

- COMPANY banner (3' x 5') will be displayed at the EVENT venue, provided by sponsor
- COMPANY name listed on EVENT NAME Web site, with link to your Web site
- Opportunity to provide item in the gift bag
- 2 tickets to the Saturday Evening Gala
- 4 tickets to the Friday Evening Reception

By signing below, you will confirm the commitment of COMPANY as articulated above.

At your convenience, please return this letter of agreement and a signed copy of the enclosed Sponsor Agreement to me in the enclosed envelope. If you have any questions or need anything at all, please feel free to contact me at PHONE or via e-mail at E-MAIL ADDRESS.

Thank you once again for your commitment to our fundraising efforts for the Charity and this important event. The EVENT NAME promises to be another spectacular event!

Sincerely,

NAME
TITLE

_____   _____
COMPANY Representative   Date

Sample Donation Form

Date _____

Name of Donor _____

Indicate how Donor would like to be listed in the event program

_____

Address _____

_____

Phone _____

Is there a gift certificate?

YES NO

If YES, please include with Donor Sheet

PLEASE INCLUDE ALL PERTINENT INFORMATION
AND DESCRIPTION FOR THE RAFFLE BELOW:

Physical Item (Note size, color, artist, etc.)

Service/Trip (Note dates, location, restrictions, etc.)

_____

_____

_____

_____

Estimated value of item: _____

All donations must be received by: _____

Solicitor's Name: _____

Please e-mail all raffle information to: _____

Resources

Better Business Bureau
www.bbb.org
Resource for vendor
background checks

Business Arts
www.BusinessArts.com
Resource for staff back-
ground checks

Dailyplan-it
www.Dailyplan-it.com
Event planner Web site

Fab Job
www.Fabjob.com
Online employment search

Free Law Library
www.free-law-library.com
Free information on employment and contracts

Hot Jobs
http://hotjobs.yahoo.com
Online employment search

Marketingpilot.com
www.marketingpilot.com
Software for event planners

Programwrl.com
www.programwrl.com
Event-planning software

Sharewareconnection.com
www.shareconnection.com
Event-planning software

Special Events
www.specialevents.com
Online resource for
event planners

United States Department of Labor
www.dol.gov
Great resource for employment questions

Index

The Everything® Career Guide Series

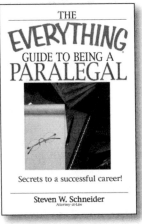

THE EVERYTHING GUIDE TO BEING A PARALEGAL

Secrets to a successful career!

Steven W. Schneider
Attorney-at-Law

Trade Paperback, $14.95
ISBN 10: 1-59337-583-2
ISBN 13: 978-1-59337-583-6

THE EVERYTHING GUIDE TO BEING A PERSONAL TRAINER

All you need to get
started on a career in fitness

Kate Kenworthy, M.Ed., A.T.C., C.S.C.S. &
Stephen A. Rodrigues, M.Ed., P.E.S.

Trade Paperback, $14.95
ISBN 10: 1-59869-227-5
ISBN 13: 978-1-59869-227-3

THE EVERYTHING GUIDE TO BEING A REAL ESTATE AGENT

Secrets to a successful career!

Shahri Masters
Author of The Everything® Homeselling Book, 2nd Edition

Trade Paperback, $14.95
ISBN 10: 1-59337-432-1
ISBN 13: 978-1-59337-432-7

THE EVERYTHING GUIDE TO BEING A SALES REP

Winning secrets to a successful–
and profitable–career!

Ruth Klein

Trade Paperback, $14.95
ISBN 10: 1-59337-657-X
ISBN 13: 978-1-59337-657-4

THE EVERYTHING GUIDE TO BEING AN EVENT PLANNER

Insider's advice on turning your
creative energy into a rewarding career

Jennifer Mancuso

Trade Paperback, $14.95
ISBN 10: 1-59869-417-0
ISBN 13: 978-1-59869-417-8

Helpful handbooks written by experts.

THE

EVERYTHING
GUIDE TO CAREERS IN
HEALTH CARE

Find the job that's right for you

Kathy Quan, R.N., B.S.N., P.H.N.

Trade Paperback, $14.95
ISBN 10: 1-59337-725-8
ISBN 13: 978-1-59337-725-0

THE

EVERYTHING
GUIDE TO
**CAREERS IN
LAW ENFORCEMENT**

A complete handbook to
an exciting and rewarding life
of service

Paul D. Bagley

Trade Paperback, $14.95
ISBN 10: 1-59869-077-9
ISBN 13: 978-1-59869-077-4

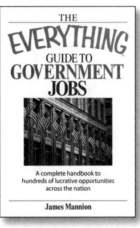

THE

EVERYTHING
GUIDE TO
**GOVERNMENT
JOBS**

A complete handbook to
hundreds of lucrative opportunities
across the nation

James Mannion

Trade Paperback, $14.95
ISBN 10: 1-59869-078-7
ISBN 13: 978-1-59869-078-1

THE

EVERYTHING
GUIDE TO STARTING
AND RUNNING A
**CATERING
BUSINESS**

Insider's advice on turning
your talent into a lucrative career

Joyce Weinberg

Trade Paperback, $14.95
ISBN 10: 1-59869-384-0
ISBN 13: 978-1-59869-384-3

THE

EVERYTHING
GUIDE TO STARTING
AND RUNNING A
RESTAURANT

Secrets to a successful business!

Ronald Lee, Restaurateur

Trade Paperback, $14.95
ISBN 10: 1-59337-433-X
ISBN 13: 978-1-59337-433-4